Outsider in the
White House

Outsider in the White House

Bernie Sanders
with Huck Gutman

Foreword by Nina Turner

Afterword by John Nichols

VERSO

London • New York

This updated edition of *Outsider in the House* first published 2019
First published by Verso 1997
© Bernie Sanders 1997, 2015, 2019
Preface © Bernie Sanders 2015, 2019
Afterword © John Nichols 2015, 2019
Foreword © Nina Turner 2019

1 3 5 7 9 10 8 6 4 2

Verso
UK: 6 Meard Street, London W1F 0EG
US: 20 Jay Street, Suite 1010, Brooklyn, NY 11201
versobooks.com

Verso is the imprint of New Left Books

ISBN-13: 978-1-78873-769-2
ISBN-13: 978-1-78478-419-5 (US EBK)
ISBN-13: 978-1-78478-420-1 (UK EBK)

British Library Cataloguing in Publication Data
A catalogue record for this book is available from the British Library

The Library of Congress Catalogued the Previous Edition as Follows:

Sanders, Bernard, author.
[Outsider in the House]
Outsider in the White House / Bernie Sanders with Huck Gutman ; afterword by
John Nichols. — Updated edition.
pages cm
Original edition published in 1997 under title: Outsider in the House.
ISBN 978-1-78478-418-8 — ISBN 978-1-78478-419-5 —
ISBN 978-1-78478-420-1
1. Sanders, Bernard. 2. Presidential candidates—United States—Biography. 3.
Legislators—United States—Biography. 4. United States. Congress. House—
Biography. 5. United States—Politics and government—1989- I. Gutman, Huck,
1943- II. Title.
E840.8.S26A3 2015
328.73'092—dc23
[B]
2015031867

Typeset in Fournier MT by Hewer Text UK Ltd, Edinburgh, Scotland
Printed and bound by CPI Group (UK) Ltd, Croydon CR0 4YY

Contents

Foreword:
The Lived Experience of Bernie Sanders
by Nina Turner

I have always believed that the Reverend Dr. Martin Luther King Jr. spoke a powerful truth when he said, "The ultimate measure of a man is not where he stands in moments of comfort and convenience, but where he stands at times of challenge and controversy." I think this is especially true when someone is running for the presidency. So I understand why people want to know more about Senator Bernie Sanders. It is one thing to cheer for the senator's speeches and policies, but it is something else to get a sense of how his lived experience has led him to be so passionately committed to economic, social, and racial justice. There is a hunger to know more about the man we all call Bernie. And it will only continue to grow.

I write this as someone who has come to know Senator Bernie Sanders very well. Our journey together began after many of the events recounted in this book occurred, but before he was the national figure he is today. And that is a good place to begin.

Bernie has become such a vital figure in our politics that it may be hard for some folks to remember that there was a time not so long ago when he was battling to be heard. I was one of those who heard him back then, and I want people to understand how powerful that was, for me and for a great many Americans like me. He had first come to light for me in a very deep way in 2010, when he filibustered for eight and a half hours against the extension of George W. Bush's tax cuts. Watching him stand strong and boldly against just about everyone else in Washington on that one issue, an issue that was so important for working people, that's when he caught my attention in a unique way. It was not until several years later, however, that I came to see him as a presidential prospect.

I had a feeling of heaviness coming off of the 2014 mid-term elections. So many of us had tried so hard. I was one of the many Democrats who had run and lost that year. As a state senator who had long been involved in voting rights struggles, I was so proud to be the Democratic nominee in the great state of Ohio for the office of Secretary of State. My campaign sought to do something that had never been done before, which was to elect an African American woman to statewide office in Ohio. We thought we could make a breakthrough that would matter in Ohio, and nationally. But it wasn't to be. The Republican wave that swept across the country that year hit Ohio particularly hard. Democrats were losing everywhere. We had always known that our campaign was going against the odds, that we were running against entrenched incumbents more monied than we were. I hated losing, but I knew that my defeat was part of something bigger—and I knew that Democrats were going to have to address it. That made me all the more attentive to the 2016 presidential race.

What was going through my mind then was a question: "How do I rally Democrats to feel better about the future?" So when I was approached to help Ready for Hillary, the group that was preparing for Hillary Clinton's 2016 presidential campaign, I was open to it. Early in 2015 it seemed as if there might be only one candidate making a serious bid for the Democratic nomination, and I wanted to do my part for my party.

Then, in came Bernie Sanders from Vermont. I was aware of the senator as someone who had been on the right side of the issues over the years. When 2015 hit and he was out there saying that he was thinking about running for president, something started percolating in me. I'll never forget that my husband had seen him on TV, and he called me. He said, "Baby, this candidate Bernie Sanders . . ." and I said, "Yeah, I know who he is." And my husband said, "He's going to run, and I think this is your candidate. This person reminds me of you."

Not long after that, I watched the senator's announcement, and I said, "Wow." There was a feeling that came over me, like a quickening, as we would say in the black church. I had an awakening. It was one of those moments when your consciousness is pierced. You can't sleep, you can't eat, you can't think. I knew I couldn't just continue to go along the path I'd been on. I had to change course—and that's what I did. I was an official in the Ohio Democratic

Party, so I called my chair and said, "Look, you know, I think I'm going to endorse Senator Sanders." I remember him saying, "Do you have to do that? Can you just wait until the primary?" I said, "No, I *have* to do this. Have to do it. I have no choice."

What Bernie Sanders was saying about the issues spoke to me so deeply. It connected with my life. I had these flashbacks about my mother, who died at a very young age. My mother died underinsured. So when he was talking about "Medicare for All," that touched me. I am a first-generation college graduate, and I know that I have the opportunities I have right now, degrees that I have right now, because I was able to become a cycle breaker using higher education as a path. I don't think I would have as much opportunity as I have to this day without it. So when he talked about "College for All," that got to me where I live.

There were all these touchpoints that just spoke to me. But what struck me most powerfully, and what makes this book so important, is that Bernie Sanders has been speaking to all of us for all these many years about how the system is rigged against poor people, against working people, against the vast majority of Americans who only want a fair chance to live a good life. We are all different, but Bernie reminds us that we all have things in common. He's been making that point for decades. It's in his heart. And it touches my heart because I come from a working-class family. I grew up in a single-mother household. I saw my mother struggle every single day to provide for seven children—to provide for our material needs, but also to provide for our emotional needs—and so I heard everything that he was saying about the poor as if he was speaking directly to me. It touched me where I live. It engulfed me and I was just automatically drawn to his truth from my lived experience.

That is part of what has made supporting Bernie Sanders a mission for me. This is the man who I believed would transform the country from that White House, who would use every lever of power that he has as president of the United States of America to create a system that, finally and truly, is fair for the working poor and for the barely middle class in this country. So I made the leap. I started working with Senator Bernie Sanders in 2015, and I have never really stopped.

When you work closely with someone, you see who they really are. Sometimes that can be disappointing, because who they are is not as impressive as their rhetoric. But with Bernie Sanders, it's the opposite: the more you know about the man, the more he opens up to you, the more you realize that this politics is *who he is*. It's who he has always been. That is part of what comes through in this book, and I value that.

Bernie's always been focused on policies. He's got this "not me, us" approach to politics. I understand that. But I also understand that people are interested in the man who formulated the policies, the man who has campaigned for them over all these years. When Bernie pauses to reflect, when he tells us about where he comes from, it's powerful.

Knowing who Bernie Sanders is, knowing where he is coming from, gives a new dimension to the positions he takes as he campaigns for president. The senator's father was a Jewish immigrant who came from Poland to the

United States in the 1920s. The senator never got to know his father's side of the family because they were killed in the Holocaust. Who better understands the notion that immigrants would try to come to this country not just for a better life but, sometimes, to save their lives? And you want to talk about white supremacy? The ultimate white supremacists, the Nazis, murdered members of his family. So does he understand why we must struggle against white supremacy now? Yes, he does. We know this from his life story. We know that he grew up in a neighborhood where his elders had to escape the Holocaust. Navigating his community helped inform his civil rights platform. His justice journey came from his family.

When Bernie Sanders went to college at the University of Chicago in the early 1960s, he joined the Congress of Racial Equality. He joined the fight against segregation and racism and bigotry in all of their forms as part of a multiracial collective of people standing up to injustice. And when they were protesting segregation and the unfair allocation of resources by the Chicago school district, he was arrested. He was chained to a black woman who was protesting with him. He stood in solidarity with that woman as she was trying to create a better future for her children, for every child. Bernie Sanders understood, all the way back then, that you had to challenge every kind of bigotry because bigotry touches us all. It hurts us all. He was ready to be arrested because of this understanding. This is what he was willing to do in times of challenge and controversy.

That was just the beginning of the senator putting himself on the line for the cause. People need to know that

Bernie Sanders has marched for civil rights, for women's rights, for immigrant rights, and for labor rights. It is such a part of him that, I think, some people don't notice. But we *should* notice that, even as a senator and as a presidential candidate, he has gone to Iowa to join the picket lines of Bakery, Confectionery, Tobacco Workers and Grain Millers' International Union members, to New York to rally with Verizon workers, to Mississippi to organize with Nissan workers, to California to rally with university workers.

Bernie Sanders has become a prominent man, a contender for the presidency of the United States. He is at a place in his life where he could make political calculations, but he continues to make moral calculations. He has taken on Jeff Bezos and Amazon, Disney, and other major corporations to elevate the cause of the living-wage movement, and these acts of solidarity have changed people's lives. The senator recognizes what is possible when we work together for economic and social and racial justice. He has always recognized this. We saw it in the 1960s and we are still seeing it today.

This is the lived experience of Bernie Sanders, the experience that he communicates in this book. It is a shared experience, one that many of us feel a connection with. That sense of connection has led me to recognize that this remarkable man is uniquely positioned for the moment in which we all find ourselves. It is why I hope and pray that he will be our next president.

Cleveland, Ohio
June 2019

Preface

When people say I am too serious, I take it as a compliment. I have always understood politics as a serious endeavor, involving the fates of nations, ideals and human beings who cannot afford to be pawns in a game. I suppose this understanding makes me an outsider in contemporary American politics. But if I am more serious about politics than those candidates who jet from one high-donor fundraiser to the next, or from a Koch Brothers–sponsored summit to the Sheldon Adelson "primary," I do not think I am more serious than the American people.

The American people want political campaigns to be about candidates' stands on the issues, not about fundraising, polls, or the negative ads that overwhelm honest debate. Elections should be influenced by grassroots movements and unexpected coalitions, not by the cult of personality or a billionaire's checkbook.

From the time I began to get involved in politics, as a student organizing for civil rights on the University of

Chicago campus, as a peace activist in the Vietnam War era, as a supporter of labor unions and peoples' struggles, what offended me most about electoral politics was the pettiness. It seemed that the media and political parties were encouraging voters to make decisions of enormous consequence on the basis of whether a candidate had a bright smile or delivered a zinger belittling another candidate—not on the basis of ideas or philosophy, let alone idealism. I never wanted to be a part of such a soulless politics. And across my years of campaigning for causes and for elective office, I think I have done a pretty good job of avoiding it.

The first edition of this book, originally titled *Outsider in the House*, was written two decades ago, after I had been elected to the U.S. House of Representatives from Vermont but long before I ever imagined I would campaign for the presidency. It tells the story of how we built an independent progressive politics in one city and then in one state. It is the story of an insurgency that won first the mayoralty of Burlington, Vermont's largest city, and then a statewide congressional seat. More importantly, it is the story of how we used the authority that extended from those victories to make changes for the better in the lives of people who don't have many allies in positions of power.

The working people of Vermont are the real heroes of this book because they stuck with the fight for economic and social justice long after the media and the political elites expected them to give up. They did not merely keep at it; they drew their friends and neighbors into the process— increasing election turnout at a point when it was declining in much of the rest of the country. I always say that our greatest accomplishment in Burlington was not our initial victory in the mayoral race of 1981—although that was a sweet victory. Our greatest accomplishments were the victories that came in the elections that followed, when increased voter turnout, especially from low-income people and young people, allowed us to beat back the combined efforts of economic and political elites to stop us. We did not overwhelm our opponents with money, we overwhelmed them with votes—like it's supposed to work in a democracy.

When I reread *Outsider in the House* recently, I was reminded of the extent to which this is a story of struggle. It is not the story of easy or steady success. It is the story of hard work, a little progress in the right direction and then a setback, of election defeats and election wins, and of breakthroughs that few of us had imagined possible—until they happened.

A politics of struggle is rooted in values and vision, and above all trust. It involves a compact a candidate makes with the people who share the values, who embrace the vision. It doesn't say, "Vote for me and I'll fix everything." It says, "If I get elected, I will not just work for you, I will work with you." The work may mean implementing a program at the local level or sponsoring legislation at the federal level, but what matters most is the connection that is made between people and their elected representatives—the connection that says there is someone on the inside who is going to fight for the citizens outside the halls of power. When citizens recognize that this fight is being waged, they are energized. They make bigger demands. They build stronger movements. They forge a politics that is about more than winning an election; they forge a politics that is about transforming a city, a state, a nation, and maybe the world.

I embraced this politics of struggle as a young activist on behalf of racial justice. I got involved in electoral politics because I believed that movement activism on behalf of civil rights and women's rights and labor rights and environmental protection and peace needed to be reflected on our ballots and in the corridors of power. I started slow, losing and learning. Eventually, with the help of friends and allies whose loyalty and commitment meant everything to me and everything to our shared success, we started winning. We did not just win elections, we won the transformational progress that only comes when political activism is focused on more than the next election. My decision to run for the presidency in 2016 was inspired by the events outlined in the original text of *Outsider in the House* and by experiences that came after its publication in 1997— in the U.S. House and U.S. Senate, and more importantly on picket lines, in marches, and at town hall meetings and rallies against economic inequality, or protesting the impoverishment of workers and communities by failed trade policies, or denouncing the neglect of the basic dignity and humanity of immigrants, or against unnecessary wars, racial injustice and environmental catastrophe.

The two decades since this book was published have not been easy for Americans. The gap between rich and poor has extended beyond the breaking point of civil society and sound economics. Instead of addressing poverty, politicians of both parties have criminalized it and accepted incarceration rates that are obscene and racist; the devastating effects of climate change have been ignored; we have accepted a warped sense of priorities that says America can always find enough money for war but that there is never enough for infrastructure or education or nutrition programs. Our democracy has been rendered very nearly dysfunctional by Supreme Court rulings that make it easier for billionaires and corporations to buy elections and harder for people of color and students to vote in them. The United States is degenerating into a plutocracy as democracy is overwhelmed by money and negative ads and the collapse of serious journalism.

When I announced I was going to run for president, I said it would take a political revolution for a democratic socialist from Vermont to win the presidency. A lot of pundits thought that was an acknowledgment of impossibility. It wasn't. It was a statement of what would be necessary to undo the damage that has been done and to reclaim our country from the oligarchs. The pundits and the political consultants still have a hard time understanding this. But the people get it. They are turning out by the thousands, by the tens of thousands, for our rallies. They are sending contributions of $5 or $10 because they understand that if we all give what we can then we might yet be able to beat the billionaire class.

I am as serious as they say I am. I have no taste for symbolic campaigns. I decided to run for president because I believed it was necessary to do so, because I believed this campaign could bring about a political revolution, and I believed we could win. We did it in Burlington. We did it in Vermont. And we are doing it in America. Change comes, even in the face of overwhelming odds. And the recognition of the changes we have already made, of what we have won, inspires us to fight even harder.

When I began to write the story of my political journey, I accepted the designation "outsider." I have stood outside the mainstream of American politics. I have rejected the status quo. I have cast some lonely votes, fought some lonely fights, mounted some lonely campaigns. But I do not feel lonely now. There are a lot of us outsiders, and we are organizing for a $15 minimum wage, for job programs that address structural unemployment, for single-payer health care, for free college education, for the renewal of our cities, for the reconstruction of our infrastructure and the creation of millions of jobs, for just and humane reform of a broken and racist criminal justice system, for comprehensive immigration reform and a path to citizenship.

The majority of Americans today are outsiders, especially in the halls of power where decisions about our economy are being made. And we will remain outsiders for as long as the political balance is tipped against the great mass of Americans, for as long as the status quo is characterized by inequality and injustice. It will take all the energy of the new movements of this new time to make the change that is needed. These movements began on the outside, but even now they are beginning to be heard on the inside— changing our politics, changing our laws, changing America. Cities and states are raising wages. They are beginning to address racial disparities in policing practices and the policies that lead to mass incarceration. They are demanding a constitutional amendment that will overturn Citizens United and restore free and fair elections. Something is happening in America, something that feels like a political revolution. I have been an outsider in the House. I have been an outsider in the Senate. Now I am a candidate for the presidency. I believe that this political revolution might just put an outsider in the White House and that, together, we can remake our politics and our governance so that none of us are outsiders anymore.

I believe we can be serious and optimistic. I believe we can recognize the overwhelming odds against us and forge coalitions that overcome the odds.

The point of beginning is not a political strategy. It is a shared sense of necessity, an understanding that we must act. I believe that Americans, battered by job losses and wage stagnation, angered by inequality and injustice, have come to this understanding. I hear Americans saying loudly and clearly: enough is enough. This great nation and its government belong to all of the people, and not solely to a handful of billionaires, their super PACs, and their lobbyists.

We live in the wealthiest nation in the history of the world, but that reality means little because almost all of that wealth is controlled by a tiny handful of individuals. There is something profoundly wrong when the top one-tenth of 1 percent owns almost as much as the bottom 90 percent, and when 99 percent of all new income goes to the top 1 percent. There is something profoundly wrong when one family owns more wealth than the bottom 130 million

Americans. This type of immoral, unsustainable economy is not what America is supposed to be about. This has got to change, and together we will change it.

The change begins when we say to the billionaire class: "You can't have it all. You can't get huge tax breaks while children in this country go hungry. You can't continue sending our jobs to China while millions are looking for work. You can't hide your profits in the Cayman Islands and other tax havens, while there are massive unmet needs in every corner of this nation. Your greed has got to end. You cannot take advantage of all the benefits of America if you refuse to accept your responsibilities as Americans."

When we declare, "Enough is enough," we are demanding a country and a future that meets the needs of the vast majority of Americans: a country and a future where it is hard to buy elections and easy to vote in them; a country and a future where tax dollars are invested in jobs and infrastructure instead of jails and incarceration; a country and a future where we have the best-educated workforce and the widest range of opportunities for every child and every adult; a country and a future where we take the steps necessary to ending systemic racism; a country and a future where we assure once and for all that no one who works forty hours a week will live in poverty.

Now is not the time to think small. We cannot settle for the same old establishment politics and stale inside-the-beltway ideas. We cannot let the billionaire class use its money and its media spin to divide us. Now is the time for millions of working families—black and white, Latino and Native American, gay and straight—to come together, to revitalize American democracy, to end the collapse of the American middle class, and to make certain that our children and grandchildren are able to enjoy a quality of life that brings them health, prosperity, security and joy—and that once again makes the United States the leader in the world in the fight for economic and social justice, for environmental sanity and for a world of peace.

Now is the time for us to make America the country that the vast majority of our people want it to be. It will take a political revolution to make the change. But I have learned from the experiences recounted in this book that political revolutions are possible. They are not made by billionaires or political insiders. They are made by workers whose jobs are threatened, by students who are overwhelmed by debt, by retirees on fixed incomes, by outsiders who recognize that enough is enough—and who recognize that they must organize and campaign and vote for something better. When we stand together there is nothing, nothing, nothing we cannot accomplish.

Bernie Sanders
September 2015

Acknowledgments

I want to thank the people of Burlington, Vermont, and the people of the state of Vermont for their support over the years. In going outside of the two-party system and making me the longest-serving independent member of Congress in American history, you have done what no other community or state has done.

Thank you very much for giving me the opportunity to serve.

Thank you, Jane. Without your love and support as my wife, much of what is described in this book would not have occurred.

Thank you, Levi. You have traveled the state with me to political meetings since you were a year old. Your love, loyalty, and friendship have always sustained me.

Thank you, Heather, Carina, and Dave. You have let me into your lives and, in doing that, have helped show me the meaning of family.

Thank you, Larry. As my older brother, you opened my eyes to a world of ideas that I otherwise would never have seen.

Thank you, Huck. Without your help and tenacity, this book would not have been written.

Thank you, Colin Robinson, for Verso's strong support for this project.

No member of Congress achieves much without the support of a strong and dedicated staff. In that respect, I have been extremely fortunate in having so many wonderful and hardworking coworkers. The following people have served on my congressional staff since 1991, and I thank all of them for their efforts: Paul Anderson, Mark Anderson, Lisa Barrett, Dan Barry, Stacey Blue, Debbie Bookchin, Doug Boucher, Steve Bressler, Mike Brown, Katie Clarke, Greg Coburn, Mike Cohen, Steve Crowley, Clarence Davis, Jim DeFilippis, Don Edwards, Christine Eldred, Molly Farrell, Phil Fiermonte, John Franco, Mark Galligan, Liz Gibbs-West, Dennis Gilbert, Bill Goold, Huck Gutman, Theresa Hamilton, Katharine Hanley, Adlai Hardin, Millie Hollis, Lisa Jacobson, Carolyn Kazdin, Nichole LaBrecque, Megan Lambert, Rachel Levin, Sascha Mayer, Florence McCloud-Thomas, Ginny McGrath, Chris Miller, Elizabeth Mundinger, Laura O'Brien, Eric Olson, Kirsa Phillips, Anthony Pollina, Jim Rader, Tyler Resch, Mary Richards, Jane Sanders, Jim Schumacher, Brendan Smith, Tom Smith, Sarah Swider, Doug Taylor, Eleanor Thompson, Jeff Weaver, Cynthia Weglarz, David Weinstein, Ruthan Wirman, Whitney Wirman, Tina Wisell.

Huck Gutman wishes to thank his wife, Buff Lindau, for

her unstinting love and her endlessly generous support. He also wishes to thank Bernie Sanders for showing Vermont, and the nation, what a progressive politics looks like when it works, successfully, in the real world.

Introduction

November 5, 1996. We won. Blowout. By 7:30 p.m., only half an hour after the polls close, the Associated Press, based on exit polls, says that we will win, and win big.

The town-by-town election results are coming in by phone and over the radio. In Burlington, my hometown, where we always do well, we are running much stronger than usual. We even win the conservative ward in the new north end. We win Shelburne, a wealthy town usually not supportive. Winooski. Landslide. We win Essex, my opponent's hometown. We're now getting calls in from the southern part of the state. Brattleboro. We're winning there almost three to one. Incredible. We're even winning in Rutland County, traditionally the most Republican county in the state. We're also winning in Bennington County, where I often lose.

By ten o'clock, Jane and I and the kids are down at Mona's restaurant, where we're holding our election night gathering. The crowd is large and boisterous. When our victory celebration appears on the TV monitor, the crowd becomes very loud. I can hardly hear myself speak into the microphones. The noise is deafening. The next day the *Rutland Herald* describes my remarks as "vintage Sanders": "We know that there is something wrong in this country when you have one percent of the population owning more wealth than the bottom ninety percent." I said a few other things as well. I was very happy.

My Republican opponent, Susan Sweetser, calls to concede and we chat for a few minutes. She then goes on television to thank her supporters and wish me well. Jack Long, the Democratic candidate, drops by to offer congratulations.

The extent of our victory becomes clear the next morning when the newspapers publish the town-by-town, county-by-county breakdown of election results: 55 percent of the vote to Sanders, 32 percent to Sweetser, 9 percent to Long. We won in every county in the state and nearly every town. Who could have imagined it? An Independent victory—much less a sweep—is rare. So rare that when *USA Today* published the nationwide tallies for congressional races, the copy under Vermont read: "At Large—56%, Democrat Jack Long—9%, Republican Susan Sweetser—33%." Apparently, "Independent" is not a category in the paper's database.

The newspaper in front of me says that "Sanders is the longest-serving Independent ever elected to Congress, according to Garrison Nelson, a political science professor and an expert on Congressional history." Gary, who teaches at the University of Vermont, knows about these things.

That's what he studies. Who would have believed it? Thank you, Vermont.

But this had been a tough race, far more difficult than the final election results indicate. Newt Gingrich and the House Republican leadership had "targeted" this election, and spent a huge sum of money trying to defeat me. Some of the most powerful Republicans in the country came to Vermont to campaign for Sweetser, including Majority Leader Dick Armey, Republican national chairman Haley Barbour, presidential candidate Steve Forbes, House Budget chairman John Kasich, and Republican convention keynote speaker Susan Molinari. As chairman of the House Progressive Caucus, a democratic socialist, and a leading opponent of their "Contract with America," I've been a thorn in their side for some time. They wanted me out—badly.

My campaign was also targeted by corporate America. A group of major corporations organized by the U.S. Chamber of Commerce, the National Association of Manufacturers, and the National Federation of Independent Businesses put me at the top of their "hit list" and poured tens of thousands of dollars into the state to sponsor negative and dishonest TV ads, as well as a statewide mailing. By the end of the campaign Vermonters were watching four different TV ads attacking me.

The wealthiest people in Vermont went deep into their pockets for my Republican opponent. They wrote out dozens of $1,000 checks (the legal maximum) and attended $500-a-plate functions. We also took on the National Rifle Association (NRA), the National Right to Work

Organization, and other right-wing and big money organizations. Never before had the ruling class of Vermont and the nation paid quite so much attention to a congressional race in the small state of Vermont—a state with just one representative.

By contrast, as an Independent, my campaign ran without the support or infrastructure of a major political party. There were no campaign contributions from our "central office" in Washington, no "coordinated campaigns" with other candidates, no photo-ops with a presidential candidate at the local headquarters, no votes from families with a long and proud record of commitment to our party's ideals. We had to fight for every vote that we got. And that's what we did.

We rose to the occasion and ran the best campaign that we had for many years—perhaps ever. Our coalition—of unions, women's organizations, environmental groups, senior citizens, and low-income people—had done a terrific job. We raised close to a million dollars, received over 20,000 individual contributions, distributed by hand over 100,000 pieces of literature, made tens of thousands of phone calls, and sent out over 130,000 pieces of mail. The campaign staff was fantastic, our volunteers dedicated—and it all came together on Election Day.

Obviously, this book is more than a manual on running a successful congressional campaign. It is a political biography. It talks about some of the victories that I and my co-workers in Vermont have had, but also about a lot of *unsuccessful* campaigns and derailed ventures. (Given the state of the left in America, how could it be otherwise?)

This is a book about hopes and dreams that will not be realized in our lifetimes. It is about the fragility of democracy in America, a nation in which the majority of people do not know the name of their congressional representative and over half the people no longer vote. It is about a political system in which a tiny elite dominates both parties—and much of what goes on in Washington—through financial largesse.

Here is a story of corporate greed and contempt for working people, of private agendas masquerading as the public good and corporate America's betrayal of workers in its drive for galactic profits. It describes a national media, owned by large corporations, which increasingly regards news as entertainment, insults the intelligence of American citizens daily, and is even further removed from the reality of everyday life than the average politician.

And Vermont. This is a book about the great state of Vermont—my favorite place in the world—and about our "big city," Burlington, with 40,000 people. It visits our small towns, where most Vermonters live, and drops by our county fairs and our parades to look at the kind of special relationship that exists between people in this small state.

It is about my eight years as mayor of Burlington, and how the progressive movement there helped make that city one of the most exciting, democratic, and politically conscious cities in America. Yes! Democracy can work. It is about the United States Congress, the good members and the not so good. It examines the two major political parties—neither of which comes close to representing the needs of working people—and the frustrations and successes of helping to create an independent progressive political movement. It reviews some of the battles in which I've participated—for sane priorities in our federal budget, for a national health care system guaranteeing health care for all, for a trade policy that represents the needs of working people rather than multinational corporations, for an end to corporate welfare, and for the protection of programs that sustain the weakest and most vulnerable among us.

Most of all, this book is about the struggle to maintain a vision of economic and social justice, and the optimism necessary to keep that vision alive.

It goes without saying that I never would have become mayor of Burlington, Vermont, or a U.S. congressman without the help of dozens of close friends and co-workers who have worked at my side for many, many years. They have energized me and sustained me. Thanks to all of them.

1

You Have to Begin Somewhere

May 20, 1996. I'm tired. It was too hot last night and I didn't sleep well. All night a raccoon chattered in the attic of the house, finally waking me up for good at 6:30 a.m., after only four hours' sleep. All night I worried about the impact of Dick Armey's visit to the state of Vermont.

Armey, Newt Gingrich's number-two man and the type of reactionary who makes even Gingrich look like a liberal, came to Vermont to endorse Susan Sweetser, my opponent in the upcoming congressional election. More importantly, he came to raise money for her. Sweetser probably made a big mistake by inviting him, since Armey, the majority leader in the House, epitomizes the congressional right wing that is every day sinking lower in the public's estimation. About thirty Vermonters demonstrated at the hotel where Armey was speaking at a $500-a-plate dinner. They are not great fans of the Gingrich-Armey "Contract with America."

The article in the *Burlington Free Press*, the largest paper in the state, gave decent coverage to the demonstrators' protest against the savagery of the Republican cuts in Congress. The press coverage raised important issues about the Republican agenda, with its attacks on the poor, the elderly, and women, and in doing so tied Sweetser to that unpopular agenda. It even quoted someone from the local chapter of the National Organization of Women (NOW), a definite plus. Still, Sweetser ended up raising $30,000 in one night, which is a helluva lot of money, especially in a small state like Vermont.

Sweetser had advertised the Armey event as a "private briefing by the Majority Leader." I wondered if Armey was going to share his wisdom with rich Vermont Republicans about how we should eliminate Social Security, Medicare, Medicaid, and the concept of the minimum wage, ideas he had voiced in the past. Or maybe he was just going to talk about the "Republican Revolution." In any case, in Vermont $500 is a lot of money for dinner. I hope these rich folks enjoyed themselves.

I feel in my gut that this is going to be a very, very tough campaign. I won the last election by only three points, and Sweetser is much better organized than my previous opponent. She has started her campaign much earlier and is going to raise a lot more money than he did. I also fear that it will be a nasty campaign, with personal attacks that will become increasingly ugly. It's going to be a brutal six months, and frankly I'm not looking forward to it.

What is really distressing is not only the negative campaigning—the lies and distortions that have already begun—but the enormous amount of time I am going to have to spend raising money and dealing with campaign operations, rather than doing the work I was elected to do in Congress. Sweetser began her campaign in *November*— less than halfway into my two-year term. That's crazy. That means that I have to keep my mind on an election for twelve months, rather than focusing on my real work.

The last couple of weeks I played a leading role in opposing the Republican Defense Authorization Bill, which supplied $13 billion *more* for defense than Clinton's budget had allocated. And Clinton's budget was already way too high. But now, instead of concentrating on the important issues facing Vermont and America, I will have to devote more and more energy to the campaign. I am going to have to start getting on the phone and raising money. I'm going to have to think about polling, and TV ads, and a campaign staff. I'm going to have to make sure that we don't repeat the many mistakes that we made in the last campaign. Basically, I'm going to have to be more *political*. It's too early for that, and I don't like it.

Most people don't realize how far Newt Gingrich, Rush Limbaugh, and their friends have shifted the debate about where the country should be moving. In terms of the defense budget, 75 House Democrats—out of 197— supported the outrageous boost in military expenditures. Of course, almost all of the Republicans (including those fierce "deficit hawks") backed the increase. The Cold War is over, we spend many times more than all of our "enemies" combined and, with very little fanfare, the defense budget is significantly raised.

In the Armed Forces Committee, the vote for increased military spending was almost unanimous. Only two members, Ron Dellums and Lane Evans, out of the fifty-five members of the committee, voted against it. That's pathetic. A little pork for my district, a little pork for yours—and taxpayers end up spending tens of billions more than is needed.

Ditto for the intelligence budget. Major Owens of New York, Barney Frank of Massachusetts, and I have been trying to cut the CIA and other intelligence agency budgets for the last five years. This year, while introducing an amendment to trim their budget by 10 percent, I read into the record a *New York Times* article that described how the National Reconnaissance Office, one of the larger intelligence agencies, had *lost* $4 billion. That's right. They lost the money. They simply could not account for $4 billion, and their financial records were a complete shambles. No problem. The intelligence agencies got their increase anyhow.

Meanwhile, the Republican Congress, with many Democrats in agreement, are cutting back on every social program that people need—for the elderly, for children, for the sick and disabled, for the homeless, for the poor. That's called "getting our priorities straight."

I always feel anxious at the beginning of a campaign, but I feel more so this time. It's bad enough to be on the hit list of Gingrich and Armey, and to have the chairman of the Republican National Committee come to Vermont to announce he will give Sweetser the maximum allowable under the law, $153,000. What is most worrying, however, is that we progressives are not generating the excitement and support we need. That's the situation even in Vermont, where independent progressive politics is as advanced as any place in the country.

I have no illusions. This is my fifth race for Congress. I lost in 1988, won in 1990, '92, '94. People are not as excited as they were when I first ran. "Reelect Bernie—Again" is not an especially stirring slogan. And there simply aren't enough progressives committed to *making* the electoral struggle. The activities of most progressives revolve around specific issues and action groups. Many are not really in touch with their communities, nor do they appreciate the hard work involved in winning a congressional seat, a governorship, or even a mayoralty. Theory and ideas are exciting, but the practical work of capturing and holding public office—that's another story. So I'm concerned about running into the same problem we saw two years ago: lack of motivation among our core supporters.

One difficulty we're up against is that, to a large degree, modern American politics is about image and technique. In case you haven't noticed, elections do not have much to do with the burning issues facing our society. Ideas. Vision. Analysis. Give me a break! Most campaigns are about thirty-second TV ads, getting out the vote, polling, and reaching undecided voters.

It is six months before the election, and the Republicans have already done their focus groups. How do I know? I can hear it in their "message," which they repeat over and over again like a mantra: "Bernie Sanders is ineffective. Bernie Sanders is out of touch. Bernie Sanders is a left-wing extremist. Bernie Sanders rants and raves on the House floor and still no one listens to him. Susan Sweetser, on the other

hand, is a sensible moderate who can work with everyone." They think that's how they can beat me. Maybe.

It is very frustrating that, because modern electoral politics is driven by technique, one needs more and more
sophisticated "experts" in order to compete in the big
league of congressional campaigns. But how far does one
go in this direction? Was I elected to Congress as the first
Independent in forty years so that I could hire a slick
Washington insider consultant who will tell me what to say
and do? Not very likely. Am I going to be shaped and
molded by a Washington insider? Not while I have a breath
in my body.

On the other hand, is it against some law of nature for a
progressive and democratic socialist to present effective
television ads, or is that just something that Republicans
and Democrats are allowed to do? No. In my view we
should do our TV well. Shouldn't we be prepared to
respond immediately to TV ads from my opponent which
distort my record? Yes. Are we betraying the cause of
socialism because we don't communicate with mimeo-
graphed leaflets and pictures of Depression-era workers in
overalls and caps? No. The world has changed, and it's
appropriate to use the tools that are available.

Still, I have reservations. From my first day in Vermont
politics, I prided myself on never once having gone to an
outside consultant. We did everything within the state of
Vermont, everything "in-house," usually in *my* house. You
should have seen how we wrote the radio ads—around my
kitchen table. John Franco, a former Assistant City Attorney
in Burlington, loud, brilliant, occasionally vulgar. George

Thabault—my assistant when I was mayor, imaginative, funny. David Clavelle, a local printer who had also worked in my administration. Huck Gutman and Richard Sugarman—college professors. Jane and me. Quite a crew. A helluva way to write a radio ad.

As for our television ads, we always went with my close friends and wonderful Burlington filmmakers, Jimmy Taylor and Barbara Potter. They were always good, sometimes brilliant, and they knew Vermont. My wife, Jane, who is the most visual person that I know, was also in the middle of things. In 1990, when I won my first congressional race, Jimmy, Barbara, and Jane produced an ad that received rave reviews. It was taped in Jimmy and Barbara's living room in Burlington. For two hours, with the camera pointed straight at my face, Barbara and I chatted informally about why I was involved in politics and what issues were of greatest concern to me. Jimmy and Barbara then edited the content down, and we aired a five-minute spot.

At a time when the vast majority of TV commercials were thirty seconds or less, this ad was not only well received for its straightforward focus on the issues, but for the novelty of its length. Later, we cut the ad into one-minute and thirty-second sections, reinforcing what the voters had already learned from the original.

In 1990, local talent was enough. It helped us win an election that most people thought we would lose. And it was more than effective in 1992 and '94. But now, in 1996, we are taking on the Republican National Committee, probably the most sophisticated political organization in the world, with money to burn. I know that we are not as prepared for the Republican assault as we should be, that we are facing the fight of our lives and we need all the help we can get.

So, for the first time, I went out of state to a real, grown-up "consultant." I figured that we really didn't have to do what they said, but that it wouldn't hurt to listen. But more on that later.

Plainfield, Vermont, fall 1971. I had just moved from Stannard, a tiny town in that remote section of Vermont we call the Northeast Kingdom, and was living in Burlington, which, with less than 40,000 inhabitants, is the state's largest city. I had originally come to Vermont in 1964 for the summer, and permanently settled there in 1968. Jim Rader, a friend from my student days at the University of Chicago, whose acquaintance I renewed in Vermont, mentioned to me that the Liberty Union Party was holding a meeting at Goddard College in Plainfield. I'd heard of the Liberty Union, a small peace-oriented third party that had run candidates in Vermont's previous election. Jim's information rattled around in my brain for a few days, and I ended up going to the Plainfield meeting.

Why did I go? I really don't know. I had been active in radical politics at the University of Chicago, where I was involved in the civil rights and peace movements, and had worked very briefly for a labor union. I grew up in a lower-middle-class home in Brooklyn, New York, and knew what it was like to be in a family where lack of money was a constant source of tension and unhappiness.

My father worked hard as a paint salesman—day after day, year after year. There was always enough money to put food on the table and to buy a few extras, but never enough to fulfill my mother's dream of moving out of our three-and-a-half-room apartment and into a home of our own. Almost every major household purchase—a bed, a couch, drapes—would be accompanied by a fight between my parents over whether or not we could afford it. On one occasion I made the mistake of buying the groceries that my mother wanted at a small, local store rather than at the supermarket where the prices were lower. I received, to say the least, a rather emotional lecture about wise shopping and not wasting money.

I was a good athlete, and there was always enough money for a baseball glove, sneakers, track shoes, and a football helmet—but usually not quite of the quality that some of the other kids had. While I had my share of hand-me-downs, there was enough money for decent clothes, but only after an enormous amount of shopping around to get the "best buy." At a very young age I learned that lack of money and economic insecurity can play a pivotal role in determining how one lives life. That's a lesson I've never forgotten.

When I was graduating James Madison High School in Brooklyn, New York, I applied for admission into college. My father had his doubts. He had dropped out of high school in Poland and come to this country as a young man, worked hard all of his life and, with vivid memories of the Depression, wondered whether a solid job after high school wasn't a safer route than spending four more years as a student. My mother, who had graduated high school in the Bronx, disagreed and thought it important that I go to college.

My parents always voted Democratic, as did virtually every other family in our Jewish neighborhood, but they were basically nonpolitical. My family went to only one political meeting that I can recall, when Adlai Stevenson spoke at my elementary school, P.S. 197, during one of his presidential campaigns. It was my brother, Larry, who introduced me to political ideas. He became chairman of the Young Democrats at Brooklyn College and, fulfilling his sibling duties, dragged me to some of his meetings. More importantly, he was a voracious reader and brought all kinds of books and newspapers into the house, which he discussed with me.

I spent one year at Brooklyn College and four years at the University of Chicago, from which I graduated with a BA in 1964. I got through college with student loans and grants and through part-time work. I was not a good student. I took some time off from my studies when a dean suggested that perhaps I should "evaluate" my commitment to higher education. The truth is, though, that I learned a lot more from my out-of-class activities than I did through my formal studies. At the university I became a member of the Congress of Racial Equality (CORE), the Student Peace Union (SPU), and the Young People's Socialist League (YPSL). I participated in civil rights activities related to ending segregation in Chicago's school system and in housing, and I marched against the proliferation of nuclear weapons. I also worked, very briefly, for a trade union, the United Packinghouse Workers. At the end of my junior year I worked in a mental hospital in California as part of a project for the American Friends Service Committee.

While coursework didn't interest me all that much, I read everything I could get my hands on—except what I was required to read for class. The University of Chicago has one of the great libraries in America, and I spent a lot of time burrowed deep in the "stacks"—the basement area where most of the books were stored. I read mostly about American and European history, philosophy, socialism, and psychology. Among many other writers, I read Jefferson, Lincoln, Fromm, Dewey, Debs, Marx, Engels, Lenin, Trotsky, Freud, and Reich. I also discovered the periodicals room.

In any case, there I was on a beautiful fall day in 1971 in a room full of strangers at a meeting of a group called the Liberty Union.

When I arrived, I soon discovered that the purpose of this meeting was to nominate candidates for the U.S. Senate and the U.S. House of Representatives. Vermont's senior senator, Winston Prouty, had died on September 10, 1971, and the state's lone congressman, Robert Stafford, had decided to give up his House seat to run for the open Senate post in a special election to be held in January. That left two positions vacant, with no incumbents contesting either race.

The small Liberty Union Party was not exactly overflowing with individuals who were interested in running for the two seats. So, full of enthusiasm for what I believed was right and just, I raised my hand and offered my views on education, the economy, and the war in Vietnam. An hour later, I had won the nomination as the Liberty Union candidate for the open Senate seat. Talk about grassroots democracy! That meeting also allowed me to meet two life-long progressives who have remained close friends ever since, Dick and Betty Clark of Chittenden.

When I say "won" I am being overly generous to myself. I was chosen as the candidate unanimously because there was no competition. By day's end, I had embarked on the first political campaign of my life. Together with Doris Lake, who was selected as the candidate for the House, I was to present Vermont voters with a political perspective from outside of the two-party system.

At the beginning of the campaign I participated in my first ever radio broadcast—a talk show in Burlington. And what a show it was. I was so nervous that my knees shook, literally bouncing uncontrollably against the table. The sound engineer frantically waved his arms at me through the glass partition between the studio and the control room. The sound of the shaking table was being picked up by the microphone. A strange thumping noise traversed the airwaves as the Liberty Union candidate for the U.S. Senate began his political career. And the few calls that came in expressed no doubt that this career was to be short-lived. "Who *is* this guy?" one of the listeners asked.

Despite such inauspicious beginnings, I enjoyed the experience of running for office very much. What excited me most was the opportunity to express to the people of Vermont views that many of them had not heard before. Although Vermont is a very small rural state, it has dozens of radio stations, eleven daily newspapers, and over thirty weekly newspapers. As it turned out, much of the local media was delighted to report the strange opinions of the Liberty Union's candidate. Again and again during that summer and fall I stressed my opposition to the war in Vietnam, and articulated my belief in economic democracy and social justice.

My political opponents in Vermont often accuse me of being boring, of hammering away at the same themes. They're probably right. It has never made sense to me, then or now, that a tiny clique of people should have incredible wealth and power while most people have none. Justice is not a complicated concept, nor a "new" idea. Tragically, most politicians do not talk about the most serious issues facing our country, or the real causes of our problems. So I do. Over and over again. This drives the media and my opponents a bit crazy, but most Vermonters seem to appreciate that I address the issues most relevant to their lives. And should we ever achieve economic and social justice in this country, I promise that I'll write some new speeches.

Just prior to the 1970 election, the Banking Committee of the U.S. House of Representatives published a report documenting the degree to which large banks in America controlled many major corporations, exerting enormous economic influence over our society. (Little would I, or anyone else in Vermont, have believed then that twenty years later I would be a member of that committee.) I lugged that report all over the state, quoting from it extensively.

I used the publication to talk about the phenomenon of "interlocking directorates," showing how a handful of very powerful people were making decisions affecting one major sector of the economy after another. I contrasted the reality of corporate domination with the lives of ordinary working people—laborers, farmers, shop owners—who had little or no say over what happened to them on the job.

Time after time, I pointed out that such disparity in the distribution of wealth and decision-making power was not just unfair economically, but that without economic democracy it was impossible to achieve genuine political democracy. The message could be reduced to a simple formula: wealth = power, lack of money = subservience. How could we change that? How could we create a truly democratic society?

For me, one of the highlights of that campaign was the public debates I had with Republican congressman Robert Stafford and the Democratic candidate, State Representative Randy Major. More often than not, the audience was sympathetic to the views I expressed—especially the call for economic justice. Although I was the candidate of a minor party, people were listening to what I had to say and they often supported my position.

The lesson I learned from those debates and the audience response—a lesson that remains with me today—is that the ideas I was espousing were not "far out" or "fringe." Frankly, they were "mainstream." They were concepts that a majority of people would support, if they had an opportunity to hear them. In short, social justice was neither "radical" nor "un-American."

But another political fact became clear to me during this first campaign: the perpetual bane of American third parties.

"I fully agree with what you're saying, Bernie," someone in the audience would invariably tell me after a debate. "But I don't want to waste my vote on a third-party candidate." How many times over the years have I heard that view?

That first campaign also provided a good introduction to the role of the media in politics. It was an unforgettable experience. The Democratic candidate, State Representative Randy Major, was not widely known and was considered a long shot in our (then) very Republican Vermont. So Major devised a plan to attract media attention by "skiing around the state to meet the voters." It was a brilliant publicity gimmick, and it worked wonderfully. Throughout the campaign, people were talking about the skiing lawmaker.

In fact, far more press attention was paid to the condition of Major's ailing feet than the "issues" facing Vermont and the nation. Here I was, giving long-winded statements to a bored media about the major problems facing humanity, and the TV cameras were literally focused on Randy's blisters. It was "new," fast-breaking news. Would he be able to continue his ski effort the next day? Tune in and find out. In any case, neither my "in-depth analyses" nor Randy's skiing made much of a difference to the election outcome. In January 1972, Bob Stafford won the special election by thirty-one percentage points. Spending less than one thousand dollars, I came in a very distant third, with only 2 percent of the vote.

But if the truth be told, I was proud of the campaign that I had run. The low vote I got did not depress me. I understood that making political change was a long process, and that we had achieved an important kind of success. The

Liberty Union, with a few campaign workers and limited financial resources, had exposed tens of thousands of people to new perspectives. Some Vermonters were seeing politics beyond the prism of the two-party system.

Six months later, in the general election of 1972, I ran for governor of Vermont. During that campaign I naturally concentrated on the state and local issues that a governor deals with. The interest in my campaign increased but my percentage of the vote declined. This time, I ended up with only one percent. Now that's quite an experience—getting one percent of the vote. However, the issues that I and other Liberty Union candidates raised during that campaign helped play an important part in the election results and eventually resulted in changes in public policy.

Thomas Salmon, a Democrat, upset the Republican candidate, Fred Hackett, and was elected as only the second Democratic governor in the state's history. During the campaign, Salmon very shrewdly and effectively picked up on two issues that the Liberty Union was fighting for: property tax reform and dental care for low-income children. Under the Salmon administration, a popular property tax rebate program was established, as well as a "tooth fairy" program that went a long way toward improving dental care for kids. Despite our paltry one percent, the Liberty Union made an impact on major legislation.

1972 was the year Richard Nixon won a landslide victory over George McGovern. During that campaign, the Liberty Union threw its support behind the presidential candidate of the People's Party, Dr. Benjamin Spock, the world-famous pediatrician. A delightful man, Spock campaigned in

Vermont on several occasions. Because he was one of the "major" candidates for president, Spock was provided with Secret Service protection and was guarded in exactly the same way as Nixon and McGovern. Some twenty-five agents watched over him, in shifts, twenty-four hours a day.

As the Liberty Union candidate for governor, and the head of our ticket, I was given the responsibility of meeting Spock at the airport when he came to Vermont. I was broke at the time, and needed to borrow a few bucks to put gas into my old VW bug just to get there. At the airport, after convincing the Secret Service that I really was a candidate for governor, I was able to welcome Spock to Vermont.

Later in the afternoon, Spock, I, and other Liberty Union candidates walked down Church Street, Burlington's main thoroughfare, and campaigned under the very watchful eyes of the Secret Service. I remember the incongruity of it all. Here I was, without a dime in my pocket, about to get one percent of the vote, being protected by a dozen well-armed agents of the federal government.

During that trip, Spock and I spoke at Johnson State College. In the midst of his speech, which was very well attended, a student ran into the auditorium and screamed out, "Is there a doctor in the house? There's been a car accident." Some drunken students had driven their car off the side of the road, and it overturned. Can you imagine their surprise when they found Dr. Spock and the U.S. Secret Service tending to their needs? Probably sobered them right up.

I ran for the U.S. Senate again in 1974. That election, in which I was vying for the seat left open when the venerable

George Aiken retired, was a very close, hard-fought contest. While most of the state focused on the major party candidates—Patrick Leahy, a Democratic state's attorney from Chittenden County, and Richard Mallary, the incumbent Republican member of the House—I doubled my highest previous vote total, now reaching 4 percent. Leahy pulled off a major upset in that election and became the first Democrat ever elected to the U.S. Senate from Vermont.

1974 was a very exciting year for the Liberty Union, and the high point of its existence. Michael Parenti, who had been dismissed from his teaching post at the University of Vermont because of his antiwar activities, ran an excellent campaign for the U.S. House and received 7 percent of the vote against Republican Jim Jeffords (who won) and a Democrat—an extraordinary showing for a third-party candidate. Michael, who remains a good friend, eventually left the state and has since become an outstanding progressive writer.

The Liberty Union also put up strong candidates that year for governor, lieutenant governor, and for a number of seats in the state legislature—and many of them did well. Martha Abbott, our candidate for governor, and Art DeLoy, our candidate for lieutenant governor, each received about 5 percent of the vote. Nancy Kaufman, a young attorney who was the Liberty Union candidate for attorney general, received over 6 percent. (Twenty years later, Martha Abbott was elected to the Burlington City Council as a Progressive, where she continues to play a leadership role in the progressive movement.)

In 1976, as the now "perennial candidate" of the Liberty Union, I ran for governor again, this time against Republican

Richard Snelling and Democrat Stella Hackel. With a solid performance in a prime-time television debate and greatly increased name recognition, I ended up with 6 percent of the vote. An increase to be sure, and an all-time high for me, but a long way from victory.

After that campaign I decided to leave the Liberty Union Party. It was a painful decision. I was proud of what a small number of people could accomplish in terms of running good campaigns, fighting utility rate increases, and supporting striking workers. We had done extremely well with limited resources, had brought a number of serious issues before the public that otherwise would not have been aired, and we affected public policy. With almost no money, our candidates received as much as 8 percent of the vote in three-party statewide elections. Further, since many of our candidates were women, we played a role in breaking down sexism in statewide politics. We also provided excellent political opportunities for working people and low-income citizens. One of our candidates for lieutenant governor, Art DeLoy, was the leader of one of Vermont's largest unions— the first time in memory that an active trade unionist had run for office.

But as is often the case for small third parties, we were not attracting new members, new energy, or new leadership. Virtually all party responsibilities continued to rest with a handful of dedicated activists—including me. Enough was enough. My political career was over. With politics behind me, I set out to make a living and began building, reasonably successfully, a small business in educational filmstrips. I wrote, produced, and sold filmstrips on

New England history for elementary schools and high schools. It was a lot of fun. In the process, I improved my writing skills and learned something about photography, marketing, and door-to-door salesmanship. I also met a lot of fine educators around Vermont.

In 1979, after discovering that the vast majority of college students I spoke to had never heard of Eugene Victor Debs, I produced a thirty-minute video on his life and ideas. Debs was the founder of the American Socialist Party and six-time candidate for president. During his lifetime, Debs had a profound impact on American politics and the lives of American workers. Many of his ideas about trade unionism laid the foundation for the growth of the CIO in the 1930s and '40s. The Debs video was sold and rented to colleges throughout the country, and we also managed to get it on public television in Vermont. Folkways Records also produced the soundtrack of the video as a record.

Debs died in 1926, but his vision and the example of his life still resonate today. Unfortunately, his ideas remain sufficiently dangerous for them not to be widely taught in schools or discussed in the mass media. He fought to achieve a truly democratic society in which working people, not big money, would control the economic and political life of the nation. He founded the American Railway Union and led a bitter strike against some of the most powerful forces in the country. He believed in international worker solidarity and spent years in jail for his opposition to World War I. In 1920, while in jail for opposing that war, he ran for president—receiving close to one million votes. Eugene Victor Debs remains a hero of mine. A plaque commemorating him hangs on the wall in my Washington office.

Although I now had a business career, in an important sense my political work had not ceased. I was educating people, not from a podium or in a radio interview, but by resurrecting the heroes of our nation's political past. The Debs video was a success, and I was now beginning to think about a video series on other American radicals—Mother Jones, Emma Goldman, Paul Robeson, and other extraordinary Americans who most young people have never heard of. For better or worse, my media production career came to end in 1980.

But forward now to 1996, when aspects of the campaign are worrying me deeply, and getting me depressed. Too many questions are unanswered, and there are too many loose ends.

How do we relate to Vermont Democrats? In Congress, I chair the fifty-two-member House Progressive Caucus, which has fifty-one Democrats and me, people with whom I have an excellent relationship. But things are different in Vermont, where, among others, Governor Howard Dean is a moderate-to-conservative Democrat.

How do we relate to President Clinton, who is rapidly moving to the right? Should we establish links with his Vermont campaign? How should I respond to the Ralph Nader presidential campaign? Nader is a personal friend and an exemplary progressive, and his supporters have asked me to endorse his candidacy.

What should the progressive movement in Vermont do for this campaign? In addition to my own race for reelection, should we put up a full slate of candidates for office? Should we at least run a candidate for governor?

In Burlington, Progressives have won seven out of the last eight mayoral elections. I was mayor from 1981 to 1989; Peter Clavelle from 1989 to 1993. After losing to a Republican in '93, Clavelle was reelected in 1995. That same year, Progressives also took control of the City Council. But how do we strengthen the progressive movement throughout the state, beyond Burlington? We have had minimal electoral success in legislative races. Over the last six years, two or three Progressives have held seats in the legislature. Terry Bouricious, who served on the Burlington City Council for ten years and has worked with me over the last twenty, was elected in 1990, '92, and '94. Dean Corren was elected in '92 and '94, and Tom Smith, also a former Burlington city councilor, was elected in '90 and '92. But although we have strong pockets of support in communities around the state, never has a Progressive or Independent from outside Burlington captured a legislative post.

These are a few of the questions that I and other progressives are wrestling with as we begin organizing in earnest for the campaign.

In terms of who to support for president, the choice is really not difficult. I am certainly not a big fan of Bill Clinton's politics. As a strong advocate of a single-payer health care system, I opposed his convoluted health care reform package. I have helped lead the opposition to his trade policies, which represent the interests of corporate America and which are virtually indistinguishable from the views of George Bush and Newt Gingrich. I opposed his bloated military budget, the welfare reform bill that he signed, and the so-called Defense of Marriage Act, which he supported. He has been weak on campaign finance reform and has caved in far too often on the environment. Bill Clinton is a moderate Democrat. I'm a democratic socialist.

Yet, without enthusiasm, I've decided to support Bill Clinton for president. Perhaps "support" is too strong a word. I'm planning no press conferences to push his candidacy, and will do no campaigning for him. I *will* vote for him, and make that public.

Why? I think that many people do not perceive how truly dangerous the political situation in this country is today. If Bob Dole were to be elected president and Gingrich and the Republicans were to maintain control of Congress, we would see a legislative agenda unlike any in the modern history of this country. There would be an unparalleled war against working people and the poor, and political decisions would be made that could very well be irreversible.

Medicare and Medicaid would certainly be destroyed, and tens of millions more Americans would lose their health insurance. Steps would be taken to privatize Social Security, and the very existence of public education in America would be threatened. Serious efforts would be made to pass a constitutional amendment to ban abortion, affirmative action would be wiped out, and gay bashing would intensify. A flat tax would be passed, resulting in a massive shift in income from the working class to the rich, and all of our major environmental legislation would be eviscerated.

The Motor Voter bill would be repealed, and legislation making it *harder* for people to vote would be passed. Union-busting legislation would become law, the minimum wage would be abolished, and child labor would increase. Adults and kids in America would be competing for $3-an-hour jobs.

You think I'm kidding. You think I'm exaggerating. Well, I'm not. I work in Congress. I *listen* to these guys every day. They are very serious people. And the folks behind them, the Christian Coalition, the NRA, the Heritage Foundation, and others, are even crazier than they are. My old friend Dick Armey is not some wacko member of Congress laughed at by his colleagues. He is the Majority Leader of the U.S. House of Representatives. Check out his views. No. I do not want Bob Dole to be president. I'm voting for Bill Clinton.

Do I have confidence that Clinton will stand up for the working people of this country—for children, for the elderly, for the folks who are hurting? No, I do not. But a Clinton victory could give us some time to build a movement, to develop a political infrastructure to protect what needs protecting, and to change the direction of the country.

This is more than utopian fantasy. First of all, there are some promising developments in organized labor. Several months ago the Progressive Caucus met with John Sweeney, the new president of the AFL-CIO, who told us that there

will be a greater AFL-CIO commitment to union organizing, and more energy and resources spent in the political
process. This has been long needed and is a very welcome
development.

The great political crisis in American society is the quies-
cence of working people. If 5 percent of unionized workers
became politically active, we could radically transform
economic and social policy in this country. Today, most
low-income workers do not vote, and many have very little
understanding of the relationship of politics to their lives.
The average American worker has come to accept that he
or she has no power on the job. The company is moving the
plant to Mexico. How can I stop it? The CEO earns 173
times more than the average worker. Who am I to contest
management prerogatives? Corporations are asking for a
give-back in health care, despite record profits. What
authority do I have to challenge big capital? In our "democracy," the vast majority of working people feel helpless—*are*
helpless given the current political structure—to protect
their economic interests or chart their future.

If you have no influence over your own working conditions, what kind of power can you have over the economics
and politics of the entire country? Why bother to vote?
Why bother to pay attention to politics? And millions don't.
In Vermont and throughout the country, the rich ante up
$500 or $5,000 at a fundraising event to support the candidate who will represent their interests. Meanwhile, the
majority of the poor and working people don't even vote.
No wonder the rich get richer and everyone else gets poorer.
Are we really living in a democracy?

Certainly, some of the more powerful unions, with entrenched bureaucracies and leaders disinclined to rock the boat, have contributed to this malaise. For many years, the AFL-CIO, under Lane Kirkland, was extremely conservative and inactive. A few years ago I was asked by some union leaders to speak with Kirkland at a dinner during the AFL-CIO convention in Florida. My mission was to radicalize him. I tried. I didn't succeed. "Lane, what about a national AFL-CIO cable TV station which could educate working people about what's going on in our society and give them information they never get on commercial TV?" I asked. "Can't be done," he replied. "What about more organizing efforts? What about more political activity?" Not much of a response. Kirkland impressed me as an intelligent and thoughtful man with no energy or interest in making change. He was totally resigned to the status quo.

During the spring, 300 Vermont workers came out to hear Rich Trumka, former president of the United Mine Workers and new secretary-treasurer of the AFL-CIO. He gave a rousing speech, which was very well received. The new president of the Vermont AFL-CIO, Ron Pickering of the Paperworkers, is doing an excellent job in reactivating the union movement in Vermont. One of the main goals of the "Sanders for Congress" campaign is to involve more and more working people in the political process. I look forward to working with Ron as the campaign progresses. We're going to receive substantial financial help from the unions, but we want rank-and-file grassroots support as well.

In June, there was a founding convention in Cleveland

of the Labor Party, an organization which, at its inception, was supported by labor bodies representing over a million American workers. These union workers see no fundamental difference between the Democratic and Republican parties—and are starting a new party. It was an important political event, yet it received virtually no media coverage. Not one word in the *New York Times*, the *Washington Post*, or the *Wall Street Journal*. Hey! Only representatives of a million workers coming together to form a new political party. And now for another story about our favorite billionaire, Ross Perot, and *his* third party.

The Labor Party convention grew out of several years of organizing by people from the Oil, Chemical and Atomic Workers, the United Electrical Workers, and other progressive unions. These union activists have long understood that negotiating a good contract for their workers is only part of their job, and that working people will continue to get the short end of the stick unless we have a government that represents *their* interests. The slogan of the Labor Party is, "The bosses have two parties. We need one of our own." Hard to argue with that.

Politicians often claim that they are running for office because "the people urged me to do it." This is rarely true. But in late 1980, it was true for me. Well, not exactly "the people." It was my good friend Richard Sugarman.

Richard, talk-show aficionado, baseball statistician, brilliant philosopher, and professor of religion at the University of Vermont, suggested that I run for mayor of Burlington against the five-term incumbent Democrat, Gordon

Paquette. In Richard, you could not have found a more unlikely political adviser. As a Hasidic Jew, professor, and writer, he is deeply involved in the interpretation of sacred texts; as a philosopher, he is immersed in the abstract thought of Plato, Nietzsche, Sartre, and Levinas. But he also has a very pragmatic side. Richard is one of the sharpest political observers I have ever known.

His idea, however, seemed more than a little farfetched. "Richard, why should I run for office when I'm happily retired from politics? How could I possibly win against an entrenched political machine? And what the hell would I do if, by some miracle, I actually won?" Those were only a few of my questions as he dragged me into the Burlington city clerk's office in late fall 1980.

With the help of an employee in the office, Richard and I discovered the musty binder that contained the official Burlington election results from way back when. We went through and analyzed the 1976 gubernatorial election results. Patiently, he showed me a ward-by-ward breakdown of the election results, indicating how city residents had voted. Richard had a point to make: even though I received only 6 percent of the vote statewide, in Burlington I carried 12 percent, and in the two working-class wards of the city, over 16 percent.

On the basis of this showing, Richard reasoned that if all of our energy were concentrated on my hometown, we might win the upcoming mayoral election. For days and nights, friends and I argued about the wisdom of running and, if I did run, what kind of strategy made sense. Finally, convinced that for the first time I might have a real chance not only to educate the public but actually win an election, I decided to run as an Independent. I collected signatures on nominating petitions, submitted them to the city clerk, and the campaign was on its way.

And what a campaign it was! Talk about coalitions. By the time Election Day rolled around, we had brought together leaders of the low-income community, college professors, the Burlington Patrolmen's Association, environmentalists, and conservative homeowners worried about rising property taxes.

This was not to be an "educational" campaign. The goal of this contest was to win. For this reason, the campaign was issue-oriented, focused on the most serious problems facing Vermont's largest city, problems ignored by city government. While I often placed these issues within the context of what was going on nationally, and made it clear that a fundamental change of priorities was needed at the national level, virtually all of my energy was spent addressing the concerns that faced the people of Burlington. I was running for mayor, not U.S. senator. The people of the city wanted to know how I would improve the quality of life at the local level if I became mayor. Those were the issues I addressed.

Our electoral strategy was straightforward, aimed at creating a broad-based, grassroots constituency. Starting with the low-income and working-class wards, I knocked on as many doors as possible. As I walked through the neighborhoods, I told people that I would do my best to represent those in the city who had long been locked out of City Hall. I listened to their concerns and supported their grievances. For instance, public housing tenants told me how unhappy they were with the ineffective leadership of the Burlington Housing Authority. They had almost no voice in decision making, maintenance was poor, and there were virtually no recreational activities for their children. In Lakeside, a working-class neighborhood in the south end, I walked a picket line with residents who had, for years, been asking the administration to repair an underpass that, in rainy weather, became impassable and left the entire neighborhood dangerously isolated from the rest of the city.

As I sat in kitchens and talked on front stoops in low-income neighborhoods, I heard the bitterness in their voices. They were well aware of the inequitable provision of municipal services. They knew that street and sidewalk paving, police protection, park maintenance, and snow clearing were less available to them than to upper-income neighborhoods. So I made alliances with neighborhood organizations in the low-income and working-class areas who believed, rightly, that their communities were not getting a fair shake from city government.

I tried to speak for those who had never had a voice in City Hall. Landlords in Burlington had all the power in tenant/landlord relations, so I pledged to the city's tenants that, for the first time, they would have a strong ally in the mayor's office. I championed the rights of tenants and came out in support of their fight for rent-control legislation.

One of my most widely noticed positions was strong opposition to a huge increase in the property tax proposed by Mayor Paquette. He calculated that with only token resistance (mine), he could slip the tax hike by without suffering any negative political effects. I kept stressing my opposition not only to this particular tax increase but also to the very concept of the property tax. Property taxes are highly regressive and hurt, in particular, low- and moderate-income citizens, especially senior citizens. During the campaign, I proposed that Burlington break its dependence on the property tax and develop a fair and progressive tax system to fund municipal services and local education. Day after day, door after door, I was pleasantly surprised by the kind of support I encountered. Either people were not being honest with me or we were going to do a lot better than the pundits expected. It turned out that Burlingtonians *were* honest.

Our campaign had a great deal of energy, but little sophistication. My campaign manager, Linda Niedweskie, an aspiring nutritionist who had recently graduated from college, had never before been involved in politics. Linda provided us with a strong sense of organization and kept everyone focused. Two low-income advocates, Dick Sartelle and John Bartlett, did a great job, and a number of former Liberty Union members, including John Franco and Terry Bouricious, also played active roles. David Clavelle, who had worked for a while for Senator Leahy, taught us how to make voter ID telephone calls. What a remarkable idea! Using the telephone for a campaign. None of us had thought of that. Together with a lot of volunteers who were energized by the remote but real possibility that we could win and develop a radically new politics for the city, we worked to canvass every home and apartment in Burlington.

The campaign itself functioned as a crash course in Burlington's problems and politics. In truth, I knew very little about Burlington city government. I had attended two Board of Aldermen meetings in my life—and had fallen asleep at one of them. They were boring. When the campaign began, I hadn't a clue where Ward 1 was, or the political difference between Wards 4 and 2. Not only did I have to become familiar with city problems and solutions, I had to learn to place those issues in a relevant context and devise viable solutions. In some ways, running for statewide office was easier than running for mayor because I was more familiar with the terrain of national and statewide politics.

Even though my campaign was geared toward lower- and middle-class people, a number of Burlington's upper-income citizens voted for me. One reason for this was that I attacked a plan to build high-rise condominiums on the city's waterfront. Burlington is a beautiful city, located on the eastern shore of Lake Champlain, with stunning vistas of the lake and New York's Adirondack mountains. A real estate developer had proposed building luxury high-rise condominiums along the choicest sections of the waterfront. When I vigorously opposed that project, many citizens concerned about the environment and preserving the natural beauty of the city decided that my candidacy was worth serious consideration. By the end of the campaign a local artist, Frank Hewitt, had designed an effective poster that boldly proclaimed, "Burlington is not for sale."

I spoke out against the planned expansion of the local hospital, primarily because it would burden the community with increased health care costs. But I also knew from going door to door that neighborhood residents were angry that the unnecessarily large expansion would replace a popular sledding hill with a large decked parking lot. So I stood up for local families who wanted children and past custom to count for more than cars and cement.

Again and again, in varying ways, our campaign reminded the people of Burlington that the incumbent mayor and his local Democratic machine were in cahoots with the downtown business community and irresponsible "pro-growth" forces, and out of touch with the concerns of the average citizen. My basic campaign message was that if I were elected mayor, I would open City Hall to *all* the people. I would run the city by responding to the best interests of working people, low-income people, and the middle class—the very folks who had largely been frozen out of the decision-making process.

But as it turned out, of all the issues I raised, the one that gave the greatest impetus to my candidacy was my support for municipal workers who were frustrated that the incumbent mayor and treasurer had refused, year after year, to negotiate in good faith with their unions.

The problem with a third-party or independent candidacy, as I had learned back in my Liberty Union days, was that although people will often agree with the candidate's position, they are skeptical of his or her "electability." So it was of major importance that, shortly before the election, the Burlington Patrolmen's Association endorsed my bid for mayor. They did so because I promised to listen to the concerns of cops on the beat and open serious labor negotiations with their union. In supporting my candidacy the police union and its leader, Joe Crepeau, showed enormous courage. If I lost (which most people expected) they would be even deeper in the city doghouse with the incumbent mayor.

Needless to say, their endorsement became a monumental campaign event and a major news story: a leftist populist, a former opponent of the war in Vietnam, had gained the support of the blue-collar forces of law and order! The coalition we had brought together—low-income people, hard-pressed working-class homeowners, environmentalists, renters, trade unionists, college students, professors, and now the police—reinforced each other in the belief that together we could win the election.

I cannot emphasize enough how important it was that we developed a "coalition politics." The way to rekindle hope in America, we learned in our small New England city, is to bring people together. After all, most people share things in common with their neighbors. They work hard to make a living, they are concerned about their children, they want to drink clean water and to feel safe in their homes. Reminding ordinary people that government can and should work for them, speak with their voice, is the great strength of coalition politics, and the hope, I believe, for America's future.

Being a congressman is tougher than you think. And it's even tougher than that when you're a serious legislator, trying to accomplish things in Washington while, at the same time, you're running for reelection in a difficult campaign. And it's even tougher than *that* when you're an Independent, taking on half the world in D.C. and the other half of the world back home. (Then again, some of my friends say I have a tendency to exaggerate.)

I come home to Vermont every weekend. That's where I live. I'm always surprised when people assume that I live in Washington. No way. I *work* in Washington. I *live* in Vermont. During the six years that I've been in Congress, I've spent two weekends in D.C. I come home to Vermont for several reasons. That's where my family and friends are. Vermont is where I want to spend my time. I couldn't be a good congressman if I weren't in constant touch with my friends, neighbors, and constituents. It's not just the many town meetings and conferences I hold or the schools and meetings that I attend. It's the walk downtown. It's the ride in the country. It's getting a sense of the weather. It's seeing the local papers rather than reading faxes. It's watching the local TV. It's getting a *feeling* of what's going on, and what people are thinking about.

I know members, especially some who have been in Congress for a while, who believe that they *live* in D.C. They go back to their districts now and then. But their hearts are in Washington. That's dangerous. When that happens you run the very real danger of forgetting where you come from, and what you're supposed to be doing.

There are great differences between being a mayor and a congressman. A mayor is a big fish in a little pond. A congressman is one body out of 535 (not to mention the president). But the main difference to me is physical proximity. When you're a mayor, you're *always* home and on the job. In fact, the problem is you can't get away for a minute. The phone rings at your house at 4 a.m. because the snowplows have blocked somebody's driveway and she can't get to work. A neighbor collars you in the produce section of the grocery store to report his annoyance with a zoning ordinance. You're running around the city checking out the condition of the streets when it snows. You're talking to kids at the Teen Center. It's very different from being in Congress. In Congress, you may be working on a multibillion dollar issue that affects millions of people, but nobody back home knows what you're doing. And you don't even know what the weather is like.

In the middle of a campaign it seems that everything comes to the fore. All your neuroses, all your fears, all your weaknesses. You're *on* all the time, and you're often tired, stressed out, prone to make mistakes. And a mistake in a campaign can be very costly. And I am tired. The past two years have been very tough. It's one thing to criticize intellectually the policies of Gingrich and the right wing. It's another thing to be locked in the day-to-day struggle, to be in a committee meeting or on the floor of the House, and to see and feel the ugliness and irrationality of much of what goes on. It is depressing and debilitating. But now I'm beginning a campaign. It's time to go forward.

I remember when I began my reelection effort for mayor in 1983. I was absorbed in city issues and neglected the upcoming campaign. The first debate was held one afternoon in a radio station. I stayed too late at City Hall and came flying into the station just in time. I was unprepared for the event and did poorly. Getting beaten in that debate immediately jolted me into the real world of politics, and into understanding the significant difference between being an officeholder and a candidate. It was a lasting discovery. No matter how hard I work, no matter what I accomplish, somebody else will always want my job. That's democracy. Okay. Time to figure out how I get reelected. Don't worry about the last two years. Don't worry about being tired. Start moving forward in this campaign. Focus. Focus. Focus.

Phil Fiermonte, a former AFT union organizer and the head of my congressional outreach effort, keeps reminding me that we should begin to organize the campaign. "It's getting a little late, Bernie," he says. "We need money. We need a staff. Gotta get moving. It's going to take some time to get a good campaign manager." "Hey, Phil. You want to be campaign manager?" "No. Definitely not. I don't like campaigns. I'll help out, but I want to stay in the congressional office."

But deep down Phil knows that he is a doomed man. He will have to jump-start the campaign, work eighty hours a week, and deal with terrible pressure. I know all of the progressives in Vermont and Phil, by far, has the best organizational capabilities and temperament for the job. Further, he knows me well and tolerates my many foibles.

We briefly consider the possibility of hiring out of state, but dismiss the idea. You just can't put an ad in the *New York Times* saying, "Wanted. Campaign manager for the only Independent in Congress. Knowledge of democratic socialism and independent politics required. Familiarity with Vermont and rural life a must. Eighty hours a week.

Terrific responsibility. Low pay." Frankly, there aren't too many folks around who would respond to that ad. I'll stick with the Vermonter.

Phil, Jane, myself, and a few close friends discuss some of the immediate challenges. As we talk, I compile a list of the major concerns we face in the campaign. It looks like this:

MONEY

STAFF

STYLE

GUNS

MEDIA

MY HEALTH

OUR "MESSAGE"

To many people this list might seem like a strange hodge-podge. Political issues, fundraising, media strategy, and my personal concerns logically should be in separate catego-ries. But when you sit down to a political meal, you don't find meat on one platter and vegetables and potatoes in separate bowls. A campaign is like a stew. Everything is in one pot. All the issues are mixed up together.

Money

When Sweetser announced her candidacy in November, she refused to discuss campaign spending limits, which meant that her wealthy friends were going to supply her with a bundle. Last campaign, we raised over $700,000. This time we'll need more, probably $900,000, which is a lot considering that my campaigns are financed primarily from small individual contributions. We also receive PAC money from labor unions, senior citizen organizations, environmental, women's, and children's groups, but the bulk of our funds come from ordinary people with limited resources. Since we have been criticized in the past for raising too much money out of state (even though we always have many more Vermont individual contributors than any other candidate), we are determined to raise substantially more in Vermont. Our supporters don't have a lot of money and we can't hold $500-a-plate fundraisers. But we can do much better than in the past.

Staff

Finding people skilled in the intricacies of campaign work is more difficult than it sounds. Most people do not sit at home for a year and a half, waiting to work on a campaign. Sometimes you luck out and get experienced, mature people in between jobs. Sometimes you don't. One of the problems with our last campaign was that our staff was young and inexperienced and they didn't get along terribly well. They were all terrific and hard-working people, but there were clashes of personality. In fact, as I later learned, chairs occasionally went flying across the room. This time we wanted to hire a more mature and compatible staff.

Style

I had not run a good campaign in 1994, and when I assessed its weaknesses I had to acknowledge that it was me, not the staff, that was the major problem. My style of campaigning had been too passive. I had been reluctant to respond quickly and vigorously when I was attacked. My attitude was: "The people aren't going to believe this nonsense. They know what I stand for. I don't have to respond to every stupid criticism." Wrong. This time we would respond immediately and forcefully. Further, we would not allow ourselves to be on the defensive. My opponent had served four years in the state senate, and had a record. We would let Vermonters know about it.

Guns

During the 1994 campaign the National Rifle Association (NRA) had played a very forceful role against me. They distributed widely a "Bye, Bye, Bernie" bumper sticker, held press conferences and public meetings, placed radio ads, made phone calls—and it was effective. There is no question that we lost many working-class men in that election because we handled the gun issue badly.

Vermont is a rural state in which tens of thousands of people enjoy hunting and own guns. During hunting season thousands of kids go out with their fathers and mothers to hunt and enjoy the outdoors. Vermont is an "outdoor" state—and hunting is a key part of that way of life. I am pro-gun, and pro-hunting. But I don't believe that hunters need assault weapons and AK-47s to kill deer. I voted for the ban on assault weapons, which brought the wrath of the NRA down on me.

For this campaign, we devise a three-pronged strategy on the gun issue. First, according to a number of polls, the vast majority of Vermonters (and Americans) *support* the ban on assault weapons. Susan Sweetser's position—the straight NRA line, which is opposition to all gun control—is way out of touch with what Vermonters believe. We are going to make that clear. Second, we will bring into the campaign a number of hunters who support my position on the ban on assault weapons. Third, we will ask friends who *disagree* with the ban to publicly support my candidacy by stating that guns are only one issue among many. As one NRA friend told me, "You can't buy an AK-47 without a job. Let's get our priorities straight."

Media

For most of my political life I've had a problem with WCAX-TV, the largest television station in the state. Pure and simple, it's a Republican station. The owner of WCAX is a wealthy, conservative Republican and major contributor to the state party. Unsurprisingly, the news division often reflects his views. The station is not a right-wing wacko operation; many of its political stories are fair and accurate, and it has a number of good reporters. But overall, and in a consistent way, there is a very clear Republican bias to its reporting, which usually becomes more conspicuous as election time draws near. And I'm not the only target. Other Progressives, liberal Democrats, Senator Leahy—all have been skewered by WCAX at one time or another. Positive stories are ignored, negative stories are played up. There is no easy way of dealing with this. It's hard to win a fight against someone behind a TV camera. We need to keep thinking about it.

Health

In modern politics, the personal becomes the political whether we like it or not. And I am facing personal difficulties that could have troublesome implications for the upcoming campaign. Ever since the end of the last campaign, my voice has been hoarse, sometimes almost inaudible. Once, on the floor of the House, I could barely complete a speech. I must drink water constantly while I'm talking, and I can't speak publicly without a microphone. More and more my voice seems unnatural and strained. Personally, it is getting to be a real drag, and I think it is hurting me politically.

Doctors have diagnosed the problem as a nodule on my vocal cords, and recommend surgery. I have never had a serious medical problem in my life. I haven't spent a night in the hospital since I was born. I don't want a doctor scraping away at my vocal cords and making me sound like Donald Duck.

I'm trying for a "natural cure." I drink all kinds of weird teas. I've taken homeopathic remedies. I'm supporting the cough drop industry. I'm trying to change my way of speaking. It's all very interesting, but none of it is working.

I don't want to do it, but if my voice doesn't get better soon, I'm going to have the surgery. I can't go through the campaign like this. A reporter recently asked me, "Do you have throat cancer?" Every time I'm on the radio someone asks me about my voice. If people think that I am in poor health, I'm not going to win this election.

Message

It may seem surprising, but of all the challenges ahead the decision of what my overall campaign message will be is the easiest to address. For two years I've been listening to the garbage of Gingrich and his right-wing friends. And for two years I've been fighting them. This campaign is going to be about the Gingrich agenda.

If elected, Ms. Sweetser will vote for Gingrich as Speaker of the House. If Vermonters want massive cuts in Medicare, Medicaid, education, veterans' programs, and environmental protection, together with huge tax breaks for the rich, Ms. Sweetser is going to be elected the next representative from Vermont. Frankly, I don't think that's going to happen.

Nonetheless, I know that Sweetser will be a very tough opponent. She is bright, articulate, attractive, and very popular. Further, she has an unusual history indicating a great deal of courage and strength. Kevin J. Kelley described Sweetser in a November article in the *Vermont Times*, a weekly newspaper:

> Susan Sweetser brings several assets to her race against Congressman Bernie Sanders. Foremost among them is her standing as one of the most popular young politicians in Vermont. After only a single term in the legislature, the 36-year-old Republican finished first in 1994 in the crowded and highly competitive field of candidates vying for state senate seats from Chittenden County. Sweetser is a rising star likely to shine brightly for many years in state—and possibly national—politics.

Sweetser is still associated in the public mind mainly with her courageous decision in 1989 to reveal that she had been raped nine years earlier. In acknowledging that she had been sexually assaulted, Sweetser defied the social taboo that requires women to remain silent and not to challenge the unwarranted sense of shame felt by many rape victims.

Having helped initiate a candid discussion on a sensitive subject, Sweetser went on to campaign tirelessly on behalf of "victims' rights." She founded Survivors of Crime, Inc., a group that advocates tougher penalties and preventive measures in regard to crimes of violence. Sweetser's effectiveness in this area also results from what Elizabeth Ready, a state senate colleague, describes as her "spunky spirit." Sweetser exemplifies the sort of determined, do-it-yourself approach to life sure to appeal to many Vermonters.

Yes, this is going to be a tough election. The early polls show that. On February 28, a *Rutland Herald* poll has me ahead by 47 percent to 32 percent. Maybe that sounds good, but it's not. I am much better known than Sweetser, and early polls almost always give an advantage to the incumbent. In fact, as the *Rutland Herald* points out, a poll which they did in late June 1994 had me almost thirty points ahead of my opponent that year, John Carroll, and I won by only three points. Sweetser is starting her campaign much earlier than Carroll did, and already has better name recognition than he did. *Roll Call*, a Washington political newspaper that analyzes congressional races, calls the race a "toss up." I can't disagree with that assessment.

*　　*　　*

Election Day, or Town Meeting Day as we call it in Vermont, was March 3, 1981. I got up at five o'clock in the morning, ready to go. As I drove down North Avenue I saw telephone poles plastered with red-and-white "Sanders for Mayor" posters. Campaign volunteers, mostly from the low-income housing projects, had been up early, and the signs served notice that our election-day effort was proceeding as planned. Their presence seemed a good omen: we were everywhere, we were ready for the final day.

As I continued the drive from my apartment to the north end of the city, I noticed a young nurse, dressed for work later that morning in her white uniform, holding up a "Sanders for Mayor" sign at a major intersection. I had not expected to see her out there, shivering in the early morning cold, symbolic of the energy and commitment that had propelled our campaign. Another good omen.

Still, I was far from confident that the day would be ours. There was a chance that we would surprise everyone and walk away with the election. A nice comeuppance for the newspaper columnist who the day before had predicted that I would lose by twenty points. Still, as had always been the case for me in the past, I could get obliterated. Conventional wisdom was with the newspaper columnist: despite the surprising endorsement of the Patrolmen's Association, despite the wide support we seemed to be drawing throughout the city, Bernie Sanders and the progressive effort could still get hammered.

What no one anticipated, but what in fact happened, was a nailbiter.

The day was a blur. I made appearances at each of the six ward polling places. I kept checking with Linda Niedweskie at campaign central to see how things were going and what the voter turnout was like. The good news for us was that voting was heavier than usual, 25 percent higher than in previous mayoral elections. Supporters wished me well. Campaign workers ferried elderly and low-income voters to the polls in the carpools we had organized.

The polls closed at seven. In each ward the votes were tallied by ward officials, most observed by members of our independent coalition. As my friend Richard had predicted months before as we pored over those musty polling books in City Hall, I did extremely well in the working-class districts. In fact, we carried Wards 2 and 3—traditionally Democratic and working class—by almost two to one over Paquette.

As the vote totals rolled in, it appeared that the election would be very close. Our strong performance in the low-income and working-class wards was being offset by a less than inspiring performance in the more affluent wards. Apparently, speaking forthrightly about the needs of working people made wealthy folks nervous. With all of the machine ballots counted, and with the absentee ballots tallied everywhere but in Ward 3, we were ahead, though not by much. Only the paper absentee ballots in that one Democratically controlled ward remained to be counted. We waited anxiously.

What seemed like an interminable amount of time passed, and still there was no word from Ward 3. Finally, surrounded by lawyers and supporters, I marched into the ward polling place to see what was going on. A few minutes later, a group of ward functionaries came out from behind a closed door, where they had been counting the ballots. Even though I had won the ward by two to one on the voting machines, it seems I had lost the absentee ballot count by the same amount.

Yet, to my surprise, to Mayor Paquette's shock, to the business community's alarm, and to the deep interest of Vermonters throughout the state, when the absentee votes were tallied in with the rest, I found myself elected mayor of Burlington—by a mere fourteen votes. For once, the old saying was really true: every vote had counted. So stunning was the upset that nine years later the state's largest newspaper would still be referring to it as "the story of the decade."

But the evening did not end with our victory and my live appearance on late-night news, ferried to the state's largest television station by a reporter with a siren on the roof of his car. With such a close election there would be a recount, and City Hall had possession of all the ballots. After a great deal of legal mumbo jumbo among my lawyer friends, meeting in the midst of total chaos in somebody's office, it was decided that we should try to get the ballots out of City Hall.

So, in the middle of the night—at three o'clock in the morning to be precise—a lawyer and I traveled down a dirt road and woke up a judge to request that the election ballots be impounded. The judge granted our request. The next morning the ballots were moved to the state courthouse.

One month later, I was sworn in as mayor of Vermont's largest city, the only mayor in the entire country elected in opposition to the two major political parties. I would be reelected three times, and then move on to the U.S. House of Representatives, the first Independent in the Congress in four decades. But that March night in 1981 was the event which made possible all that came after.

We were a coalition of ordinary people, none of whom had any real access to power in the conventional scheme of things, but we had contested an important election—and we had won. If an independent progressive movement could win in America's most rural state—and until recently, one of America's most Republican—then it might be possible for progressives to do likewise anywhere in the nation.

2

Socialism in One City

"They're playing you for a fool and they've already taken away your right to representation in Congress. Who are 'they'? The leftists, extreme liberals and radicals all over the country. From Berkeley, California to New York's Greenwich Village, thousands of these people, that's right, thousands of them, have been contributing to and working hard for the election of Bernard Sanders to Congress."

This, from a fundraising letter widely distributed throughout Vermont, is the gist of Sweetser's campaign strategy: a slightly retooled version of '50s-style redbaiting. The people of Vermont have been duped. Bernie Sanders does not represent their interests. He owes his allegiance to left-wing "outsiders" who control him through their purse strings.

Every campaign has an official beginning. Mine was May 27, 1996, the day I made the formal announcement of my candidacy. The first of five such announcements scheduled for each region of Vermont took place in Burlington, my hometown and the state's largest city. Symbolically, we held the event in the Community Boathouse on the waterfront, one of the major accomplishments of my time as mayor. We organized the announcement as we had two years ago. The campaign staff—Tom Smith, John Gallagher, and Brendan Smith—brought together leading representatives of our various constituencies, the backbone of our support. Each of them spoke for a few moments about issues of importance to them and reasons why they wanted me reelected. Tom Smith, a former Progressive in the state legislature, emceed the event. We had a very good crowd, over 150 people at noon. It was a beautiful Vermont spring day.

Ron Pickering, the head of the Vermont AFL-CIO, was there, representing 20,000 union workers and retirees. So were Representative Bobby Starr, the chairman of the House Agriculture Committee and a leading voice for family farmers in the state legislature, and Sally Conrad, a former state senator and one of the strongest advocates for women and the poor. Stan LaFlamme, a disabled Vietnam veteran who was a member of my Veterans Council, delivered a very poignant speech. Ned Farquar of the Sierra Club spoke for the environmental community, Mira Fakiranada for the low-income community, and Alice Cook Bassett for senior citizens. We heard from Will Rapp, the owner of Gardener's Supply and a successful and environmentally conscious small businessman. Liz Ready, a progressive Democrat in the state senate, recalled her encounters with Susan Sweetser. And Peter Clavelle, who was director of economic development in my administration and was now in his third term as the Progressive mayor of Burlington, talked about my mayoral record.

These folks, many of them personal friends, represented the progressive coalition that we had worked hard over many years to bring together: workers, family farmers, women's advocates, low-income people, veterans, senior citizens, environmentalists, and small businesspeople. Together, they stood for the vast majority of the people in Vermont. Together, we would win this election.

I wrote my announcement speech the night before. As usual, when I was speaking my voice was hoarse and strained, and I had to stop a couple of times to down some water. In the speech, I tried to frame the central issues of the campaign. This is how it began:

Six years ago, I asked the people of Vermont to do something that had never been done before in the history of our state, and had not been done for forty years in the United States of America. And that is to send an Independent to Congress—someone not affiliated with the Republican Party or with the Democratic Party.

When I first ran for Congress, I asked the people of Vermont to send me to Washington so that I could fight for those people who can't afford to attend $500-a-person fundraisers like the one my opponent recently held; and who can't afford to have well-paid lobbyists in Washington protecting their interests. That's the promise that I made, and that's the promise that I've kept.

I asked the people of Vermont to send me to Congress so that I could stand up to a Republican president when he was wrong, and a Democratic president when he was wrong; to stand up to a Democratically controlled Congress when they were wrong and a

Republican controlled Congress when they were wrong. And that's what I've done.

Mostly, I asked the people of Vermont to send me to Congress so that I could fight for justice—a concept we don't hear too much about anymore. To fight for justice for working families and the middle class—80 percent of whom, since 1973, have experienced a decline in their standard of living or, at best, economic stagnation—while at the same time the people on the top have never had it so good.

During the 1980s, the top one percent of wealth holders in this country enjoyed two-thirds of all increases in financial wealth. The bottom 80 percent ended up with less real financial wealth in 1989 than in 1983—and that trend continues. Today, tragically, the United States has the most unfair distribution of wealth and income in the entire industrialized world.

Justice. An economy in which all people do well, not just the very rich. And that's what I've been fighting for.

I then described some of what I had seen in Vermont as I traveled around the state during the two preceding years.

I talked about the meeting I had with a woman in Danville, who told me that both she and her husband were working sixty hours a week in order to save money to send their daughters, excellent high school students, to college. But despite their back-breaking efforts, they didn't know if they would succeed—given the high cost of college and the enormous debt they would have to sustain.

I talked about the young farmer I had met in Troy. She and her husband go out milking at 5 a.m., seven days a week. But despite their hard work and their love of the land, they didn't know if they would be able to stay on the farm because of the collapse of milk prices.

I talked about the senior citizens I met throughout the state who, despite Medicare, were unable to afford their prescription drugs. And how some of them were forced to choose between adequately heating their homes in the winter or buying the food they needed.

And I talked about the young workers who had no health insurance and dead-end jobs.

My point was that while the economy might have been working well for the people on top, it was leaving many, many people far behind.

Next came my legislative achievements. For years my opponents had been telling Vermonters that as an Independent I couldn't pass major bills or amendments. It was important to set the record straight. In fact, I had an impressive legislative record.

I had helped lead the effort to raise the minimum wage and to pass the Northeast Dairy Compact, legislation of great importance to Vermont farmers. It was my amendment that passed the House and told the president that he couldn't put $50 billion at risk bailing out the Mexican economy on behalf of Wall Street investment banks. Another amendment of mine stopped an outrageous example of corporate welfare—a $31 million Pentagon bonus for the board of directors and CEO of Lockheed-Martin for merging their companies and laying off 17,000 workers. In Vermont it gets cold in the winter, very cold, so my office led the effort in the House to stop Gingrich's attempt to eliminate the fuel assistance program, LIHEAP, restoring almost full funding for it, as well as seeing through a major amendment for affordable housing. Further, I passed legislation that prevented insurance companies from discriminating against battered women, and an amendment stating that an HMO or insurance company could not force a woman and her newborn baby out of the hospital before they were ready to go. And there were other successful amendments and bills that I had authored. The important point was to show Vermonters that an Independent could pass legislation relevant to our state and to the nation.

But then came, perhaps, the most important point that I wanted to make. I continued:

> What this election is about is whether Newt Gingrich, Dick Armey, and the Republican Party are going to have another two years to push through the most reactionary, extremist agenda in the modern history of America—or whether we stop them cold right now and tell them that greed and bigotry and scapegoating are not what America is all about.
>
> What this election is about is whether Gingrich and Armey and the Republican Party are going to be successful in slashing Medicare, Medicaid, education, environmental protection, veterans' programs, nutrition, affordable housing, and a dozen other programs impacting tens of millions of Americans—while at the same time they give huge tax breaks to the rich and large corporations, and build B-2 bombers and Star Wars gadgets that the Pentagon doesn't want.

Finally, I concluded by emphasizing what is too frequently ignored in politics: that despite all of the problems and pettiness that take place every day in the political world, it is imperative for progressives to maintain a vision—a vision that has been carried forth generation after generation after generation—a vision that cries out for social justice and the attainment of the true potential that this country can become.

I ended my remarks by stating:

It is vitally important to the future of this country and our state that we defeat the Republican agenda, and that we prevent the Republicans from recapturing the Congress and taking the White House. That is enormously important. But it is even more important that we as progressives and as Vermonters hold on to that special vision that has propelled us forward for so many years.

A vision which says that in this richest of all nations all of our people, and not just the wealthy, should enjoy the fruits of their labor with decent jobs and benefits that allow them to live in dignity. That we cannot continue to have the highest rate of childhood poverty in the world, while the number of millionaires and billionaires continues to increase. A vision which says that every man, woman, and child in this country is entitled to health care as a right of citizenship, and that the United States must join the rest of the industrialized world by enacting a national health care system, a single-payer health care system. A vision which says that lifelong quality education is the essence of what being alive is about, and that all of our citizens, no matter what their incomes, should be able to receive a higher education.

A vision which says that we respect the struggles that women have been waging for so many years, and that the very personal decision of abortion must be decided by the woman herself—and not Newt

Gingrich or the United States government. A vision which says that we judge people not by their color, their gender, their sexual orientation, their nation of birth—but by the quality of their character, and that we will never accept sexism, racism, or homophobia.

A vision which says that there is no conflict between respect for the environment and job growth, and that, in fact, our economy improves when we stop environmental degradation. A vision which says that a society is ultimately judged by how we treat the weakest and most vulnerable among us—the children, the elderly, the sick, the disabled. And that we do not cut back on programs which help the weak and the powerless, in order to give tax breaks to the rich and the powerful.

The announcement event in Burlington was a terrific success. It was great to see so many of my old friends again, people who had been part of our efforts in Burlington when I was mayor, people who had worked with me for years. I was honored and humbled to be part of a coalition of such good, decent, and down-to-earth people. It was a completely different world from the backbiting of Washington. I was very proud to be a Vermonter.

But the warm feelings lasted only until the evening news was broadcast. We were then reminded very pointedly that in politics there's reality, and there's perception of reality as portrayed on television. The official campaign had just begun, and voters were forming their first impressions. And what they saw on TV was very different from what had actually taken place.

My Republican opponent, Susan Sweetser, held a press conference immediately after my announcement. Her attack on me for attacking her (which I didn't—I never even mentioned her) dominated the news. She was particularly successful at turning our announcement to her advantage on the largest television station in the state, WCAX-TV, which gave as much time to Sweetser's response as to my speech. In the midst of their coverage, they felt it necessary to report, incorrectly, that I had spent almost $200,000 more than my Republican opponent in the *last* election—they simply "forgot" to mention the independent expenditures made on his behalf by the Republican Party, including money paid to WCAX.

Stuart "Red" Martin, the conservative Republican who owns WCAX, had already contributed $2,000, the maximum amount allowed by law, to the Sweetser campaign. Recently Peter Freyne, a columnist on the Vermont weekly newspaper *Seven Days*, quoted Martin as saying that he wanted "to chip in as much as I can . . . I feel I'm doing a public service if we remove Bernie Sanders." From the beginning, we had worried about how WCAX would cover this campaign. Now we knew. We were off to a very bad start.

In effect, my opening announcement on TV became a pro-Sweetser promotion. The strategy of her campaign handlers is the essence of modern TV-oriented campaigning: when your opponent makes a speech, respond very quickly so that the television report focuses more on the response than on the original statement. In general, sound-bite television likes the idea of "conflict" more than the simple reporting of information. This works especially well when a TV station is sympathetic to a particular point of view.

Increasingly, both with regard to the campaign and my congressional duties, I worry about the role of television "news" in the life of our country—regardless of the political orientation of the station. The simple fact of the matter is that no one, not Bill Clinton, not Bob Dole, not Bernie Sanders, can deal with complex issues in a seven-second sound bite. The rapid pace of TV "action news" makes it virtually impossible for there to be serious reflection on important issues. Further, there is little sense of proportion in the coverage given to issues. TV news wants *new* developments, and smart press secretaries cater to this craving by concocting gimmicks and photo ops—anything to get their bosses on the tube.

Meanwhile, the deepest and most profound issues facing the country rarely get discussed because they don't fit the format. Several years ago, I attended a meeting with the head of a network news division. He described the extraordinary commitment of labor and money to coverage of an airplane crash—routine procedure for a disaster story. Someone asked him about his network's reporting of the savings and loan scandal (a real disaster). His reply: "We didn't do much. It wasn't good television. Too boring."

Every night, television news offers colorful, fast-paced, and exciting coverage—but of what? Ultimately, Americans who depend on TV for information learn very little about how and why things really happen in their country. Good entertainment? Yes. Knowledge for a democracy? No.

There is no question that Sweetser's people will be doing a lot of instant response "spin." Pretty sophisticated stuff for a small state like Vermont. Much better than I've done in past campaigns. I didn't even know until later that her campaign manager was at my announcement with a tape recorder. It is now clear what their strategy will be. Every time I speak they will be there, almost literally "in my face." On the other hand, whether that sort of attack strategy will succeed in Vermont remains to be seen. Vermont is not California or New York. I'm not so sure that Vermonters will enjoy the spectacle of an in-your-face style of campaign.

While my opening announcement was poorly covered by television, the newspaper coverage was excellent. The three major print media, the *Burlington Free Press*, the Vermont Press Bureau (representing the second and third largest papers in the state, the *Rutland Herald* and the *Times-Argus*), and the Associated Press (which covers for all the papers), described the event accurately on their front pages and provided ample coverage of my remarks. In print, Sweetser's statement that "Bernie Sanders represents the tired failed ideology of left-wing extremism" didn't play as well as it did for the television cameras, especially given that I was surrounded by representatives of the vast majority of the people of Vermont. Her attack on my support for the needs of working people and the middle class sounded as if she were unaware that a majority of Vermonters are not as supportive of Gingrich as she is.

I wish I could say that I was enthused once the campaign had begun officially. After all, it was great to see so many old friends show up, people who have been with me through so many struggles. But even that had its down side. It reminded me that a major challenge of this campaign is not only to get people involved, but to get them involved in a meaningful way. In the 1994 campaign, we recruited very few new campaign workers. No one wants to sit around an office waiting for orders from on high. How do we develop a structure that attracts volunteers and gives them significant work to do? How do we develop a sense of excitement? That's tough. But we must do better than in 1994.

It's also tough being an incumbent. Yes, I know. You're not feeling sorry for me. Incumbents, you say, have all kinds of advantages. You're right. We have staff, access to information, an ability to make news and play the "Rose Garden strategy" by simply doing our jobs. That's true. But there are also serious disadvantages.

One of the very real problems I have in this campaign, one I felt severely two years ago, is that I have to spend much of my time in Washington while my opponent has seven days a week in the state of Vermont. She's on local radio shows. She's constantly talking to groups. She's getting interviewed by reporters in small towns. Meanwhile, I'm stuck in Washington, dealing with congressional business (my job, after all) that isn't likely to be reported in the local news, or facing tough votes which will offend one or another constituency.

But I'm not the only member of Congress having to worry about the incumbency predicament. Gingrich's freshman class of "revolutionaries" want to go home too. They're in trouble, and they want to campaign in their districts. The good news, therefore, is that we may get out of the Capitol earlier this year than last election.

*   *   *

The recount was completed two weeks after the election. My lead dropped from fourteen to ten votes. But still, I am elected mayor of Burlington, the only candidate in America to buck the two-party system, the only socialist mayor in the country.

I was inaugurated in April 1981, before a huge crowd at City Hall. I was pleased with the speech I delivered, tying local issues to the broader national and international context. For the first time in anyone's memory, local radio carried a mayor's speech live. Later, a reporter asked me for a copy of the speech, and I handed her my pages of scribbled notes on a yellow legal pad. That's too bad. I wish I had that speech today.

Hysteria reigned. The establishment was in total shock. The director of the hospital later wrote that when he heard the news on the radio, he nearly drove his car off the bridge he was riding over. The local bankers, who had scheduled a meeting for the day after the election, tried to figure out how they would communicate with the new mayor. Did anyone know this guy? I got a call from the Democratic lieutenant governor. "Don't do anything rash," she said.

I became a celebrity, of sorts. The local media was ecstatic: this election was the biggest Vermont political story in years. And it went beyond Vermont. The *New York Times*, the *Boston Globe*, and many other national papers featured stories on the "socialist mayor." Phil Donahue invited me to be on his show for a full hour. I declined, choosing not to be the spokesperson for the American socialist movement. I did accept NBC's offer to fly Jane and I to Chicago for a ten-minute Donahue interview on the

Today Show. And there was Canadian television, and the BBC. Somebody told me that I was even broadcast on Chinese radio.

Garry Trudeau of Doonesbury fame came to Burlington and we had breakfast together. This was just after the Socialist Party and François Mitterand had taken power in France. Not long after a Doonesbury cartoon appeared that read, "As goes Burlington, so goes France." And then there were T-shirts, with several variations on "The People's Republic of Burlington." All and all, it was a very heady experience for a guy whose last bid for public office garnered only 6 percent of the vote.

An immediate crisis involved purchasing clothes suitable for a mayor. At the time, I didn't own a suit, just one or two corduroy sports jackets and a few ties. While it wasn't my intention to become the best-dressed mayor in America, or even to wear a tie all that often, I thought a little sprucing up wouldn't hurt. Overnight, my wardrobe doubled.

More importantly, I had to put together an administration. Under Burlington's charter, the mayor has the right to appoint a city attorney, clerk, treasurer, constable, and a number of other positions. I needed to find competent, experienced people who shared my political views. And beyond this more immediate concern was the monumental task of transforming city government.

How would we implement our campaign promises? How would we democratize Burlington politics and open up city government to all the people? How could we break our dependency on the regressive property tax? How could we protect the environment and stop unnecessary road construction? How would we address the needs of low-income and working-class neighborhoods? How would we bring women into a city government that had been dominated by an old boys' network? What could we do for the kids and teenagers of the city, and for the seniors? How could we treat city employees fairly, not only through decent wages and working conditions, but by involving them more in the decision making of their departments? How would we make Burlington a city in which all people have access to the arts, not just those with money? Above all, how could we accomplish all of this with only two supporters on a thirteen-member City Council, and virtually no support on the various commissions that directed most of Burlington's departments?

My "shadow cabinet" and I organized a series of task forces to begin addressing these questions. Essentially, we opened the doors of City Hall and invited all interested people to come in and suggest the best ways forward. We were delighted by the response. Hundreds of people from all walks of life attended a wide variety of meetings. Many of them had great ideas.

Out of these task forces came a number of Mayor's Councils: on youth, the arts, women, senior citizens, health care, and tax reform, among other issues. Over the years, and after great political struggle, some of these councils were incorporated into the structure of city government. In the early days of my administration, however, they served almost as a parallel government.

Those early days at City Hall were exhilarating, but very tense. To be more accurate, there was a civil war taking place in Burlington city government. Conservative Democrats had controlled Burlington city government for decades and, with their Republican allies, they were surely not going to give up their power without a fight. The Board of Aldermen (as it was then called) consisted of eight Democrats, three Republicans, and two supporters of mine—Terry Bouricius and Sadie White.

At twenty-seven, Terry became the first Citizen Party candidate in America elected to public office. I had known Terry since his student days at Middlebury College, where he participated in the Liberty Union and helped in my 1976 gubernatorial race. While Terry ran his aldermanic campaign more or less independently of my mayoral race, he was a strong socialist and a natural ally, and he is a leader of the Vermont progressive movement to this day. After five terms on the Board of Aldermen, Terry was elected to the state legislature, where he is now serving his fourth term.

Sadie White, at seventy-nine, also defeated the Democratic machine to become an alderwoman. But her story is quite different from Terry's. For many years Sadie had been a Democratic state representative in the legisla-ture. Her independence and willingness to stand up for her working-class constituents earned her the enmity of the machine, and they dumped her. Sadie had the last laugh, however. She came back with a vengeance, winning elec-tion to the Board as an Independent. Despite enormous pressure to return to the Democratic Party fold, she has remained an unwavering ally and good friend, during her stint on the Board and to this day.

At my first official meeting as mayor, the Board of Aldermen fired my secretary, the only person I had been able to hire. They claimed I hadn't hired her in the proper way. (They allowed me to rehire her soon after.) Two months later, on the day that the mayor formally announces his choices for administration posts, the Board rejected all of my appointees. The situation was absurd: I was expected to run city government with the administration of the guy I had just defeated in a bitter election, and a group of people who vigorously opposed my political goals. We were outflanked by the opposition on every major decision. The votes were always the same: eleven to two, the eight Democrats and three Republicans on one side, Terry and Sadie on the other.

The Democrats' strategy was not too complicated: they would tie my hands, make it impossible for me to accomplish anything, then win back the mayor's office by claiming that I had been ineffective.

And what was our strategy? First, we were going to do everything that a mayor could possibly do without the support of the City Council. Second, we were going to expose the local Democrats and Republicans for what they were—obstructionists and political hacks who had very few positive ideas. Third, and most important, we were going to build a third party in the city to defeat them in the next election.

During this first term, I discovered that the city was wasting substantial sums of money on its insurance policies. Local companies, year after year, were getting the city's business at substantially higher than market rates. I instituted a radical socialist concept, "competitive" bidding, which saved the city tens of thousands of dollars. We were showing that to be "radical" did not mean that we wasted taxpayer dollars. Quite the contrary. For those of us committed to the idea that government should play an important role in the life of our community, it was absolutely necessary to show that we could run a tightfisted, cost-effective administration. There is no excuse for wasting taxpayer money.

We also started a successful Little League program in the city's poorest neighborhood, and began what was to become a citywide tree-planting program that transformed block after block in Burlington. We began a very popular summer concert series which drew thousands of people to a beautiful waterfront park, where they listened to great music and watched the sun set over Lake Champlain. We did all this and more by scratching together a few bucks here and a few bucks there.

As the year progressed, it became clear that the only way we could carry out effective policy for the city was by electing a majority of Progressives to the Board of Aldermen—which meant the creation of a new political entity. In the beginning we called it the Independent Coalition. Later, it was renamed the Progressive Coalition. The Coalition existed only in Burlington. While not a political party under state law (because it is not a statewide organization), it operates in Burlington as if it were exactly that.

In the winter of 1981–82, we recruited aldermanic candidates from each of the city's wards for the election in March. Rik Musty, a psychology professor at the University of

Vermont, was our candidate in Ward 1; Zoe Breiner, a young worker at IBM, in Ward 2; Gary DeCarolis, a mental health worker for the state, in Ward 3; Jane Watson, an attorney, in Ward 4; Joan Beauchemin, a long-time community activist, in Ward 5; and Huck Gutman, coauthor of this book and UVM professor of English, in Ward 6.

It gets very cold in Vermont in the winter, with lots of snow and ice. Frankly, it's not always fun knocking on doors when the weather is below zero. But that's what we did. Without exception, all of our candidates mounted vigorous campaigns, knocking on almost every door in their wards. I went out with our candidates as often as possible. We were motivated, to say the least. The themes of the campaign were crystal clear. First, our candidates ran on a progressive platform. Second, they were taking on Democrats and Republicans who were preventing the mayor from doing his job.

Voter turnout for the aldermanic elections hit an all-time high, and on election night, March 2, 1982, we had one wild celebration. Ward 1—victory. Ward 2—victory. Ward 3— victory. Ward 4—defeat. Ward 5—a runoff election between the Progressive and the Democrat as neither candidate received 40 percent of the vote. The Republican was defeated. Ward 6—a runoff between the Progressive and the Republican. The Democrat was defeated.

If my mayoral victory one year before had been regarded by some as a fluke, there could be no mistaking what was happening now. A political revolution had occurred in Burlington. The people had spoken, loudly and clearly. With a very high voter turnout, the citizens of Burlington informed the Democrats and Republicans that they wanted change—*real* change. Progressives were on the move.

As expected, the Democrats and Republicans combined their efforts for the runoff elections in Wards 5 and 6. The Republicans supported the Democrat in Ward 5, and the Democrats backed the Republican in Ward 6. Although our candidates ran very hard, both Joan and Huck lost.

Consequently, we did not capture a majority of the thirteen-member Board. (And we never did in my eight years as mayor.) But with the votes of Rik, Zoe, and Gary added to Sadie's and Terry's, we now at least had veto power. We could block any Democratic-Republican initiative. They had no other choice but to work with us. There was a new balance of power, and we could go forward.

My life as mayor was immediately made easier when the Board of Aldermen, suddenly seeing the light of day, decided to accept my appointments to various city positions. After a year as mayor, I finally had an administration. No longer would the mayor's advisers have to meet around my kitchen table to write the budget as volunteers. Now we could actually work at City Hall, and they would get paid for their work.

I was able to bring in a topnotch financial analyst, Jonathan Leopold, as treasurer. Jonathan revamped the city's entire financial operation, saving Burlington substantial sums of money. Barr Swennerfelt as assistant treasurer, Peter Clavelle as personnel director, Jim Dunn as assistant city attorney, Jim Rader as city clerk, David Clavelle as constable, and Steve Goodkind as city engineer rounded out my early appointments.

The Sanders administration and the Progressive Coalition were aggressive on all fronts. We were a very activist city government. The property tax, the major source of funding for education and municipal services in Vermont, is regressive because it is not based on ability to pay. Many senior citizens and working people were (and are) paying far more in property taxes than they can afford on their limited incomes. For seven straight years I did not raise the general property tax for homeowners in Burlington. At the same time, I fought hard for more progressive forms of taxation.

While I had strong backing from city residents in this fight, I did not have the support of the state legislature. In Vermont, municipalities must get approval for charter revisions from the state legislature. Time and again the legislature refused to approve the progressive charter changes that the people of Burlington had voted for— sometimes overwhelmingly. It was very disheartening, and one of the reasons I ran for governor in 1986. But more on that later.

Nonetheless, we did become the first municipality in Vermont to develop alternatives to the property tax. After a major struggle against many of the restaurant owners, we implemented a one percent room-and-meal tax. We also passed a classification system of taxation which raised to 120 percent the tax rate on commercial and industrial property. After a court battle, the utilities were forced to pay for the damage done when they tore up our streets for utility work. Following a heated battle with a cable TV company, and an effort on our part to create a municipally owned system, we managed to get substantial revenue from them and reduced rates for seniors.

The large tax-exempt institutions in the city, the University of Vermont and the Medical Center Hospital, successfully resisted most changes to the status quo. However, we did substantially increase payments from them for police and fire service. As a result of opposition from the governor and legislature, we were unable to generate the revenue we wanted from the municipally owned airport in South Burlington. But by taking over the administration of the large parking lot there, and deploying our own police officers for security, we did improve our cash flow.

Needless to say, our administration and movement were about more than progressive tax policy and efficient government. We were also about involving people in the process, about community, empowerment, fun, and excitement. For instance, the Mayor's Council on Women, which soon became the Burlington Women's Council, brought together women's organizations representing diverse professions and political orientations, from radical gay feminists to conservative businesswomen. Initiatives by the Women's Council included legislation, far ahead of its time, on domestic violence and specialized training for the police department, a study of "comparable worth" that resulted in a financial upgrading for many female municipal employees, and funding for a very successful program which trained low-income women in male-dominated, non-traditional types of employment, such as the building trades.

Jane O'Meara Driscoll, who later became my wife, headed up our Youth Office—first on a volunteer basis, later on the payroll. Jane launched a very successful municipally funded child care center, as well as a Teen Center. Everyone yells at teenagers and tells them to stay out of trouble and not do drugs. We offered them a social space, and opportunities for music and dance. Jane developed an afterschool program for younger kids, a youth newspaper, a theater program, a youth employment program, a summer garden project, and a public access TV show. She also implemented Operation Snow Shovel, a wonderful service program through which young people cleared snow for the elderly and disabled.

We started a number of cultural activities that took art into the streets. A jazz festival—with free concerts and music on our buses. A blues festival. A reggae festival. A country music festival. A chew-chew festival. Free summer concerts in the park. A First Night event on December 31, attended by thousands of people. Almost all of these events continue to this day.

One of my favorite evenings was a poetry reading in which Allen Ginsberg joined Burlington schoolchildren to read their poems in Burlington City Hall. Noam Chomsky, perhaps the best-known radical author in America, spoke to a full house in City Hall. Studs Terkel visited us during a Workers' Rights celebration. Abbie Hoffman, Dave Dellinger, and I spoke on a panel in what turned out to be a very amusing evening. Ella Fitzgerald showcased a jazz festival. Burlington was becoming one of the most exciting and culturally alive small cities in the country.

These brief descriptions of the councils' work imply that implementation of their programs was a breeze. But the creation of the councils was a major political struggle, complete with blood, sweat, and tears. Almost every funding request was accompanied by vituperative and vicious debate. Everything was partisan. Nothing came easy.

I remember a letter to the editor written by an older man that said: "I don't know anything about this socialism, but Sanders is doing a good job repaving the streets." My administration never lost sight of the fact that, while broadening the scope of city government and developing new policy were important and satisfying, we could never forget about taking care of the basics. And in this area, we out-Republicaned the Republicans.

We expanded and improved the Police Department, and began the process of paying our officers a living wage. Ironically, one of my major allies in improving the Police Department was Tony Pomerleau, the chairman of the Police Commission and one of the wealthiest people in the state. (It was Tony's disastrous high-rise condominium waterfront development project that I had campaigned against in 1981.) Tony became such a good ally on police matters that he lost the support of the Democrats and Republicans and had to be reappointed with Progressive votes.

We upgraded the very expensive and life-saving trucks and apparatus used by the Fire Department. We merged the Street and Water Departments, and created a much more efficient Public Works Department, with new and more capable leadership. We developed and implemented a major street repaving program. We purchased an entirely new fleet of snow removal vehicles, and developed a new and more effective snow removal plan. And we brought in competent managers to run the city departments.

We instituted the largest and most costly environmental improvement program in the state's history: a $52 million city-state-federal project to rebuild our sewer system, upgrade our wastewater plants, and stop the pollution of Lake Champlain. We shut down the environmentally unsound landfill, and killed a proposed trash-burning plan that would have been both an environmental and fiscal catastrophe.

We initiated an extensive waterfront beautification plan. The previous mayor had supported a disastrous high-rise condominium project for the downtown waterfront. After an enormous amount of public discussion and fierce debate, we ended up with a very successful people-oriented waterfront of public parks, a nine-mile bike path, and a community boathouse. Today, cyclists can travel from one end of Burlington to the other. Swimming is free of charge at any one of four public parks. We've got some nice athletic facilities as well.

We also developed some very innovative concepts in affordable housing. Against opposition from a segment of the local real estate industry, we became the first city in America to fund community land-trust housing. Through the Burlington Community Land Trust, working-class people were able to purchase their own homes at a lower cost than offered on the commercial market. The housing remains affordable in perpetuity because the owners must agree not to resell the property at market rates, accepting only a reasonable and limited return on their investment.

Working with a tenant organization and nonprofit housing groups, we prevented the largest subsidized housing development in the state, Northgate, from being converted into expensive condominiums. With a federal grant secured by Senator Leahy, and other sources of funding, we managed to convert that development into a cooperatively owned housing project—and saved 336 units for people with modest incomes. Through a variety of mechanisms, we were also able to build a number of units of affordable housing.

We also improved life for low-income people in Burlington's public housing. Every year I was able to appoint one new member to the Burlington Housing Authority. At the end of three years we finally had a majority, at which point we brought in an outstanding new director, Mike McNamara, who made major improvements in city-run low-income and senior citizen housing.

While we were able to pass the most sweeping tenants' rights legislation in the state, we were not successful in our major pro-tenant initiative, rent control. In 1982, the landlord organization defeated us decisively in a citywide vote on that issue. They raised a substantial sum of money, hired a consultant, and outpoliticked us.

In 1983, working with a citizen's committee led by local businessman Tom Racine, we managed to bring minor league baseball to Burlington. After interminable discussions with the owner of an AA Eastern League franchise and the Cincinnati Reds, minor league baseball returned to Burlington after a hiatus of thirty years. We worked out a deal with the University of Vermont to use their field, and the Vermont Reds became a huge success. In their first year, they drew over 120,000 fans. The team won three straight Eastern League championships and, amazingly, were one of the great minor league teams of their time. At least a half dozen players on the Vermont Reds became major leaguers, including such stars as Kal Daniels, Paul O'Neill, Chris Sabo, Jeff Montgomery, and Jeff Treadway.

I happen to think that Burlington is one of the most beautiful cities in America. But the truth is that a number of cities have nice waterfronts, good streets, honest police departments, and even minor league baseball. But how many cities of 40,000 have a foreign policy? Well, we did.

As you may recall, I was not the only elected official in America during the 1980s. There was that other fellow, Ronald Reagan. Many Burlingtonians, including myself, supported the Sandinista government in Nicaragua. President Reagan did not. We disagreed with him. We expressed our displeasure.

Somewhere in the Reagan archives, or wherever these things are kept, is a letter from the mayor of Burlington on this subject. There are also official proclamations from the Burlington Board of Aldermen, made after long and emotional public hearings. "Stop the war against the people of Nicaragua! Use our tax dollars to feed the hungry and house the homeless. Stop killing the innocent people of Nicaragua."

This was an issue that many of us in the progressive movement felt very strongly about. Not only was the war against Nicaragua illegal and immoral, it was an outrageous waste of taxpayer money. As a mayor, I wanted more federal funds for affordable housing and economic development. I did not want to see taxpayer dollars going to the CIA for an appalling war. While most of the Democrats and Republicans on the Board of Aldermen disagreed, to us this was very much a municipal issue.

In 1985, I was invited by the Nicaraguan government to visit Managua for the seventh anniversary of the Sandinista Revolution. I was—believe it or not—the highest-ranking American official present. The competition wasn't too keen. I think the only other elected American official was a school board member from Berkeley, California.

The trip to Nicaragua was a profoundly emotional experience. Along with other "foreign dignitaries," I was introduced to a crowd of hundreds of thousands who gathered for the anniversary celebration. I will never forget that in the front row of the huge crowd were dozens and dozens of amputees in wheelchairs—young soldiers, many of them in their teens, who had lost their legs in a war foisted on them and financed by the U.S. government.

During the trip I had an opportunity to meet with Daniel Ortega, the president of Nicaragua, as well as other government officials. I also met with some of the opposition, including Jaime Chamorro, the editor of the opposition newspaper, *La Prensa*. Father Miguel D'Escoto was then the Nicaraguan foreign minister. I met him in a small church in Managua where he was lying in bed, fasting in protest against U.S. support for the contras.

This trip took on special significance because I was accompanied by a reporter from our local newspaper, the *Burlington Free Press*, the largest paper in the state. The reporter, Don Melvin, covered the City Hall beat. He found out that I was going to Nicaragua and somehow managed to convince his editors that if his job was following the mayor, then that meant following him to Nicaragua. Don filed a story each night from Nicaragua that made the front pages of the paper. Our relationship remained entirely professional, and I had no clue as to what he was writing until I returned home. As it happened, he did an excellent job of describing what he saw, and his articles succeeded in countering a lot of the lies and distortions about Nicaragua trotted out by the corporate media.

One of the most moving experiences of the trip occurred on our very first day there. Shortly after we arrived in Managua, we boarded a small plane and flew to the town of Puerto Cabezas, on the Atlantic coastline. Before I left Burlington, the city had agreed to develop a sister-city program with Puerto Cabezas. I went there to meet with local officials and work out the details. News had just reached the town, which had a heavy Miskito Indian population, that some people who had returned to their home on the Rio Coco had been killed, and their bodies were being transported back to Puerto Cabezas.

Eighteen hours earlier, Don and I had been breakfasting together in Burlington. And now, on that same unbelievably long day, somewhere in an Indian village on the Atlantic coast of Nicaragua, we listened to the wailing of family members who received their dead relatives back into the village. It was an unforgettable experience.

The sister-city program with Puerto Cabezas was very popular and continues to this day. Out of that program came many trips back and forth of Vermonters and Nicaraguans, and the development of many friendships. The people of Burlington provided a significant amount of material help in terms of medical supplies, school equipment, and other desperately needed goods. In return, we had the opportunity to learn about a courageous people and a very different culture.

On May 28, 1988, Jane and I were married. The marriage ceremony was held—where else?—in North Beach, a public park on Burlington's waterfront. A lot of people attended.

On the next day we began a quiet, romantic honeymoon. We went to Yaroslavl, in the Soviet Union, along with ten other Burlingtonians, to finalize our sister-city relationship with that city. Trust me. It was a very strange honeymoon.

Like the Puerto Cabezas project, the sister-city program with Yaroslavl has been very successful. Each has different constituencies of support. Puerto Cabezas mostly attracted the energy of left-wing activists who were initially involved because of their support for the Sandinista Revolution and opposition to U.S. intervention in Central America. The Yaroslavl project received more broad-based backing, including from a number of business people in the city.

In 1987, the Leningrad Youth Choir gave a magnificent concert at Memorial Auditorium, our largest facility. The audience was especially moved when the young people from Leningrad performed alongside high school students from throughout Vermont. We also played host to a number of Soviet students who visited Burlington High School as part of an exchange program.

Jane and I visited Cuba in 1989. I had hoped to meet with Castro, but that didn't work out. But I did meet with the mayor of Havana and other officials.

Burlington had a foreign policy because, as progressives, we understood that we all live in one world. We understood that just as actions taken outside of our city affected us, we could have an impact on national and international developments. If children in Nicaragua were suffering because of U.S. policy, it was our responsibility to try to change that policy. If children in the United States were going hungry because the federal government was spending more than was necessary on the military, we also had a responsibility to work on changing that.

As the mayor of Burlington, and someone committed to grassroots democracy, I saw no magic line separating local, state, national, and international issues. How could federal cuts in education not be a local issue? They affect our public schools. How could environmental degradation not be a local issue? It affects the water we drink and our health. How could issues of war and peace not be a local issue? It is local youngsters who fight and die in wars. Ultimately, if we're going to revitalize democracy in this country, local government will have to assume a much stronger and more expansive role.

I think back on my eight years as mayor of Burlington with enormous satisfaction. We had shown that good people could come together, take on very powerful special interests, and successfully fight for social change. We had shown that if you open the doors to City Hall and are prepared to fight for the interests of ordinary people, they will come in and join the struggle.

But let me be very clear: a major factor in our success was that we worked *extremely* hard. We had to in order to survive. Year after year. Yes, the movement was filled with bright people who had loads of creative ideas. Yes, we ran attractive and articulate candidates, and enlisted people who became excellent administrators. But unless you are ready to hit the streets, knock on doors, and communicate with your constituents, you're not going to be successful.

We did not accomplish all that we set out to do, and we made our share of mistakes. But no one, not even our worst enemies, could accuse us of being armchair radicals. We outworked our opponents in every campaign. Remember that in Burlington, elections are held every year when half the Board comes up. That's a lot of work.

In 1983, the *Burlington Free Press*, the city's daily newspaper and voice of the business community, urged the Democratic and Republican parties to join forces around one candidate in order to defeat my reelection bid. Gee. Here I was, year after year, telling people that there wasn't a helluva big difference between the two major parties, and the *Burlington Free Press* agreed with me.

But the two parties did not combine in 1983. Instead, they ran separate candidates. Judy Stephany, a leader in the Vermont House of Representatives, ran as the Democratic candidate; Jim Gilson, the chairman of the school board, was the Republican candidate. The election night results were Sanders 52 percent, Stephany 31 percent, and Gilson 17 percent. The Progressives were also successful in reelecting two members to the Board of Aldermen.

In 1979, before the progressive movement was active in Burlington, 7,000 people had voted in the mayoral election. In 1981, when I was first elected, participation went up to 9,300—a 30 percent increase. In 1983, when I was reelected, 13,320 people voted, almost twice as many as in 1979. The citizens of Burlington had seen a local government working for their interests, and they came out in large numbers to support it. In the low-income and working-class wards, I won close to 70 percent of the vote in a three-way race, and our aldermanic candidates won landslide victories.

Interestingly, as Burlingtonians paid more and more attention to local elections in March, they also voted in far larger numbers in the national elections in November. In 1984, 18,129 Burlingtonians voted in the presidential elections, a 23 percent higher turnout than in 1980. In the national election, the city voted strongly Democratic.

In 1985, I ran for a third term against the former lieutenant governor of Vermont, Democrat Brian Burns. The Republican candidate was Diane Gallagher, a member of the City Council. In that election, I received 55 percent of the vote, Burns 31 percent, and Gallagher 12 percent.

When I announced for reelection for a fourth term in 1987, I stated that, if I won, this would be my last two years. In that election, somewhat belatedly, the Democrats and Republicans finally heeded the advice that the *Burlington Free Press* had given them in 1983. They rallied around one candidate, Paul Lafayette, who was a Democrat on the City Council. Needless to say, taking on the combined parties wasn't easy, and Paul ran a smart campaign. When he was nominated by the Democrats in a contested caucus, close to a thousand people, a huge turnout, attended the meeting. After six years out of the mayor's office, the Democrats were very anxious to regain City Hall. We were very happy, therefore, when we defeated Lafayette, 54 to 46 percent.

Despite a poll showing me with a very high favorability rating and no serious opposition, I left office in April 1989. Eight years was enough. At the end of the month I attended my last Board of Aldermen meeting as mayor of Burlington. I was very happy that this meeting ended on a better note than my first. The Democrats, Republicans, and Progressives presented me with a beautiful newspaper collage, highlighting some of the outstanding events of my tenure.

I was also delighted that my replacement as mayor would be Peter Clavelle, a Progressive. Peter had served in my administration for a number of years, most recently as the director of economic development, where he did an outstanding job. Peter became mayor by defeating a candidate supported by both the Democrats and Republicans. I was leaving the city in good hands.

This whole campaign fundraising situation stinks to high heaven. In the past, I have fought hard for campaign finance reform which limits the amount of money that can be spent in an election and which emphasizes public funding of elections and small individual contributions. Ordinary Americans should have a chance to win elections, not just the rich or representatives thereof. If reelected, I will accelerate my efforts in this area.

Ironically, Susan Sweetser is attacking me on the issue of fundraising. She criticizes the fact that I do not list every contribution under $200. (Federal Election Commission law mandates only that contributors of $200 or more be itemized.) And in press conferences and press releases, she points out that I receive much of my support from out of state. Hence the strategy of tying me to a national cabal of left-wing extremists.

For years, Vermont Republicans have been furious that I have been able to raise money and run strong campaigns. They understand, as I do, that a winning campaign is well nigh impossible without adequate financial resources. In 1988, it is likely that if I had been able to spend as much as my Republican opponent, Peter Smith, I would have won. In 1990, while we were outspent again by Smith, we raised enough money to mount a forceful campaign—and win. I was not outspent in 1992 or '94.

As the only Independent in Congress, I face unique fundraising handicaps that my campaign works very hard to overcome. Unlike Democrats and Republicans, I do not receive any funds from a political party. I do not benefit from the coordinated campaigns that Democrats and Republicans utilize. My campaign does not get support from a party organization that provides staff, polling, literature, offices, mailings, voter checklists, and other services. Further, as a Progressive, I have adamantly refused financial support from Big Money interests. Throughout my political career, I have never accepted one penny from a corporate PAC. (Of the Banking Committee's fifty-two members, only two, including myself, receive no PAC funds from interests associated with the corporate financial community.)

Most importantly, the vast majority of my contributors do not have a lot of money and are unable to give large amounts. In campaign after campaign, I receive *more* individual contributions from Vermont than my opponents, but *fewer* total dollars. Our average campaign contribution is less than $35. My Republican opponent will always have a much higher average contributions. Sweetser, for instance, is collecting many $1,000 checks from some of the richest people in the state, not to mention the $30,000 she raised at the $500-a-plate function attended by Dick Armey.

So, how have we raised money in the past, and what are we doing this campaign? Simple. We play to our strengths. While our average campaign contribution is small, we receive an enormous number of contributions from middle-class and working people, in Vermont and throughout the country. This campaign we hope to receive some 20,000 individual contributions, an incredible number. As the only Independent in Congress, and as a progressive, working people from every state have contributed to my campaigns. If the Republicans think I'm embarrassed by this, they can think again. I'm proud to have the support.

Raising money from so many people takes an enormous amount of work and record keeping. We have to record every contribution that comes in and make certain that our bank deposits are correct. We also have to fill out the FEC reports several times during the campaign—and make sure that they are right. Tineke and Jerome Russell and Sara Burchard have volunteered for this massive undertaking for the last two campaigns. They have done an extraordinary job.

It is unlikely that we will ever be able to raise as much money in Vermont as a strong Republican like Sweetser. The arithmetic is simple. If 400 wealthy individuals made an average contribution of $500, Sweetser would raise $200,000 in Vermont. That is much more than we have ever raised, or are ever likely to raise. You just can't accumulate that kind of money when your average contribution is less than $35, and when you get thousands of contributions from people who are doing the best they can by sending a check for $10 or $20. I would need close to 6,000 contributions averaging $35 to match her $200,000, not to mention the greatly increased costs and the labor associated with actually raising that much money from so many people.

While I will not accept PAC money from corporate America, I gladly accept PAC contributions from organizations fighting to improve life for ordinary people. Over the years, my campaigns have received strong financial support from PACs associated with organized labor, the environment, women, senior citizens, human rights, and the needs of children. That is continuing in this campaign.

The general ignorance surrounding the issue of campaign financing is frustrating. My opponents call me a "hypocrite" for accepting PAC money. How can I accept PAC money, they say, and then claim that I am fighting against "special interests"? Isn't a PAC, by definition, a "special interest"? Aren't all PAC contributions the same? Does it make any difference who the PAC represents?

Such questions, which are repeated ad nauseam in the media, reflect a lack of understanding of the role of money in politics. So, let me be very clear about this. I do *not* believe that working people are a special interest. I do *not* believe that hungry kids are a special interest. I do *not* believe that fighting for the right of women to control their own bodies is a special interest. I do *not* believe that protecting the environment is a special interest.

Believe me. The problem with Washington, and politics in the United States, is *not* that ordinary people have too much power and influence. It's not that too much attention is being paid to low-income children. It's not that the needs of the rich and large corporations are ignored.

The problem, for those who have just crawled out from under a rock, is that groups representing the wealthiest people in this country are able to decisively influence the legislative process so that public policy reflects the interests of the privileged few and not the needs of the general population. And if you don't understand this simple fact, you haven't a clue as to what politics in America is all about.

In this campaign, my opponent has been promised $153,000 from the Republican national party, which will come directly from some of the richest people in America. She has already received, and will undoubtedly continue to get, heavy contributions from some of the largest corporations in America and from groups that represent multi-billion dollar corporate interests. She is obtaining significant support from some of the wealthiest people in Vermont. She indicated at the very beginning of the campaign that she did not want a limit on the amount that could be spent.

Bottom line. If people, including the media, do not understand the difference between one candidate who receives the bulk of his support from organizations and individuals who represent working people and the middle class, and another candidate who receives the bulk of her support from the wealthy and large corporations, then they do not know much about what goes on in Congress. I am going to do my best to prevent the wealthy and corporate interests from buying this election.

3

The Long March Forward

In 1986, I ran for governor as an Independent. I was still in my third term as mayor of Burlington. I ran because the state legislature continually denied Burlington and other communities the democratic right to reform their regressive property tax system. We voted for change but, despite all the lip service to "local control," the legislature and the governor refused to allow us to change our city charter and implement progressive legislation. They simply nullified what we were attempting to do. In Burlington, we were showing that grassroots democracy could work. In the state capital, they were thwarting our efforts and trying to destroy our momentum.

I also ran for governor because I feared that the "Burlington Revolution" would suffocate if we didn't expand beyond one city. People all over the state believed in progressive politics and wanted to be involved in electoral activity. We needed new energy. We also needed to make a political connection between the rural and urban areas of the state.

Madeleine Kunin, the former Democratic lieutenant governor, had been elected the first woman governor of Vermont in 1984, and was running for reelection in 1986. Peter Smith, the lieutenant governor, was the Republican candidate. Kunin was a liberal, strong on women's issues and the environment. We had very serious disagreements, however, not only on the issue of "local control" and the need for Vermont to break its dependence on the property tax, but on health care, child care, utility rates, the needs of the poor, and involving working people in the political process. In any case, I mounted a campaign to become the first Independent governor in Vermont's history. The campaign was a near disaster, and came very close to ending my political career.

The major tactical error that we made was transferring our campaign office from Burlington to Montpelier, where we had a strong but inexperienced base of support. I wanted to physically separate my work as mayor from that of the campaign office, and allow a new group of progressive activists to play leading roles. I also wanted Vermonters to feel that this was a statewide effort, not something emanating from the Burlington progressive community.

It just didn't turn out the way it was supposed to. Our central Vermont activists were smart, hard working, and dedicated, but they lacked the day-to-day experience of running a campaign. Further, and even more importantly, the race against Kunin was very difficult. Liberals were angry that I was running against a female Democrat, as were some environmentalists.

Midway through the campaign, as we were running out of money and going nowhere in the polls, my campaign manager resigned. There was a growing feeling from supporters, and the media, that I should and would drop out of the race. This was the lowest point in my political career. What to do?

I did not quit the race. After a lot of soul-searching and planning, what was left of the campaign limped back to Burlington and regrouped. The campaign was now back in the hands of people who had been with me through the mayoral elections.

Jane and I flew to California, where I gave speeches in Los Angeles and San Francisco. Through the efforts of such progressives as Sherri and Leo Frumkin and Peter Camejo, we were able to raise $6,000. Not a great deal of money, but it all helped. Our fundraising in Vermont also began to pick up.

Some of the people who worked with me at City Hall decided to use their free time to help out. Forty hours at City Hall, forty hours on the campaign. A long week. Jane, city treasurer Jonathan Leopold, Sue Trainer, and a few others jumped head first into the campaign. They were joined by Jeff Weaver, a young man from St. Albans, Vermont, who had been expelled from Boston University for protesting racial discrimination. Jeff would work with me for much of the next eight years.

Slowly the campaign rejuvenated. There were a number of debates, some on television, and I did well. We held lively rallies. Despite the fact that the polls put me far behind and that conventional wisdom suggests that a third-party candidate will fade under such circumstances, we kept gaining momentum right up to Election Day.

Kunin received 48 percent of the vote, Smith 37 percent. I ended up with 14.5 percent. We had lost badly, but, if the truth be known, we felt pretty good. We raised the right issues, won the support of many working-class people from all over the state, and had come back from near political death. It could have been a lot worse.

In 1988, Senator Robert Stafford retired after sixteen years, and Republican Congressman Jim Jeffords ran for the vacant post. Vermont's sole seat in the U.S. House was open, and I decided to run for it. Peter Smith, who finished second in the governor's race against Kunin in 1986, was the Republican candidate, and Paul Poirier was running for the Democrats after winning a tough three-way primary.

In many ways that congressional campaign was the turning point for me in statewide politics. I began the race as the "spoiler." (Oh, how I love that word, with all its implications about the sacrosanct nature of the two-party system.) Would I take enough votes away from the Democrat to elect the Republican? But a funny thing happened on the way to Election Day. I wasn't the spoiler after all. The Democrat was.

Looking back, the 1988 campaign was actually a lot of fun. Smith was a moderate Republican who had received positive recognition for helping to start the Vermont community college system. Poirier was the majority leader in the Vermont House, a moderate-to-liberal Democrat. He was a former teacher and was widely considered a decent, down-to-earth guy. And then there was me.

Vermont is a small state, and Smith, Poirier, and I knew each other pretty well. In fact, we liked each other. That campaign was what Vermont politics should be about. The three of us had strong differences of opinion, but we ran civil, issue-oriented campaigns. The debates were respectful and there was no negative advertising, no desire to "destroy" the other person. Boy, does that seem like a long time ago.

That fall, Harry Reasoner and the crew of *60 Minutes* came to Vermont to film me and the campaign. They had heard that an Independent, and a democratic socialist, had a chance to win a congressional race. It was a good story for them. While they were there, I held a press conference about agricultural issues on a farm in central Vermont. The Associated Press, the most important print media organization in the state, did not show up—which was getting to be a habit with them.

When you're a politician dealing with the media, life is difficult. If you're getting screwed by the media, you don't have much recourse. Who can you complain to? They own the camera. They print the news. What are you going to do about it?

Finally, for the one and only time in my life, I did have recourse. I had *60 Minutes* following me around. I could expose the AP to the world. A politician's dream come true.

"Come on guys," I told my staff. "We're going to visit the AP and talk about fair news coverage." Ten minutes later I was walking up the stairs of the AP office in Montpelier, the camera and microphone of *60 Minutes* right behind me. This time *I* was asking the questions. "Okay, how come you never cover my press conferences? You have time for the Republicans. You have time for the Democrats. Why not an Independent?" The AP had heard it all before. Except this time the cameras of *60 Minutes* were rolling, and AP was on the defensive. It was delicious.

I had a lot of fun that afternoon. Of course, I paid for it later. You never beat the media. After I was elected in 1990, the AP chief went to Washington to do a long series on whether or not I was an effective congressman. Guess what he concluded?

But that's all over now. It's water over the dam. It's hardly worth remembering. The AP and I are friends now, and we have a truly professional relationship. Right? Right? Hello. Hello.

While I was heavily outspent by Smith, our campaign did a good job of raising money. Unfortunately, we ran out of funds one week before Election Day and were going to have to take our TV ads off the air. Jane and I discussed the matter, went to the bank, took out all the money we had—$10,000—and gave it to the TV stations.

On the evening before the election I bumped into Smith as we were campaigning in Montpelier, our state capital. We embraced and congratulated each other on a good campaign. Election night was an emotional roller coaster. The returns first came in from Burlington and surrounding towns, where I usually do well. We were ahead by ten points. Then, as the night wore on, our lead dropped to five points. Then we were in a dead heat. Finally, three points behind. And that's where we stayed, hour after hour. Three points. At one o'clock in the morning, I called Smith and conceded. We were very disappointed, but we had run an excellent campaign. The final results: Smith 41 percent, Sanders 38 percent, Poirier 19 percent. I would never again be called a spoiler.

Needless to say, *60 Minutes* did not run the profile on Bernie Sanders. This is America. Winner take all. Who wants a story about a guy who *almost* became a congressman?

Aside from my own campaign, 1988 was an interesting political year for me because I became a Democrat—for all of one night. This was the year that Jesse Jackson waged an exciting and strategically important battle for the Democratic nomination for president. Within the progressive movement in Vermont, there were differing opinions as to what our role should be in Jackson's efforts. While almost everyone was impressed by his campaign, some progressives thought that we should not get involved because Jackson was running within the Democratic Party. On the other hand, strong Vermont progressives like Ellen David Friedman, Liz Blum, Chris Wood, and others had formed a Vermont chapter of the Rainbow Coalition, which was working hard and effectively for Jackson. After a good deal of debate, the Burlington Progressive Coalition decided to endorse Jackson.

The Rainbow Coalition garnered significant support for Jackson statewide. In central Vermont, they mobilized a huge crowd for his appearance in Montpelier. Burlington and Chittenden County progressives also worked hard, and I campaigned with Jackson when he visited Burlington. On the evening of the nonbinding Vermont Democratic Party caucus, which was held in towns throughout the state, I participated in a formal Democratic Party function for the first and last time in my life. (In Vermont the primary process was then absolutely open. Anyone could identify with any party.) Along with many other progressives, I attended the Democratic Caucus in Burlington.

As mayor of the city, I gave the nominating speech for Jackson. Governor Madeleine Kunin, who also lived in Burlington, gave the nominating speech for Dukakis. Given that progressives had replaced Democrats as the governing party in Burlington, not everyone there greeted my presence with enthusiasm. In fact, a number of old-line Dems staged a silent protest by standing up and turning around as I delivered my speech. And when I returned to my seat, a woman in the audience slapped me across the face. It was an exciting evening. By the way, Jackson won the Burlington caucus overwhelmingly. He also carried the state.

By the spring of 1989, my term as mayor of Burlington was over. I was unemployed and began looking for a job. Unlike some former elected officials, I was not flooded with invitations to prestigious institutions. Actually, I didn't get *any* job offers. My particular skills, it seems, were not too marketable. Panicking a bit, I sent off letters to every college in the country. I was interested in both speaking engagements and a teaching job. I also had illusions about writing a syndicated column.

In the fall of 1989, I taught at the Institute for Policy Studies at Harvard University's Kennedy School of Government. They offer a sensible program that brings real-life politicians (not infrequently folks who have lost their last election) to the campus to give students a sense of real-life politics. I taught a course on third-party politics that was well attended. Jane took some courses at the Kennedy School, and two of our children, Carina and David, attended the local public schools. I went to more football games that fall than I had in twenty years, and became addicted to the cinnamon raisin buns at Au Bon Pain at Harvard Square. I know that conservatives worry a great deal about Harvard. They see it as a bastion of progressive thought, the brain trust for the revolution. Trust me. They can stop worrying. Harvard has many wonderful attributes, but the revolution will not start at Harvard University.

In the spring I went to Hamilton College in Clinton, New York. Dennis Gilbert, a professor of sociology there, arranged for me to teach in his department for a semester. I taught one course on politics and another on urban issues. Dennis has since become a very good friend, and remains a part of our political family. I also taught a course for adults at a satellite location through the State University of New York in Binghamton.

In May 1990, I had to make a decision about my future. I had three options. The first was to do what almost any sane human being would choose—drop out of politics. I had served eight of the last twenty years as mayor. I had run in ten elections with my name on the ballot, and I had played an active role in another five or six. I could give the people of Vermont, myself, and my family a break—and return to producing radical educational media, which I had enjoyed so much in the years before I became mayor. The idea of making videos, records, and tapes was attractive. I loved the work, and could probably bring in a decent income. I could also teach, lecture, and write—and spend time with my wife and four kids. All in all, this was a very appealing option.

My second option was to run for governor. In 1990, Governor Kunin decided not to seek a fourth term. Former governor Richard Snelling became the leading candidate and a number of Democrats were considering a run. Within the progressive movement, there was a lot of interest in having me run for governor. The truth is there was (and is) a lot more interest in what happens at the state level than in that faraway place called Washington, D.C. A "Sanders for Governor" campaign would create a great deal of excitement, bring together the various elements of the progressive coalition, sharply raise political consciousness in the state, and might very well result in victory in a three-way race. It was an option that I, and other progressives, gave serious consideration.

The negatives of a run for governor were that it would be, in Yogi Berra's words, déjà vu all over again. If the Establishment had gone berserk when I was mayor, what would they do if I were governor and the stakes were much higher? We would most certainly face enormous political and economic opposition, and some of us wondered whether we had the statewide political infrastructure and strength to sustain ourselves against such an onslaught.

If I won we could expect that the Democrats and Republicans who controlled the legislature would vigorously oppose the progressive initiatives I brought forward. Would

I be able to win more than a few votes on our key pieces of legislation?

There would also be enormous opposition from the big money interests. If we demanded that the wealthy and large Vermont corporations pay their fair share of taxes, would some of them leave the state and throw Vermont workers out on the streets? As we fought for a statewide health insurance program for all Vermonters, would the insurance companies and health care establishment sabotage our efforts and cut back on medical services? Would Wall Street lower Vermont's bond ratings and plunge us into a financial crisis? Would we be able to get our point of view out through the conservative media organs? Most importantly, did we have a strong enough political organization to keep our supporters mobilized and fighting? Could we hang in for the long haul, or would they blow us away after two years?

There was also a practical consideration: it was unlikely that I would carry 50 percent of the vote in a three-way race. The Vermont Constitution mandates that if no candidate wins 50 percent, the legislature elects the governor. While there would be a tremendous uproar if the legislature failed to seat the candidate with the most votes, it was a distinct possibility. Many Republicans and Democrats in the legislature would *never* cast a vote for Bernie Sanders.

My third and final option was to run for Congress against Peter Smith, again. While it is very tough to knock off an incumbent, I had lost the last race by only three-and-a-half points. Given the fact that the Democrat in 1988 had come in a distant third, it was unlikely that a strong Democrat would enter the race. It was probable, therefore, that I could get the lion's share of the 19 percent that Poirier had received. Further, the developing savings and loan fiasco—which in the end cost taxpayers hundreds of billions of dollars—had revealed the degree to which both parties in Congress worked to represent the interests of wealthy special interests, and exemplified what I had been talking about for years.

Should I run for governor? Should I run for Congress? After a great deal of discussion with progressives all over the state, and amid enormous media speculation, I decided to make another run against Smith.

If the congressional campaign of 1988 had been friendly, positive, and issue-oriented, the election of 1990 was the very opposite. It was one of the most bitter campaigns in Vermont history. It was not fun.

But there were a number of key elements in my favor. First, Smith had voted for the 1990 budget reconciliation bill, which proposed major cuts in Medicare. He had to make a tough choice, and he made the wrong one. I strongly opposed that legislation, and the bill was unpopular in Vermont. Senior citizens in Vermont were strongly Republican or Democrat, and not necessarily comfortable with a progressive Independent. After Smith's vote, however, I began to win more support among seniors.

Second, the 1990 congressional session went on and on and on. Smith was trapped in Washington for much of the campaign. Unlike in 1988, when I had the responsibility of being both a mayor and a candidate, I could campaign full time in Vermont. I didn't have to spend half my time running a city. That was a clear advantage, which allowed me to get around the state and meet voters.

Third, the National Rifle Association turned against Smith. In 1988, the NRA had supported both Smith and Poirier, and had opposed me. During that campaign, I was very clear that while I opposed the Brady bill because I felt that a handgun waiting period could be dealt with at the state level, I supported a ban on certain types of assault weapons, which was clearly a national issue. Both Smith and Poirier adopted the anti–gun control position of the NRA.

A few months after taking office, Smith suddenly announced that he would now vote *for* the ban on assault weapons. The NRA and other elements in Vermont's sportsmen community were furious at his about-face. They felt betrayed and worked hard to defeat him. While the NRA has never endorsed me or given me a nickel, their efforts against Smith in 1988 clearly helped my candidacy. (I should add here that in 1992, '94, and '96, the NRA strongly opposed me.)

Fourth, as I expected, no strong Democrat entered the race. Dolores Sandoval, a professor at the University of Vermont, ran a weak campaign with little party support.

Fifth, many Republicans thought Smith had been rude and disloyal to President Bush, who flew into Vermont to stump for him. At a big Republican fundraiser in Burlington, with the president at his side, Smith announced that he disagreed with Bush and supported increased taxes on the rich. Since everyone in Vermont knew that this had been my position from day one, many Republicans felt that

Smith was being opportunistic, and should not have embarrassed the first sitting president to visit Vermont in many years. Republican support for Smith turned tepid.

Last, the political climate in Vermont and America was changing. The excesses of the 1980s were becoming more and more apparent, and it wasn't just the savings and loan scandal. The rich were getting richer, the middle class was shrinking, the new jobs being created were low-wage jobs, and the people of Vermont were increasingly dissatisfied with status quo politics. The idea of going outside of the two-party system became more and more appealing. In this context, an Independent candidate began to look attractive.

Throughout the campaign, polls indicated that the race was close, with Smith slightly ahead. After Smith voted for the budget bill and the cuts in Medicare, however, the momentum shifted to us. Several weeks before the election, we were up by four to six points. Smith then panicked and made the biggest mistake of his campaign: he listened to his Washington consultants and produced the most negative television ads that anyone in Vermont had ever seen. One of the ads, taking a statement of mine out of context, described me as becoming "nauseous" upon hearing John F. Kennedy's inaugural speech. Another redbaited me by putting me on a split screen with Fidel Castro.

A week before the election, Dennis Gilbert, who was rapidly becoming a very adept pollster, put together a quick tracking poll. Not being "sophisticated" and having the poll done by big-time operators in Washington, we were able to tabulate the polling information immediately. In fact, Dennis and I counted some of the results in my car after picking up the raw data from one of our volunteer phone banks. The poll confirmed what we had been feeling out on the streets: Smith's ads were backfiring, and we were winning big. The people of Vermont did not like ugly, negative advertising.

Our momentum was palpable. Everywhere I went there was tremendous support. As I walked down streets, people honked their horns and shouted from their cars, "Give 'em hell, Bernie," "Shake 'em up." Hester McKinney, our office manager, was fielding calls of support from all over the state. Our campaign slogan was "Making History in Vermont." That's what we were about to do—and everyone knew it.

Election night was euphoric. As television stations reported victories for us in town after town, what stuck in my mind was how two years before we had been ahead early in the evening, but had ultimately lost. The last thing in the world I wanted was to show up at the celebration, presume victory, and then lose. So my family and I, along with some close friends, waited out the long night at home.

But 1990 was not 1988. Our support was amazingly strong all over the state, and we carried thirteen of Vermont's fourteen counties. The final results were Sanders 56 percent, Smith 40 percent, and Sandoval 3 percent. When we finally headed off to the celebration, well over a thousand people had already filled the basement of Memorial Auditorium. There was pandemonium. I could barely fight my way to the podium.

It is hard to describe my feelings at that moment. We had come such a long way, against such incredible odds. So many wonderful people, from one end of the state to the other, had come together to make this victory possible. Twenty years before, I had run for statewide office and had received 2 percent of the vote. As I climbed onto the platform for my victory statement, I was now the congressman-elect from the state of Vermont, the first Independent elected to Congress in forty years. It was almost incomprehensible.

All of us were exhausted, but the adrenalin of victory kept us afloat for many days. There were people all over the state to visit and thank, and a million phone calls to make. There were radio, TV, and newspaper interviews to do all across the country. I was a true novelty: the only Independent in Congress *and* a socialist. Whatever "socialist" might mean to the media, it was sure new and different. Media heaven. Among other shows, I appeared on *Nightline* with Ted Koppel. Paul Wellstone, who had just been elected to the Senate, and Gary Franks, the first black Republican in Congress, were also on that night. I did the show from the ABC affiliate in Burlington, and it was the first time that I had to answer questions while staring into a blank camera. It was a disconcerting experience. A short time later I appeared on Larry King's radio program. King and I reminisced about Brooklyn, where we had both grown up.

A new member of Congress, whether a socialist Independent or a right-wing Republican, must deal immediately with housekeeping chores. I headed for Washington and jumped in. First, I had to familiarize myself with a congressman's annual budget, about $877,000, and the legal guidelines for allocating funds to staff, mailings, general office expenses, etc. Along with other new members, I had to select an office in one of the House office buildings— Rayburn, Cannon, or Longworth—by drawing a number out of a box. I ended up with an office in Cannon, on the fifth floor. Coincidentally, this same office was used a few decades before by an aggressive young congressman from California, Richard Nixon. Now where did he hide those tape recorders?

Bells sound in the office buildings fifteen minutes before a vote, and it's down the elevator, through the halls, and across the street to the Capitol. On a vote-heavy day, you can spend an hour on trips to the Capitol and back. It's one way to stay in shape. The best offices (in the Rayburn building) are closest to the Capitol. Needless to say, new members don't get them.

The next order of business was organizing district congressional offices, along with assembling a competent staff, installing telephones, figuring out which outrageously expensive computer system worked best for my needs, and requisitioning furniture from the General Administrative Services. (We inherited some of Peter Smith's old desks.) Burlington is the largest city in Vermont, and that's where I decided to open the main district office. However, during the campaign I had promised the people of Bennington, who are in the southern tip of the state and often feel slighted by Vermont government, that if I were elected I would also establish an office there. That we did.

Unless you're a total nut who wants to make some kind of weird political statement by sleeping in your office (as some freshmen Republicans did in 1995), you need to find a place to live. Jane and I wanted to live on Capitol Hill and be able to walk to work. We found an apartment about five blocks from the office that turned out to be too big and expensive. We later took an efficiency one block from the office.

Now that I was a congressman, I had to establish goals for the next two years and decide what I could realistically accomplish. An important component of this agenda-setting was selecting the appropriate committees to serve on. This involved an enormous amount of political maneuvering.

Dealing with all of these matters at the same time must be difficult for any congressman. But they are even tougher without a party apparatus behind you and when you're the lone representative from your state. (Vermont, Alaska, Delaware, Montana, North Dakota, South Dakota, and Wyoming are the seven states with a single representative in Congress.) Patrick Leahy, Vermont's senior senator, kindly offered me the use of his offices during the transition period, and I began tackling what needed to be done.

Jane, who became an unpaid "special assistant," and Jeff Weaver took turns covering the orientation for Chiefs of Staff, sifted through hundreds of resumés, and interviewed potential staff members. A young man named George Stephanopolous, who at that time was an aide to Dick Gephardt, proved very helpful in showing us the ropes in Congress. He later went on to become George Stephanopolous.

To head the D.C. office, I brought in Doug Boucher, a former college instructor and environmental writer, who was extremely knowledgeable on foreign policy issues and

Latin America. Ruthan Wirman, a veteran on Capitol Hill, came aboard as our office manager, and John Franco and Jeff Weaver took on the legislative work. A remarkable young woman named Katie Clarke was assigned phone duty, and within a few years became our legislative director. Carolyn Kazdin, who had worked on several of Jesse Jackson's campaigns, focused on economic issues and our relationship to organized labor.

For the Vermont staff, I hired Anthony Pollina, the founder and director of Rural Vermont, as district director. Saving the dwindling number of family-owned dairy farms in Vermont was a priority, and Anthony is one of the most knowledgeable people around on agricultural issues. He also has a great deal of expertise on environmental matters. Rachael Levin, who had helped manage the campaign, came on board as our office manager. (Rachael's mother Ruth had been a member of the Liberty Union twenty years before, and I remembered Rachael as a baby.) Jim Schumacher, who had been active in Burlington city government for many years and served very effectively as our field director during the campaign, became our outreach director. Liz Gibbs-West took over scheduling and general office management.

In Vermont, we put together a strong office, which placed a great deal of emphasis on constituent services. Whatever else I and my staff would accomplish, I wanted the senior citizens, veterans, and working people of Vermont to know that if they were having trouble getting what they were entitled to from the federal government, our office would be there for them. While constituent services is not a very sexy issue, it's something that my office has always taken very seriously, and every year we respond to the concerns of thousands of constituents. Lisa Barrett, who had been a poverty lawyer for many years, did a great job in organizing that office. In recent years, David Weinstein has done an outstanding job.

Initially, I decided to break with congressional precedent and not hire a press secretary. Why should I pay someone to talk to reporters for me? It was a waste of taxpayer money and an ego trip. I would do it myself. Was I wrong! Six months later, I hired Debbie Bookchin, who had written for the *Rutland Herald*. Tina Wisell, who had done radio work in northern Vermont, eventually replaced Debbie and has been with me for several years.

In December, Jane and I borrowed some money from a friend (we were flat broke) and went to Mexico for a week. Away from the political turmoil, I was able to think about what my office would focus on, and how we could be most effective.

A delightful surprise of my first few weeks in Washington was the wonderful "Welcome to D.C." party put on by the progressive community there. With Jesse Jackson and Ralph Nader as the main speakers, some 500 people crowded into the Eastern Market. Clearly, for many of those people, I was more than the congressman from Vermont. All over the country there was a growing dissatisfaction with politics-as-usual and the two-party system, and the turnout reflected that.

Until recently, the House leadership sponsored a bipartisan orientation for incoming freshmen, usually held at Harvard. The purpose of this was to provide new members with boilerplate information on the workings of Congress as well as expert opinion from leading thinkers on the economy, social issues, and foreign policy. While there is a time and place to hear opposing points of view, this was not one of them. I personally was offended to hear from some of the leading scholars in the Reagan administration. I had not come to Congress to hear about the virtues of supply-side economics. Other new members, with different political perspectives, had similar objections. Ironically enough, it was Newt Gingrich who called a halt to the bipartisan orientations in 1994. He was quite right.

The orientation did, however, give me a first taste of my new status as a member of Congress. It was a bit heady, to say the least, to fly from Andrews Air Force Base via military transport into Boston, have my bags delivered by the military, and then ride to the hotel in a bus escorted by local police cars with lights flashing.

Although I didn't get much out of the lectures except for a few arguments, I did have the opportunity to establish friendships with members of my class, the 102nd Congress, including Neil Abercrombie (Hawaii), Maxine Waters (California), Pete Peterson (Florida), Jim Backus (Florida), Bill Jefferson (Louisiana), Rosa Delauro (Connecticut), Chet Edwards (Texas), Jim Moran (Virginia), Bud Cramer (Alabama), Tim Roemer (Indiana), Eleanor Holmes Norton (D.C.), Collin Peterson (Minnesota), and John Cox (Illinois). While most of my congressional friendships, then and now, are based on shared political views, I have grown to like a number of members with whom I have very little in common politically.

As part of orientation, the new members were invited to the White House for a social occasion to meet with President and Mrs. Bush and Vice President and Mrs. Quayle. Both the president and his wife were gracious and friendly to Jane and me, and seemed quite familiar with my victory. Jane had a long chat with Mrs. Bush, who said something to the effect that "Oh, your husband defeated that man who was so rude to the president." Go figure. On the other hand, Dan and Marilyn Quayle were decidedly unfriendly. Also, in case you're interested, the food was terrific.

My primary concern during the orientation period was how I would be treated with regard to committee assignments and seniority. I was the first Independent in forty years. What would they do with me? Committee assignments are sorted out by the parties, and I was affiliated with neither of them. Would I get on *any* committee? In Congress, the longer you serve the higher up you move in the committee structure. Would I move up if I were reelected or would I always be at the bottom of the pecking order—the last to speak, never gaining a chairmanship or ranking position?

During the campaign, I had publicly stated that I would seek entry into the Democratic Caucus, while remaining an Independent. I had spoken to some of the caucus leaders, and they were not unsympathetic to such an approach. Unfortunately, not all Democrats were in agreement. Charlie Stenholm of Texas, a leader of the conservative Blue Dog Democrats, led the opposition. He was of the opinion that having a socialist in the caucus would not sit well with folks back home.

Stenholm distributed a document containing some of my less than flattering observations on the Democratic Party. Frankly, I was surprised by the quality of his research (my introduction to Lexis Nexis)—the quotes were accurate. Over the years I had been extremely critical of the Democratic Party and its tepidness about fighting for the working families of this country. While party liberals were willing to support my entry into the caucus, the conservatives dug in their heels. At this point I worked out a compromise with Speaker Tom Foley and Majority Leader Dick Gephardt, which remains in effect today: I would not become a member of the Democratic Caucus, but in terms of committee assignments and seniority, I would be treated as if I were a Democrat, as the last-ranking member of my class.

Freshmen members are entitled to pick one "major" and one "minor" committee. I selected Banking and Community Development (very major) and Government Operations. I made those choices because both committees were chaired by progressive Democrats, and more importantly, because their jurisdictions dovetailed with my interests. The savings and loan fiasco had figured largely in my campaign speeches: it was my opinion that working people should not have to pick up the tab for the bailout, and that legislation should be passed to protect them. As a former mayor, I was also interested in creating affordable housing, maintaining community development programs, and developing other progressive initiatives for cities and towns. All of this fell within the domain of the Banking Committee, which was chaired by Henry Gonzalez, one of the strongest progressives in Congress.

The Government Operations Committee has oversight responsibility for all departments and agencies of the federal government. This committee can determine whether and why a department or agency is not adequately performing its mandate. It has wide investigative capabilities. Government Operations was then chaired by John Conyers of Michigan, with whom I had shared podiums as mayor of Burlington. I respected John, a longtime progressive, and looked forward to working with him.

Most Americans don't know the seating arrangements for members of Congress. I didn't before I arrived. In the Senate, each member has his or her own desk, and the Republicans and Democrats are on different sides of the room. I assumed the House was organized in the same way, and wondered whether a new section would have to be created for me. But House members are not assigned permanent seats; we sit wherever we want. The Democrats usually face the Speaker's chair on the left side, while the Republicans take the right. I sometimes hang out with the Illinois crowd on the Democratic side.

The Democrats and Republicans each have a "cloakroom," located just off the floor. I use the Democratic room. It's a place where you can make a phone call, grab a sandwich, watch TV, or sack out on the couch if it's 2 a.m., you need a nap, and you don't want to make the trek back to your office.

Posted on the walls of the Capitol and House office

buildings are directories listing the rooms and phone numbers of members of Congress. Question: How do you tell a Democrat from a Republican from an Independent? Answer: The Democrats are in roman type, the Republicans are in italic, and there I am, all by myself, in SMALL CAPS. My election also created problems for C-Span. They had to add a new line to their congressional record graphics. Now, when C-Span records House votes, there is a line for Democrats, a line for Republicans, and a line for the Independent. Back home everyone says, "Bernie, we always know how *you* vote." Lucky me.

4

We Win Some Victories

On August 2, 1996, the House finally gets a chance to vote on raising the minimum wage, and the measure passes overwhelmingly.

After months and months of dealing with destructive and reactionary legislation—slashes in Medicare, Medicaid, and education; the evisceration of important enviromental legislation; limiting a woman's choice regarding abortion; and punishing children—the U.S. House of Representatives finally passed something to *improve* the lives of tens of millions of Americans who are in desperate need of help.

I have worked to raise the minimum wage from almost my first day in Congress. In 1993, I introduced a bill which would have immediately raised the minimum wage to $5.50 an hour and indexed it to inflation. The only other person in the House to introduce similar legislation at the time was Marty Sabo of Minnesota.

It's easy to forget what real life is about when you make $133,000 a year as a congressman. It's easy to forget what low-income workers feel when you're one of the twenty-nine millionaires in the Senate. It's easy to forget that most people don't drop $50 on lunch when you hang out at the country club with people whose income makes *you* look like a minimum-wage worker.

But there are 12 million American workers earning less than $5.15 an hour, or $10,712 a year. And no, these are not all middle-class teenagers earning a little mad money. Three-quarters of them are adults, mostly women, trying to keep themselves and their families alive. These are people who take on two and three jobs, because forty-hour-a-week jobs are hard to come by, who have to walk to work or wait long periods for a bus because they can't scrape together enough money to buy a car, who sleep in emergency shelters or in campgrounds because they can't pay the rent.

The national minimum wage today, in terms of purchasing power, is 26 percent less than it was twenty years ago. If the minimum wage had kept pace with inflation from 1968, it would be $6.45 today. The increase passed by Congress—$4.70 on July 1, 1996, and then to $5.15 on July 1, 1997—is totally inadequate, but it is at least a step forward. Further, millions of workers making slightly more than the minimum wage—$5.00 to $6.00 an hour—will also get a bump upward.

Since the 1930s, when minimum wage legislation was first enacted, much of the business community and their representatives in Congress have fiercely opposed raising the minimum wage. Executives make millions of dollars a year in income, and yet they oppose a $2,000 a year increase for a fellow American making $8,840. They send forth their lobbyists to do battle—from the U.S. Chamber of Commerce, from the National Federation of Independent Businesses, from the National Association of Manufacturers. Pathetic.

The way the debate on the House floor shaped up was nothing new. Same old lies. Same old bullshit. Same old empty sound-and-fury. Suddenly Dick Armey, Newt Gingrich, and others who had received millions in contributions from corporate America and the rich were deeply concerned about the well-being of low-income workers. Raising the minimum wage, they declaimed with melodramatic handwringing, would *hurt* the poor, not help them. So deeply pained were they by the plight of low-income workers, they could barely hold back the tears. The right-wing think tanks, which are funded by corporate America, had come to the same conclusion, based on "scientifically" assembled empirical data: raising the minimum wage would result in job loss. Companies would not be hiring young workers.

After these same congressmen had just passed legislation to throw millions of poor people off welfare, to make major cuts in food stamps, to slash affordable housing, forgive me for thinking that their sudden display of concern for low-income workers seemed a bit insincere. The theatrics bordered on the comic. Armey vowed to fight an increase in the minimum wage with every fiber of his being. And he did. The Republican leadership stalled a vote for as long as possible. John Boehner, chairman of the House Republican Conference, threatened to kill himself if a minimum wage increase was passed. He didn't. Where is Republican honor when you really need it?

But there was a new, even more insidious, element in this year's debate. In 1989, President George Bush signed a minimum wage increase that had the support of most Republicans, including Newt Gingrich. It was a reasonably bipartisan effort. It is an indication of how fast and far Congress has veered to the right that in the early phase of the 1996 debate virtually no Republicans would back a minimum wage increase. Even more incredible, there were now a significant number of Republicans who wanted to *abolish* the concept of the minimum wage altogether, and grant American workers the "freedom" to work for $3.00 an hour. What had once been the dream of the lunatic fringe had now moved into the mainstream of the Republican Party.

The law of the jungle, the survival of the fittest. Employers want to pay workers bottom dollar, and workers are too desperate to refuse. Voilà. The "magic of the marketplace" at work, brought to us by people who make $133,000 a year. How very civilized.

Millions of Americans are now working for starvation wages. To add insult to injury, these low-wage jobs cost *taxpayers* huge amounts of money in corporate welfare. When fast-food chains, grocery stores, and service industry employers pay $4.50 or $5.00 an hour, their employees often need additional support in order to eat, pay the rent, and take care of their kids. These are the workers who receive Medicaid, food stamps, subsidized housing, and other resources through government programs.

In 1993, when I introduced my minimum wage legislation, I was only able to secure fifty cosponsors, almost all
progressive Democrats. No Republicans signed on.
President Clinton was also opposed, as I discovered at a
meeting with him in the Oval Office. Clinton confers regu-
larly with the congressional leadership of the Democratic
and Republican parties. In a phone conversation, I suggested
it might be appropriate for him to meet with the leadership
of the "Independent Caucus" as well. He was kind enough
to schedule me for a fifteen-minute session. I stayed for half
an hour.

Our discussion centered on three issues. First, I tried to
win his support for raising the minimum wage. He said
that he was not unsympathetic to the idea, but that it
couldn't be done while his health care proposal was being
debated. Second, I commiserated with him about the
savage attacks he had been receiving from the media. He
and Mrs. Clinton were being ripped apart by Rush
Limbaugh and other right-wingers every day of the week.
I asked him to think about the very serious problem of
corporate control of the media and what, if anything,
could be done about it. Lastly, I asked for his support of
the Northeast Dairy Compact, which would greatly assist
Vermont's dairy farmers. Vermont farmers are going out
of business in large numbers because they receive a very
low price for their milk. The Compact, which is supported
by all six New England states, would allow the Northeast
region to set a fair price for the milk their farmers produce.
Clinton understood the concept and indicated that he was
not unsympathetic.

Despite the importance of the issue and the desperate straits of a core constituency of the electorate, there was practically no discussion in 1993 by the Democratic Party about raising the minimum wage. Now, in 1996, with a presidential election coming up, and tired of being on the defensive over the Republican agenda, the Democrats finally recognized it as a good political issue: polls showed that over 80 percent of the people were sympathetic to raising the minimum wage. The Democrats correctly perceived that making a pitch for low-wage workers would boost their campaign against Gingrich and Bob Dole, and their woeful record on the needs of working people.

To give the Democrats due credit, once they decided to push the issue, they did a very effective job. House Majority Leader Dick Gephardt organized an impressive press conference at which low-wage workers had an opportunity to air their views. It was unusual and refreshing for workers to have a platform on Capitol Hill. Ted Kennedy, Paul Wellstone, and a few other senators spoke, as well as a number of us from the House.

From then on, the Democratic leaders placed the issue at the forefront of their agenda. They had members raise the issue during the "one minutes" at the beginning of the day, and worked hard and creatively to get the legislation attached to various other bills that the Republican leadership was bringing up. For once, they were focused and determined to press a piece of legislation to its conclusion.

In one of the few instances since Gingrich ascended to the Speaker's chair, the Republicans couldn't hold their members in line. Faced with the unpleasant task of explaining to low- and moderate-income workers in their districts why they were not willing to support a long over-due increase in the minimum wage, six northern Republicans broke away from Gingrich and backed the legislation. Soon after, another fourteen Republicans were prepared to bolt, with more waiting in the wings. Finally, a majority of the House supported raising the minimum wage—and Gingrich and Armey, kicking and screaming, were forced to call a vote.

The debate itself was quite extraordinary. In effect, Republicans argued that miserable wages are good for America because they keep the country competitive. For workers, of course, this "competition" means a race to the bottom: responding to wages paid in China, sometimes as low as twenty cents an hour.

But the major battle on the floor involved the Goodling amendment, designed to exempt businesses with $500,000 or less in profits from paying the minimum wage. By itself, this amendment would have taken away minimum wage protection from new applicants for some 10.5 million jobs. More importantly, it would have paved the way for the eventual elimination of the minimum wage concept altogether. The proposal to remove minimum wage requirements for small businesses was defeated on a close vote of 229 to 196. One hundred and eighty-nine Republicans voted for it.

During the debate, the only valid point that the Republicans made was to ask why the Democrats, if they were so concerned about low-wage workers, had not passed a minimum wage increase two years earlier when they had the majority in the House and Senate? I agreed, and got some time from Scott McInnis, a Republican from Colorado, to express my views.

While Republicans were incorrect in claiming that a small increase in the minimum wage would lead to job loss, their argument hid a more important issue. The major crisis of the current period is not unemployment, but the rapid decline in working-class wages. While unemployment remains too high—and it is far higher than "official" statistics indicate—the more serious problem is that real wages for American workers have declined by 16 percent over the last twenty years. In 1973, the average American worker was earning $445 a week. Twenty years later, that worker was making $373 a week in real dollars.

The situation is even more acute for low-wage workers and workers who lack a college degree. Real wages for male high school graduates in entry-level jobs plummeted a full 30 percent in the past fifteen years, while wages have fallen 18 percent for young women. During the 1980s, about three-quarters of the new jobs created in America were poverty-level jobs, many temporary and part-time.

"Welfare reform" has deepened the crisis. What happens to wages when millions of the working poor lose their safety net and are forced to compete with other low-wage workers? What happens to public employees and their wage scale when they are replaced by former welfare recipients forced into workfare programs?

The minimum wage bill passed by a vote of 354 to 72. Interestingly, 160 Republicans ended up voting for the bill, when just a few months before none of them had supported it. Many people might find this conversion puzzling. In fact, it is the predictable result of an important political dynamic.

The forces of reaction work most effectively behind closed doors, hidden from public scrutiny. When debate on an issue is pushed into the open, in this case, onto the floor of the House, when the close link between special interests, the wealthy, and their "representatives" in Congress is threatened with exposure, the opposition will often surrender rather than resist.

Force a vote, so that the public can see the position of their representatives, and often the common good will prevail. This is what happened, to my great surprise, with an amendment I introduced in September 1995, seeking to eliminate outrageous corporate bonuses at Lockheed-Martin.

One of Burlington's largest employers was Martin Marietta. When that defense contractor merged with Lockheed to form Lockheed-Martin, I was more than usually attuned to the implication of that deal—the downsizing of 17,000 American workers. For making the "tough decision" to fire all those workers, the executives of the newly merged company decided to pay themselves $91 million in executive bonuses. Ninety-one million dollars as a reward for obliterating 17,000 jobs.

Some of the major recipients of that bonus were the CEO of the company, Norm Augustine ($8.2 million); former Tennessee governor and presidential aspirant Lamar Alexander ($236,000); former secretary of defense Mel Laird ($1.6 million); and retired general and former member of the Joint Chiefs of Staff John Vessey ($372,000).

Now, a $91 million bonus for executives who were laying off 17,000 workers is obscene enough. Even worse, Bill Goold, my legislative director, discovered that fully one-third of that money, $31 million, was to come from the Pentagon as "restructuring costs." As soon as I learned about this outrageous federal give-away, I drafted an amendment to prevent the Pentagon from paying the bonus. Imagine: workers thrown out of their jobs paying taxes so that the bastards who fired them could stuff their pockets. Bill termed the legislation the "payoffs for layoffs" amendment.

When I brought that amendment to the floor, I thought I'd have a very hard fight on my hands. But to my surprise, John Murtha, the ranking Democrat on the Defense Appropriations Committee and consequently the person responsible for Democratic strategy on the bill, said they were going to support it. He discussed the amendment with Bill Young, the Republican chairman of Military Appropriations, who signed on without hesitation. The amendment passed by voice vote.

Here was a controversial piece of legislation—challenging corporate America, and in particular the right of the wealthy to pay themselves handsomely for eliminating the jobs of working people—which was being endorsed by both parties. The truth is, nobody wanted to defend, either on the floor of the House or especially to constituents, the government's use of taxpayer money to pay bonuses to executives (already making millions) who had just laid off thousands of American workers.

In politics, if you are not continually learning, you lose ground fast. I learned something from that success, both about the political process and about the rivers of "corporate welfare" that pour out of the Pentagon. Those lessons, along with some excellent work on the part of my staff, later enabled us to pull off another truly significant coup.

We learned, after much probing, that the Pentagon bonuses to Lockheed-Martin executives were merely the tip of the iceberg in terms of corporate welfare for the defense industry. Clinton's secretary of defense, William Perry, had instituted a new policy under which the Pentagon provides "restructuring costs" to companies that undergo a merger. Through this policy, the federal government offers corporations huge sums of money to encourage mergers in the defense industry. Corporate "efficiency" is the ostensible goal; there is no concern with the mergers' inevitable result, the laying off of many thousands of American workers.

Further, there is absolutely no evidence that fewer companies and diminished competition within the defense industry will save taxpayers one nickel. Lockheed-Martin already controls a dangerous 32 percent of defense business. Increased concentration by large companies will not lower our taxes, nor enable the Pentagon to purchase products for lower prices.

In any case, this is a perverse sort of government involvement in the economy. I subscribe to the concept of industrial policy, where the government plays a role in *creating*, with the private sector, decent-paying jobs. I do not believe that the government should offer incentives to lay off tens of thousands of workers.

In studying this issue, we learned that Lockheed-Martin alone had close to a billion dollars of "restructuring costs" in the pipeline. Another company had already received $200 million, and there were thirty-two other corporations in the process of applying for money to subsidize "restructuring." Needless to say, despite the huge amount of money involved, this was an issue that had not received much attention, either by Congress or the media.

We managed to create a very interesting left-right alliance on the issue. New Jersey representative Chris Smith is a conservative Republican with whom I had been only slightly acquainted. He is best known as one of the foremost opponents of abortion rights in Congress. But Lockheed-Martin closed down a plant in his district, a plant that had employed 3,000 workers. Smith believed that the shutdown was encouraged by the Pentagon's financial assistance. After I introduced an amendment to end the incentive program, Smith supported it. That made it the Sanders-Smith amendment. Then a moderate Democrat, David Minge from Minnesota, a progressive, Peter DeFazio from Oregon, and others, signed on as original cosponsors. The amendment would come before the House with truly broad-based support.

Again, both John Murtha, ranking Democrat on the Defense Subcommittee of the Appropriations Committee, and the Republican leadership accepted the amendment without a fuss. Nobody wanted to oppose such a sensible amendment—not on the floor, in any case—especially with tripartisan support. Nobody wanted to have to explain how using taxpayer dollars to lay off workers would benefit America.

The only controversy regarding the amendment was what it would be called. Would it be the Sanders-Smith amendment, or the Smith-Sanders amendment? Smith's version was similar to mine, but mine was stronger. But Smith is a Republican in a Republican-controlled House. We agreed that my version would be adopted, but it would be called the Smith-Sanders amendment. The legislation attracted significant attention. A substantial article in the *Los Angeles Times* called it a "major defeat" for the defense industry. Of course, getting it through the House was only the first step. It had to survive conference committee and pass the Senate. The next day, to my delight, my office received four calls from senators requesting information on the amendment: Barbara Boxer, John McCain, Chuck Grassley, and Tom Harkin. Two Republicans and two Democrats—a good sign.

By developing that amendment, I touched on a major issue that had been well hidden, and that had apparently never before been discussed on the floor of the House. To my mind, I was doing what, as an Independent, I had been elected to do. I have come to understand that one of the most important roles I can play in Congress is to raise issues that, for a variety of reasons, other people choose not to deal with. Just shifting the framework of debate can have enormous consequences.

Frankly, the big money interests do not intimidate me— not the medical-industrial complex, not the military-industrial complex, not Wall Street or the American Bankers Association. Exposing the outrageous practice by which the Defense Department subsidized corporate mergers and the laying off of tens of thousands of workers is precisely what I was elected to do.

Still, when the total Defense Authorization bill came to the floor, I ended up voting against it, even though it included the Smith-Sanders amendment. Sometimes it's difficult to explain this sort of action to people who do not follow Congress. Simply put, I try to make each and every bill better by drafting and, hopefully, passing good amendments. When the final bill comes up, I weigh the good elements against the bad and, sometimes, even if I've improved it with amendments, I still end up voting against it. In this instance, the bill contained far too much money for the military—$10 billion more than the president had wanted, and he wanted too much.

Susan Sweetser's new Federal Election Commission report has just been made public. Lockheed-Martin has contributed $10,000 to her campaign, the maximum allowed by law. What a shock.

So much to do. So little time to do it in. On Friday, after the week's battles in Congress, I fly from Washington to Hartford, Connecticut, where Phil Fiermonte picks me up and we drive to Brattleboro, in southern Vermont, for the second of my campaign announcements. This one is much like the Burlington event, but features speakers from Windham County. All the seats are filled in the Town Hall by a crowd of about sixty or seventy people. A good sign. Also, the media coverage is good.

The highlight of the Brattleboro event is an electrifying speech delivered by a young high school student, Acacia

Fanto. I am so engrossed by what she says that I don't mind being upstaged.

I first met this young woman when she came to the Vermont youth conference sponsored by my office last year. The conference brought together students from ten different high schools to give talks on issues they felt Congress should be addressing. The presentations, which in a number of cases required substantial research by the students, were excellent. The idea for the student hearing came from Tim Kipp, a personal friend who teaches social studies at Brattleboro Union High School. Acacia was his student, and her message is simple but profound: in order to preserve democracy, it is imperative that young people be actively involved in the political process. Without them, democracy will not survive. Her short speech is cogent and deeply touching.

Traveling through Vermont, I try to schedule opportunities to speak in the schools whenever I can. Over the past five years, I have spoken in almost every high school in the state as well as many elementary schools. It's important that young people get a chance to talk to their congressman, to express their concerns and opinions. Many of these students have very little understanding of the relationship of politics and government to their lives. Teachers tell me that it is surprising how many kids become more interested in the political process after meeting their congressman face to face.

Peter Shumlin, the Democratic minority leader in the state senate, endorses my candidacy at the Brattleboro meeting. Peter has not been publicly supportive in the past, but feels it is important to play a role in defeating the Gingrich agenda. After spending the night with Tim Kipp and his wife, Kathy Keller, at my longtime home away from home in Brattleboro, Phil and I drive to Bennington on Saturday morning for another opening announcement. Bennington and Brattleboro, the two major towns in southern Vermont, are only forty miles apart over the Hogback mountains, but they are as different as night and day. Brattleboro is the most countercultural town in the state, while Bennington is solidly working class.

The turnout at the meeting in Bennington is respectable, especially considering it is the kind of beautiful spring day when Vermonters hate to be inside. After a long Vermont winter, indoor meetings on a beautiful spring day are not usually a big draw. A highlight of the announcement is the talk by Mark Santelli, the former president of the UAW local at the Johnson Controls battery plant in Bennington.

On a Sunday in August 1993, I had marched with the UAW at the Battle of Bennington parade. The next day, workers learned that Johnson Controls was closing their plant, and 269 decent-paying union jobs would be lost when production was shifted to Mexico. Mark's valiant effort to keep the plant in Vermont had failed. My office was helpful in getting the laid-off workers some additional benefits under the NAFTA legislation. Mark is not only a respected union leader, he is also active in the hunting community and, like me, does not believe hunters need AK-47s to kill a deer. His support is much appreciated.

Next stop, Rutland. A political campaign is always full of surprises. This time it is a veteran, Jeffrey Hatch, who gives a terrific speech. As it happens, I had never met him before. He is very articulate and direct. "I'm a Republican, I'm a veteran, and I'm supporting Bernie Sanders because he's been good on veterans' issues." In Rutland, the speeches are wonderful, but the turnout poor.

Now it's on to St. Johnsbury, the third and last stop of the day. St. Johnsbury is the "capital" of the Northeast Kingdom, the most rural, the most rugged, the poorest, and in some ways the most beautiful part of Vermont. Our activist support in the Northeast Kingdom is almost all working class: low-income advocates, family farmers, veterans. Two couples, Bob and Kay Perkins and Marvin Minkler and Mary Strole, organized the event. A number of seniors attend, but the crowd is small. One of my favorite people in the state, Jenny Nelson, a farmer from Ryegate, gives a terrific speech. Jenny and her husband, Bill, own a beautiful farm, which has been in the Nelson family for generations. Like many other Vermont farmers, they work incredibly long hours and are fighting hard to hold onto their land. Jenny, who is one of the leaders of Rural Vermont, a progressive family farm organization, talks about how we have worked together over the years on a number of projects to save family farms.

Phil and I rack up 500 miles on the odometer that weekend. Every mile is worth it. The campaign kickoffs in Brattleboro, Bennington, Rutland, and St. Johnsbury bring our supporters together and receive generally good news coverage. But they are also important because they remind me on a deep, emotional level why I am a congressman, and how fortunate I am to have such great people behind me.

Having all those people supporting our effort is a source of great pride. It sustains me when I go back to the inside-the-beltway mentality of Washington.

Along with 434 others, on January 3, 1991, I was sworn in as a member of the United States Congress. On that day, as is customary, new members hosted receptions in their offices for friends and family who came by to wish them luck. We held a reception in our office, too. Unfortunately, I was unable to attend. I was at meetings trying to prevent a war.

On August 2, 1990, Saddam Hussein, a former ally who was well supplied with American equipment, invaded Kuwait. On August 9, U.S. troops sent by President Bush began arriving in Saudi Arabia to prevent further Iraqi aggression. Now, in early January, Bush was seeking congressional authority for an all-out war with Iraq. I was opposed to giving him that authority.

From the very beginning of the Persian Gulf crisis, I was of the belief that the United States could push Saddam Hussein out of Kuwait without having to resort to war. Diplomacy, economic boycott, isolation, financial leverage: we had many means for reversing the invasion. I was not only opposed to the war because of the potential destruction and loss of life, but also because I believe it *is* possible for the major countries of this planet, and a virtually united world community, to resolve crises without carnage. If this matter could not be solved without massive bombing and killing thousands of people, then what crisis could ever be solved peacefully?

Further, I was angry that the Iraqi situation was deflecting attention from the serious domestic crises that we
faced, problems that I was anxious to tackle. (Some would
argue that deflecting attention away from domestic injustice is one of the major functions of war.) Twenty percent
of our children live in poverty, millions of Americans lack
decent housing, workers' standard of living is in free-fall,
and we need a major overhaul of our health care system to
ensure affordable medical care for everyone. And now we
were going to spend months engaged in a war with a
two-bit tyrant.

In those early days of the 102nd Congress, several
members, among them Ron Dellums and Tom Foglietta,
organized an antiwar caucus in the House. What should our
overall strategy be in trying to prevent the war? What
alternatives were available to get Saddam Hussein out of
Kuwait without bloodshed? How could we affect public
opinion? How could we win more votes in Congress for
our position? These were some of the questions we wrestled with at meeting after meeting in the first days of the
new Congress.

In Vermont, I spoke at a large antiwar demonstration
at the state capital. About 1,500 people attended. In
Washington, I was appearing in the national media as a
critic of the drift toward war.

In early January, I attended a meeting in which Speaker
Foley and the Democratic leadership—Gephardt, Bonior,
and others—talked about the upcoming vote. At that time
the Democrats had a strong majority in the House and
Senate. Simply stated, if the Democratic leadership wanted

to block the war, they had the votes to do it. My friend Tom Andrews, a fellow antiwar freshman from Maine, asked a straightforward question: Would the leadership impose party discipline on this vote, and refuse to give Bush the authority to declare war? Foley looked straight at Tom and told him that there would be no party discipline. While he, and every other member of the leadership, was going to vote against giving the president the authority to send our troops into battle, he was not going to demand that all Democrats support that position.

At that moment, I knew the war was inevitable. Ostensibly, the Democrats controlled the House. Yet, on the most important issue facing the country, the Republicans were going to win. It was clear that there would be enough Democrats joining the Republicans to give Bush the necessary votes.

On January 15, just before the war broke out, I spoke on the floor of the House: "Mr. Speaker, let me begin my saying that I think we all agree in this body, and throughout this country, and throughout virtually the entire world, that Saddam Hussein is an evil person, and what he has done in Kuwait is illegal, immoral, and brutal. It seems to me, however, that the challenge of our time is not simply to begin a war which will result in the deaths of tens of thousands of people, young Americans, innocent women and children in Iraq, but the real challenge of our time is to see how we can stop aggression, how we can stop evil in a new way, in a nonviolent way.

"If ever there has been a time in the history of the world when the entire world is united against one small country, this is that time. It seems to me a terrible failing, and very ominous for the future, if we cannot resolve this crisis, if we cannot defeat Saddam Hussein in a nonviolent way. If we are not successful now, then I think all that this world has to look forward to in the future for our children, is war, and more war, and more war."

My speech, and many other fine speeches, had little impact. Bush had the votes. On January 17, 1991, American planes attacked Iraq with a massive show of force.

On January 18, 1991, I once again spoke on the House floor: "Mr. Speaker, a few months ago the entire world rejoiced that the Cold War had finally ended, and that the hundreds of billions of dollars being spent on bombs and tanks and missiles could finally be used to improve human life, not to destroy human life.

"Mr. Speaker, a major war in the Persian Gulf, costing us thousands of lives and tens of billions of dollars, could well be a disaster for the people of our country—especially the working people, the poor people, the elderly, and the children. I predict that this Congress will soon be asked for more money for guided missiles, but there will be no money available to house the homeless. I predict that this Congress will soon be asked for more money for tanks, but there will be no money or effort available to develop a national health care system, guaranteeing health care for all of our people—as virtually all of the industrialized world has.

"I predict that this Congress will soon be asked for more money for bombs, but there will be no money available to reindustrialize our nation so that our working people can have decent-paying jobs. There will be no money available for education and for our children—25 percent of whom live in poverty. There will be no money available for the environment, or to help the family farmer—many of whom are being forced off the land today in my state of Vermont and throughout this country.

"Mr. Speaker, I predict that in order to pay for this war, there will be more cutbacks in Medicare for the elderly, and even an effort to cut back on Social Security payments."

For me personally, this was a very depressing period. I am not a pacifist. I believe that there are times when war is legitimate, when the alternative is existence under a horrendous status quo. I think those instances, however, are much rarer than most government leaders admit.

It would seem that after thousands of years in which one group or country has resolved its problems by killing the people of another group or country, the human race should be ready to learn something about resolving differences nonviolently. I had been a vocal opponent of the Vietnam War, an opponent of the war against the people of Nicaragua, an opponent of the U.S. invasions of Grenada and Panama. Now, as a U.S. congressman, I had voted against the Persian Gulf War.

As the bombs began falling and American troops entered combat, I learned a very painful lesson about congressional politics.

A resolution was brought before the House on January 18—a Republican-drafted document endorsed by the Democratic leadership. The resolution urged congressional support for our troops in combat and simultaneously commended "the efforts and leadership of the President."

An amendment on March 5 praised the president for "his decisive leadership, unerring judgment, and sound decisions with respect to the crisis in the Persian Gulf." I was incredulous. Unerring judgment? Not only did this phrase sound like some Stalinist propaganda of the 1930s, it directly contradicted what 183 members had said through their votes against the war less than two months earlier.

It was one thing, now that the war had begun and American troops were fighting for their lives, to express support for them. I was ready and willing to do that. But it seemed to me that it was a very different thing to declare that President Bush had been right all along regarding the situation in the Persian Gulf, and that war had been the only solution. After all, almost half of Congress had opposed the president's militarism. Sending in the troops and bombers changed the situation for soldiers, but it did not nullify our basic argument that peaceful solutions are preferable to military ones. We had not been wrong, but that is exactly what the resolution asked us to say.

In the face of a growing and massive media campaign to justify and celebrate the war, it was hard to vote no this second time. A week earlier, 183 members had voted to support a continuation of economic sanctions, and against a war. Now, as I looked up at the vote tally board, *everyone* was voting yes. I remember putting my card into the machine—we vote on the floor by using a card with a magnetic strip to activate a voting machine, and then pressing either the yes or no button—and thinking to myself, "This is going to be a short congressional career." I pressed the no button. Only five other members did the same. The vote was 399 to 6.

That vote would haunt me. In every election since, political opponents charge, "In the middle of a war, Bernie Sanders did not vote to support the troops." It's a lie and a distortion of reality, but it works well in a thirty-second radio ad.

I had been in Congress for less than a month, and already I was feeling awfully lonely. But how I was feeling personally or politically was a lot less important than what was happening in the country.

And what was happening was frightening. A more or less totalitarian system was kicking into effect. Even a longtime critic of the media like myself was stunned by the servility of the media, by how quickly they fell into line behind the militaristic imperatives of the president and Pentagon. Their obedience paid off. When I returned to Vermont, there was a yellow ribbon on what seemed like every house and tree. The media had succeeded in creating a national war mood.

Television gave virtually no coverage to people who opposed the war. Reporting was tightly controlled and totally one-sided. A study done several years later found that pro-war National Football League players got more air time to discuss their views on the Persian Gulf War than the whole antiwar movement put together. During the early days of the war, Jesse Jackson led a large march on Washington, and it received almost no coverage. Simply stated, there was massive censorship of dissent, criticism, debate.

Clearly, the government had learned a lesson from the Vietnam War. This time, the media would not play a role in providing information to support any sort of antiwar sentiment. No Americans would be televised coming home in body bags. No photos of American atrocities would reach the evening news. No critics would be heard above the din of the president's pumped-up war rhetoric.

And it was not just the national television. It was the radio, the newspapers, the magazines. I tried to get news in Washington from the supposedly liberal National Public Radio network, but they were as bad as everyone else. In fact, there was no pretense at objectivity. The government *announced* that it was censoring the news. Instead of contesting this flagrant violation of the public's right to be informed, the media submitted to the blackout and lapped up the government's doctored reports. Before Congress had voted to give the president authority to send troops into combat, polls showed the country was pretty evenly divided on the wisdom of U.S. involvement. Three weeks into the war (and a massive media campaign), the overwhelming majority of Americans supported it.

One of the very few newspapers courageous enough to oppose the war was located in my own state. Stephen Faye, the editor of the *Brattleboro Reformer*, withstood criticism from some of his advertisers, and wrote forceful editorials against the war week after week. Tragically, in those emotional days, there were very few journalists with that sort of courage.

Six years after the war, I wonder how many Americans have seen even one story about the enormous loss of life suffered by the women and children of Iraq. An estimated 200,000 noncombatants died in that war, killed by our "smart bombs." This figure does not include the terrible loss of life incurred after the war as a result of hunger, contaminated water, lack of health care, and the destruction of the Iraqi infrastructure. Though brief, the war caused enormous slaughter and suffering for the ordinary people of Iraq. No, our "smart bombs" did not avoid "collateral damage." No, it was not just Iraqi soldiers who died.

The president and the Pentagon claimed the war was a success: we achieved our objectives with very little loss of American life. What they did not tell us was that some 70,000 American soldiers returned with a variety of ailments commonly referred to as Persian Gulf syndrome. In fact, ever since the war, the Pentagon has lied and attempted to conceal almost all information about the devastating effects of the war on American soldiers. It took five years for the military to even acknowledge that American troops had been exposed to chemical warfare agents when they blew up an Iraqi munitions depot in the town of Khamiseyah. Even today, it is difficult for those of us in Congress who are demanding adequate treatment and compensation for these hidden casualties of the war to get the truth from the Pentagon.

And let me be very clear. Given their enormous success in selling the Persian Gulf debacle, there is no reason to expect that the government and the media will behave any differently when the next war comes. If they could win massive public support for defending "freedom" in Kuwait, they can use the same techniques to build support for *any* war. After all, Kuwait was, and is, a country controlled by billionaire emirs. Kuwait is not so free that it allows women to vote, or even to drive automobiles. It is not so free that the Christian and Jewish soldiers we sent to defend Kuwait were allowed to celebrate Christmas or Hanukkah when they were there.

Hard as it was to be in Washington in those days, it was even harder to be in Vermont. I recall, with deep hurt, seeing off a unit of the Vermont National Guard as they departed for the Gulf. I was booed by a few people there, one of the few times in my political career that had ever happened to me. War is a very strange phenomenon. I do not claim to understand its psychological effects. Here I had done my best to prevent young Vermonters and other Americans from getting killed, and I was being booed for my efforts. One day I was at the airport waiting for a flight to Washington, and a woman said to me, "My son is over there. I'm appalled that you're not supporting him." That wasn't true, but nothing I said would convince her otherwise.

On a more optimistic note, a poll came out during that period which found my "favorability" ratings reasonably high. Apparently, a number of Vermonters respected my standing up for what I believed, even if they disagreed with my position on the war.

Those early days in Congress were very tough. I even managed to make a fool of myself at a nationally televised Washington event. To this day, whenever the subject of that night comes up, my wife, who saw it on TV in Vermont, involuntarily winces and shakes her head. I was invited to speak before the annual dinner hosted by the National Press

Club. Of course, I didn't know it at the time, but this is a major event on the Capitol calendar, attended by everybody who is anybody: Supreme Court justices, leading business people, major politicians, celebrities, and, of course, all the Washington media. Four new members of Congress, including me, had been invited to speak.

But they wanted more than a speech. We were expected to be funny, too. It was supposed to be a lighthearted and amusing evening, with everyone guaranteed a good time. I had three problems with the event. First, I have no talent for stand-up comedy before hundreds of strangers with whom I have nothing in common. Second, I was in no mood for jokes when a war I vigorously opposed had just broken out. And third, this was a black tie affair and I didn't have a tuxedo or a black tie (and I had no intention of ever buying either).

For those reasons and a few more, I called the organizers and told them that, on reflection, I didn't think I should attend. They strongly disagreed. The invitations had already gone out with my name as one of the speakers: everybody would be *terribly* disappointed. I just *had* to be there.

The upshot was that I allowed myself to be talked into going. The evening was a disaster. There I was, morose, telling lame jokes that a few of us in the office had cooked up minutes before I left for the event, my performance beamed by C-Span back to Vermont and across the country. The only consolation was that Senator Paul Wellstone, another invited speaker, was equally bad. This was a miserable night for me during a miserable period.

*   *   *

Yesterday, the *Burlington Free Press* published a story analyzing Vermonters' opinions on whether Barbara Snelling should continue her candidacy for governor. Snelling, an old friend who is currently the Republican lieutenant governor, suffered a massive stroke a month ago. What that tells me is that the *Free Press* conducted a poll, and that means they asked more than one question. So I assume that in today's paper there will be a poll on the congressional race. That worries me, because it will undoubtedly show that the gap is closing. We're not going to win this election by the twenty-one points predicted in their last poll. Sweetser will then roll out the patter used by all challengers: "We're closing the gap, we're gathering momentum, the Sanders camp is panicking"—the usual stuff.

I hate polls. If you're the incumbent and better known, you're supposed to be ahead. If the race gets closer, as it invariably does when the challenger becomes better known, then you're "in trouble." It is a no-win situation for a well-known incumbent. But what is particularly amazing about the *Free Press* poll is that I am so preoccupied with it. I even wake up in the middle of the night thinking about the damn poll. Yet, tomorrow I will have surgery on my vocal cords. Here I am, having surgery for the first time in my life, and I don't think about that at all. No nightmares. No anxiety attacks. Instead, I'm worried about a stupid poll five months before the election.

The operation is intended to correct a problem I've had with my voice. It's a scary business. I assume the doctors know what they're doing and they seem to think it's a minor procedure. Still, if they make a mistake, it's my voice for the rest of my life.

The idea of surgery has plagued me for months in a low-key, persistent way. The problem with my voice began a year and a half ago, toward the end of the 1994 campaign, when I developed a cold and was hoarse for a few days. In the midst of a campaign, you do what you have to do, so I continued giving speeches. Eventually the cold went away, but the hoarseness remained. Since then, I have had problems speaking: my voice sounds gravelly at best, and there are times when it rasps so much I have difficulty finishing a sentence.

The truth is that I've handled this voice situation stupidly. I've been a healthy person all my life: I was a mayor for eight years and have been in Congress for six, and in all that period I have missed less than five days of work. When I get a flu, I still go to work. Being sick is not part of my life. So when my throat became hoarse, I thought it would take care of itself. It didn't.

After a number of months without my voice improving, I consulted a specialist at Bethesda Naval Hospital. He told me I had a benign nodule on my vocal cords, and recommended an operation to remove it. I hoped there might be an alternative treatment, so I tried all sorts of nonsurgical remedies: throat lozenges, resting my voice, herb teas. Although my voice is marginally better than it was a year ago, it is still far from normal. All sorts of advisers, from my wife to close friends, tell me that my voice is the major point of discussion about me in the state. There's even some speculation that I have throat cancer.

The condition doesn't cause me any physical discomfort and I can forget about it most of the time. But no one else seems to be able to. On the radio last week, the last question on a call-in show was, "So, Bernie, how's your voice doing?" By now each Vermont newspaper has published several articles on the subject, including front-page stories. My medical condition is making Vermont's throat specialists famous. There has been more coverage of my vocal cords than any of the work I've been doing in Congress.

A month ago I went back to Bethesda and then to the medical center at Georgetown University. After sticking a tube down my throat and looking at my vocal cords on a TV monitor, the Georgetown doctor agreed that I could not escape surgery. The next day, I made an appointment for the operation at Bethesda. One has to remain silent for four days after the surgery, so we scheduled it for a time when it would be least inconvenient.

Naturally, I have fears about the operation, with so much at risk. It is through the voice that each of us communicates to our fellow human beings, be they wives or children or political constituents. Further, for me, an activist and a politician, speaking is an essential tool for what I need to do.

I hope to God this guy doesn't make a mistake. He seems to think it is a routine operation, no big deal. He tells me they do it all the time. I asked him, "What rate of failure do you have?" He told me there is success the overwhelming majority of times. We'll see.

Two weeks later: The operation is a success. For the first time in fifty-four years—my entire life—I have had surgery. I was very well behaved. They told me not to talk for three to five days afterward so, breaking the habit of a lifetime, I didn't. I fear, though, now that almost two weeks have passed, with all the demands on me, I am probably overdoing it. I shouldn't have given that speech to the regional United Electrical Workers convention a few days ago. So I am going to be cautious again. I've got to be very disciplined, because the worst thing I can do is to blow it now, which is what Governor Pete Wilson of California did when he had similar surgery. I do not want to go through this again, the voice I can't control, the fears, yet more surgery.

Jane thinks I am more relaxed now, which is probably true. Not knowing what sound was going to pop out of my mouth was nerve-racking. In order to compensate for the hoarseness, I had a natural tendency to raise the decibel level. On one occasion on the floor of the House, my voice went completely dead and only a glass of water brought to me by a colleague enabled me to finish my remarks.

Consequently, it is a strange experience to go to the podium for the first time following surgery. For a year and half I have had to shout into the microphone, but this time, coming forward to speak for an amendment, I am astonished. My voice is so clear and smooth that as I begin to speak, I actually *lower* it, and for the first time I appreciate the quality of the sound system in the House chamber. My voice resounds all over the hall, without any need to shout. Only now do I realize what a strain it has been.

Every year Burlington restaurants sponsor a remarkable festival called the Green Mountain Choo-Choo, bringing out thousands of Vermonters interested in sampling the wealth of dishes that the restaurants provide for the occasion. A large crowd always attracts my campaigner's instincts, so here I am, shaking hands and saying hello. Over and over again people tell me that my voice sounds great, that they are glad to see me back to my old self. I'm astonished that this matter attracts so much attention— more than any political issue I've ever worked on. But it's gratifying to find out how many Vermonters are concerned about my well-being.

Meanwhile, there have been some major developments in the campaign. Jack Long, a Democrat, will be entering the race. Long is the former state commissioner of environmental protection. Instead of a two-way race between Sweetser and me, there will now be a three-way campaign. Sweetser is delighted. She and many others believe that Long's candidacy will draw votes away from me. I'm not so sure. If he does well, he will hurt me. If he doesn't get many votes, Sweetser will probably lose as much as me. The Democratic candidate only received 3 percent of the vote in 1990 and 6 percent in 1992. In 1994 there was no Democrat.

Long, a lawyer and former state administrator, is more credible than past Democratic candidates. Governor Dean is supporting him, but states publicly that he doesn't think Long will get more than 10 percent of the vote. Clearly, I will lose some votes to Long from Democrats who would have voted for me because they dislike Sweetser. But Sweetser will lose votes from moderate Republicans who think she's too conservative and would never support me. Who knows how it will all shake out?

Long is staking out the "moderate" position. He says: "I think if I decide to run I will easily differentiate myself from Mr. Sanders and Ms. Sweetser. They are on the extreme ends, extreme right and left. There is no moderate candidate representing the views of moderate Vermonters."

Another troubling development: a new *Burlington Free Press* poll shows that Sweetser has narrowed the gap. In March, according to their poll, I was ahead by 45 to 26 percent. By late May, my lead is down to 41 to 25. It's not good news. At this stage an incumbent should be doing better. We've got a lot of work to do.

The struggle never ends. If it's not one fight, it's another. If it's not the perversity of those who represent the wealthy, it's the absurdity of congressional politics. Right now, for instance, I am fighting very hard to maintain the Northeast Dairy Compact. The Compact is an attempt to save dairy farms in Vermont and throughout the Northeast.

I was born in Brooklyn, and did not know one end of a cow from the other when I arrived in Vermont twenty-seven years later. Today, while I am by no means an expert on agricultural economics or dairy farming, I do know it is absolutely imperative that we save the family farms. They are a vital part of our state's economy, they protect our environment, and they connect us to our heritage. Vermont can be many things without its farms, but it would not be what any of us know as "Vermont."

Over the years I have developed an almost emotional attachment to the state's dairy farmers and have fought hard for them against overwhelming odds. Today there are fewer than 2,000 dairy farms in the state, a number that declines annually. The work is not attractive to young people, since the hours are long and the work week usually runs seven days. No wonder our farm population is aging.

Most people who see lovely red barns and cows grazing in pastures do not understand the economy behind the pastoral vista. Farmers have a great deal in common with workers in urban areas. Like low-wage workers everywhere, many are able to survive only because of food stamps and other programs for low-income families. And like both unionized and nonunionized workers, farmers are at the mercy of huge corporations. Agribusiness dominates the feed industry and is rapidly taking over milk production and processing. Now it is even trying to turn cows into an extension of the corporate production process.

Several years ago I led the effort in Congress against Monsanto's bovine growth hormone (BGH), which treats cows as if they were chemical factories for producing milk. The last thing that Vermont farmers need is the production of *more* milk to drive prices even lower, and the addition of new costs, not for hay or equipment but for genetically engineered chemicals. The last thing that consumers need is milk produced with artificial stimulants that make cows sick. But Monsanto, a multibillion dollar corporation, has enormous political influence with the Food and Drug Administration as well as in Congress. There was very little support in Congress for my efforts to stop the introduction of BGH.

Each of New England's six states passed legislation to create the Northeast Dairy Compact. Briefly, the Compact would enable representatives from the six states to set a fair price to farmers for the milk sold within the region. Because it is an interstate compact, it requires the approval of the United States Congress. Vermont's two senators, Patrick Leahy and James Jeffords, have worked hard and effectively on the issue, as have a number of us in the House. Finally, against great odds, the legislation has been passed. It is now awaiting the signature of the secretary of agriculture, Dan Glickman, whom I knew from his days in the House. Glickman has to decide whether the legislation meets the criteria of "compelling public interest."

The Northeast Dairy Compact legislation is on his desk and we are waiting for him to sign it . . . and waiting, and waiting. I am worried. There is strong political opposition from midwestern Representatives who mistakenly believe that the Compact will hurt their dairy farmers. There is also opposition from the powerful forces that want cheap milk—the chocolate companies, the food processing industry, and the milk processors—whose profits go up when milk prices go down. On several occasions, I have spoken to President Clinton about the legislation. He appeared supportive, but certain people in his administration were definitely unsympathetic. I also spoke to his chief of staff, Leon Panetta, and to Glickman himself.

Clearly, the Northeast Dairy Compact was more than an agricultural issue. Politics were involved. There's a presidential election coming up. Vermont has three electoral votes. Wisconsin, Minnesota, and other midwestern states have a lot more. I wonder if Clinton's folks will abandon us in the end. Glickman reassures me that the Compact will be signed. Still, I worry.

Now, right at the end of this enormously convoluted legislative process, one of those ironies that are so commonplace in politics occurs: Wisconsin's David Obey, a friend and a fellow progressive, offers an amendment in the Appropriations Committee to kill the prospective legislation. Obey represents Wisconsin, and they're opposed to the Compact. But here is another twist that underlines the strangeness of congressional politics: Bob Livingston, a Louisiana conservative and Gingrichite, chairs the Appropriations Committee. His job is to push through the Agriculture Appropriations bill, which contains the Compact. The Republican leadership is nervous that, because the legislation contains so many compromises, it could easily unravel. They want to keep the bill whole, and, at that late date, it doesn't matter any longer what is in it.

In theory, the Compact—which allows heavy government regulation of the price of milk in the Northeast—runs directly counter to all that Livingston, a free-market conservative, stands for. On the other hand, it is consistent with Dave Obey's general outlook. Dave is a progressive, who has long advocated a strong role for the federal government to protect working people.

Fortunately for us, on this one, Livingston wins and Obey loses. The Northeast Dairy Compact, as part of a major agricultural bill, is shepherded to victory by an antigovernment conservative. We take it any way we can get it.

5

The Scapegoating Congress

The last couple of weeks in Congress have been particularly depressing and ugly. After all the fine-sounding intellectual rhetoric about "philosophy" and "contracts," after all the books, conferences, and position papers by Republican think tanks, the Gingrich political strategy that we see on the floor of the House as we head into the election comes down to gay bashing, immigrant bashing, racism, sexism, and attacks on the poor.

Nothing new here. A slight variation on very old themes. The same garbage that the right wing always rolls out. If you have no rational analysis of the causation of social problems, if you represent the rich and powerful and *can't* address the needs of ordinary people, then the surefire route to political success is to manipulate people's fear and ignorance, to play off one group against another—to *scapegoat*.

For a hundred years, the white workers of the South were the most exploited white workers in America. They were paid the lowest wages, they endured the worst working conditions, their housing was abysmal, their kids went to the most backward schools, and very few could send their children to college. But what *did* they have? They were given "niggers" to hate and look down on, "niggers" who couldn't vote, drink at their water fountains, use the same bathrooms, or sit up front in the buses or movie theaters.

The political, economic, social, and educational systems of the South enforced those divisions and continually fed the antagonisms. Above all things, white workers were encouraged to despise, and protect themselves from, their black neighbors, or face losing what little they had. The rich folks in the South—the bankers, the manufacturers, the cottonfield owners—laughed all the way to the bank.

During that period, some of the bravest people in the history of America risked their lives fighting the system that perpetuated racism. In illegal meetings throughout the South (it was against the law for blacks and whites to sit in a room together), these political activists and union organizers brought black and white workers together to fight for justice. They did this not only because they believed in civil rights and equal opportunity but also because they understood that real economic and political transformation would never be achieved as long as whites and blacks were busy fighting each other—rather than their common oppressors.

Some things never change. Some struggles never end.

Today, the Republicans understand that tax breaks for the rich, cuts in Medicare, Medicaid, education, and environmental protection, and support of NAFTA, GATT, and other disastrous trade policies are not exactly a winning ticket.

Of course, it *is* the agenda of rich folks and corporate leaders, and what the Republicans are paid to deliver. But there are only so many millionaire voters, and Republicans know that this agenda is not going to win points among middle-class and working people—the people who determine the outcome of elections. Slashing Medicaid and allowing corporations to pollute our drinking water are not the kind of achievements that can be celebrated in thirty-second campaign ads for all the world to see.

Given that their real ideology—not the sham philosophy of "states' rights" or "personal responsibility" created for public consumption—reflects the interests of a tiny and very privileged segment of the population, Republicans are faced with the same dilemmas that vexed the ruling elites of the South: How to convince working people and the middle class to vote *against* their own best interests. Or, equally important, how to get them not to vote at all. Further, how to deflect attention *away* from the issues that affect the vast majority of people and around which they could *unite*.

Sound strange? It may to you, but I see it every day of the week. That's what the politics of scapegoating and "wedge issues" is all about. White against black and Hispanic. Straight against gay. Working class against the poor and welfare recipients. Men against women. Native born against immigrant. People on the outside against jail inmates. On and on it goes.

The Republicans of 1996, who undertake massive polling, understand very well the legitimate fears and anxieties that millions of Americans feel. And they are prepared to spend huge sums of money to exploit those anxieties, to divide working people and set them at each other's throats, to blind working people to the fact that instead of justice they are getting scraps from the rich man's table.

Most importantly, the Republican strategy is designed to keep working people from looking at the *real* causes of their problems, from examining who owns and controls the system and who benefits from current policies, and from seriously considering how the current political and economic structure can be changed. The Republicans pit people with little power against those with no power. Meanwhile, scarcely anyone looks at who's pulling the strings.

For the last twenty years, the average American has been working longer hours for lower wages. As real wages have dropped by 16 percent, millions of workers are now stressed out because they are working 160 hours a year more than they did just two decades ago.

And millions of Americans say, "When will it end? How hard do I have to work to pay the bills? Saturdays, Sundays, overtime? Two jobs? Three jobs? Surely I'm entitled to some vacation time. Surely I'm entitled to some fun—to see a movie, to hunt, fish, read, enjoy my children."

All over this country, women who would prefer to stay home with their children have been forced into the workplace because families now need two paychecks in order to survive. Millions of single people are fighting desperately to support themselves and to raise families alone.

And throughout the country Americans are wondering, "Am I a good parent? How can I plan for a family when my job will not allow me to take a leave? Has my boss ever had to get up ten times a night and feed a baby? Haven't his kids ever been sick? How do I get decent and affordable child care? Why was it that my father alone was able to bring home enough money to support the family?"

Most of the new jobs that are being created are low-wage jobs, paying $5.00 or $6.00 an hour. Many of these jobs are part-time or temporary. Parents know that if their kids are going to become self-sufficient, they will need a college degree, but they also know that there is little chance they can afford to pay for college fees out of wage rates that are so low.

And millions of Americans say, "But how do we send the kids to college when it costs $15,000 or $20,000 a year and we only earn $25,000? How do we save money for education when we can barely pay the mortgage or the interest on the credit card? No. We can't go $50,000 into debt. What are we supposed to do?"

More and more Americans have no health insurance or are underinsured. *Medical debt is the primary cause of personal bankruptcy in this country*. Despite Medicare, a large number of senior citizens are unable to afford the prescription drugs that they need.

And millions of Americans are asking, "Who can afford $5,000 a year for adequate health coverage? Who can go to the doctor when the deductible is so high? Three thousand dollars a day in the hospital, when you're making $20,000 a year. It might as well be a million bucks a day. Let's hope no one in the family gets sick this year."

For the self-employed, small business person, payroll taxes are often higher than income taxes. And then there are property taxes for schools and municipal government, and state taxes. Taxes. Taxes. Taxes.

And millions of American's say, "Doesn't anyone understand? I can't afford to pay more taxes. I can barely survive on what I earn today. Why doesn't the government stop spending so much of my money? Why do these politicians always want more and more from me in taxes?"

Every night on television, we see reports of horrible crimes. Murder, rape, assault, robbery. Some of them are so utterly senseless. Drive-by shootings, kids killing each other for a pair of sneakers, parents doing unspeakable things to their own children.

And millions of Americans demand an explanation. "I obey the law. I play by the rules. Why do I have to live in fear when I walk down the street? Why can't my kid be safe when she goes to school? Why is it costing me a fortune in taxes to pay for extra police or to send these people to jail? Why can't they get a job, and be decent citizens? And why does the government want to take away my guns at the very moment when I most need them to defend and protect my family?"

In summary, many Americans are thinking: "This world is changing very fast. I am confused, I am frustrated, and I am *angry*—and I'm frightened about the future."

Well, relax. Newt Gingrich, his pollsters, and his colleagues hear you. And they are prepared to *act*—boldly, forcefully, and swiftly on the floor of the House.

No, there will be no rational discussion in Congress of the *cause* of your problems and concerns. There will be no serious debate as to why the middle class has collapsed, why the gap between the rich and the poor has grown and is now wider than in any other industrialized country, why two-thirds of the increase in family wealth goes to the richest one percent, or why that same one percent now own more wealth than the bottom 90 percent.

There will be no serious debate as to why the United States has gone from first in the world in terms of wages and benefits to thirteenth, why CEOs of large corporations now make almost 200 times what their workers earn, or why we now lag behind every major industrialized country on earth in the amount of paid vacation time and parental leave our workers receive.

Nor will there be any serious discussion as to why we have record-breaking trade deficits, why our industrial base has suffered a major decline, and why the United States has lost millions of decent-paying jobs as profitable corporations close down plants here and move to countries where they pay their employees twenty or thirty cents an hour.

There will be no serious debate about tax policy that has significantly lowered taxes for the rich and large corporations, and raised taxes for the middle class, or why company after company threatens states and local communities with job loss if they don't get tax breaks, which result in higher local taxes for individuals and homeowners.

There will be no serious debate as to why the United States continues to have the most expensive and wasteful health care system in the world, and is the only major nation on earth that does not guarantee health care as a right of citizenship.

There will be no serious debate as to why the United States now has, by far, the highest rate of childhood poverty in the industrialized world, and how that poverty is translated into the highest per capita rate of incarceration of any major nation; or why two-thirds of the inmates in jail are functionally illiterate, or why more people are shot to death in two days in this country than in a year in Japan.

No. These and similar issues will not be discussed by Gingrich and his colleagues. If they were, they might bring people *together* to find solutions that would benefit the vast majority of Americans. Imagine. Black and white, Hispanic and Asian, straight and gay, middle class and low income, native and immigrant coming together to create an economy that worked well for the majority, not just the rich; a health care system that guaranteed health care for all, not huge profits for insurance and pharmaceutical companies; federal funding for education, not B-2 bombers; a tax system that favored workers, not the wealthy and multinational corporations. People coming together for the common good. Newt Gingrich's nightmare.

No. Gingrich, his colleagues and corporate sponsors can't discuss or resolve the real problems facing the average American, but they can certainly deflect attention from them. They can pass legislation that will make some of us feel better, by making others feel worse. They can divide the middle class from the poor, and all of us by race, gender, national origin, and sexual orientation. They can beat the hell out of the weak and the powerless. It's a mean, ugly kind of politics. But it's a kind of politics that wins elections.

And I see the fallout in Vermont. At a town meeting in Addison County, a woman says, "Bernie, I'm working hard and I can't afford health insurance. Why is it that my kids don't have health care, but the children of welfare recipients do? It's not right. What are you going to do about it?"

And I reply that I'm going to fight so that everyone in this country has quality health care through a national health insurance program. And she says, "No. I'm not asking you to provide health insurance for my family. I just want you to take it away from those welfare people."

Similarly, at a festival in Orleans County, a woman says, "I work at a grocery store. I'm disgusted. I see these people with food stamps come in and buy steak and better food than I can afford. Do something about it."

I hear comments like this all over the state.

As Congress winds down and prepares for the November 1996 elections, the Republican leadership introduces wedge-issue legislation, bills designed to divide the American people against each other, and so win votes for the Republicans.

On July 12, 1996, the so-called Defense of Marriage Act is brought to the floor of the House. It's a "good" issue for the Republicans. Gays constitute a small percentage of the population, and most of them do not vote Republican. Tapping into homophobia and the sexual insecurity of Americans is an effective, time-tested, vote-getting strategy.

In the early days of the Clinton administration, there was a very divisive discussion about gays in the military.

While tens of thousands of gay men and women have served this country with honor and dignity and many have died defending it, President Clinton's attempt to bring the issue out into the open—and acknowledge what already existed—created an uproar. The Republicans, as well as conservative Democrats like Senator Sam Nunn, had "done well" by exploiting the issue, and Clinton suffered a serious political setback. If gay bashing worked well in the past, why not revive it?

Homophobia is a very serious problem in this country—even within the ranks of Congress. Representative Bob Dornan (R–Calif.) spends much of his time on the floor delivering homophobic diatribes and, while his extremist views are atypical, he is rarely rebuked or controlled by the Republican leadership. Last year, Dick Armey, the Republican Majority Leader, referred to openly gay congressman Barney Frank as "Barney Fag" during a press conference. He later simulated an apology. Just a "slip of the tongue," he explained. During a debate on the floor totally unrelated to any issue concerning sexual orientation, I was stunned when Representative Duke Cunningham of California made a gratuitous comment about "homos" in the military. I demanded that he withdraw his remarks. Shouting ensued. "Sit down, you socialist," he yelled. The next day, after gay rights groups convened a press conference to condemn his remarks, he apologized, promising never to use the term "homo" on the House floor again.

These flagrant displays of homophobia have a political rationale. Dornan and company are playing to a particular constituency. Gay bashing has become a cornerstone of the agenda advanced by the Christian Coalition, a powerful element in the Republican "revolution." During the 1994 election, the Coalition distributed millions of pieces of literature ranking candidates on their "family values" yardstick. Homosexuality is, by their definition, "antifamily," and so is support for gay rights.

Again, I see the alarming results in my home state. Peter Clavelle, who followed me as mayor of Burlington, did a courageous thing in 1992 when he approved the provision of health benefits for domestic partners of city workers, including gay couples. This was one of the reasons Clavelle lost his reelection bid that year—and that was in the liberal city of Burlington.

The Defense of Marriage Act is a preemptive response to the Hawaii State Supreme Court's anticipated decision in favor of the right of gays to be legally married. The proposed federal legislation would make gay spouses ineligible for federal benefits and would allow a state to refuse recognition of gay marriages legally performed elsewhere. The bill is introduced by Representative Bob Barr (R–Ga.), who personally has a great deal of experience with the institution of marriage. He has been wed three times. Representative Enid Waldholtz (R–Utah), Acting Speaker in this debate, is also well versed in the intricacies of marriage. She is currently pressing charges against her former husband, Joe Waldholtz, who is cooling his heels in the slammer. And Mr. Gingrich himself is no slacker when it comes to marriage. His former wife, whom he divorced after her cancer operation, turned to the local church for help when Gingrich refused to pay child support. These are some of the main defenders of marriage taking the floor in the debate.

The Defense of Marriage Act is supported by *every* Republican except Wisconsin's Steve Gunderson, who is openly gay. In fact, Gunderson provides some of the strongest and most emotional arguments on the floor against this absurd piece of legislation, as does Barney Frank. Conservative Republican Jim Kolbe from Arizona votes for the bill. Several weeks later, because of anger against his vote by members of the gay community, Kolbe is about to be "outed." This rather quiet, fifty-four-year-old Vietnam veteran, who served in the House for twelve years, suddenly announces to his Arizona constituents that he is gay.

After much sanctimonious breast beating, the Defense of Marriage Act carries on the floor by a vote of 342 to 67. One hundred eighteen Democrats vote for the bill. Sixty-five Democrats and one Independent vote against it. Many people in the House are speculating about the TV ads that the Republicans will develop for use in the upcoming election against anyone who offers support for gay marriage. So does President Clinton. He endorses the legislation.

On August 1, 1996, the Republicans bring their "English Only" bill before the House. This legislation is just one part of their ongoing anti-immigrant strategy, which capitalizes on racial bigotry and general ignorance about immigration. Needless to say, most anti-immigrant prejudice is not directed at British, French, or Canadian individuals who want to become American citizens.

Unfortunately, many Americans don't know the difference between legal and illegal immigrants and, as in other countries with economic problems, xenophobia is intensifying. The issue for some can be summarized by the writing I recently saw on a T-shirt: "If you can't speak English, get the fuck out of the United States." In California, *Time* magazine reported on a nurse from Woodland Hills who "was pelted with rocks and anti-Hispanic epithets at a high school she has walked by for 10 years without incident."

The "English Only" bill mandates that all official communication by the federal government be in English. This means that members of Congress from a heavily Hispanic or Polish district, for instance, would be prohibited from communicating with their constituents in Spanish or Polish. Election, tax, and other information needed by millions of citizens would be available only in English. President Clinton indicates that he will veto this legislation, and the bill will not go anywhere—not even to the Senate. But it passes in the House by a vote of 259 to 169. Eight Republicans, 160 Democrats, and I vote against the bill.

The major scapegoating effort of the Republican leadership, however, is not gay bashing or immigrant bashing. It is not the attack on affirmative action or the bills limiting women's access to abortion.

The crown jewel of the Republican agenda is their so-called welfare reform proposal. The bill, which combines an assault on the poor, women and children, minorities, and immigrants, is the grand slam of scapegoating legislation, and appeals to the frustrations and ignorance of the American people along a wide spectrum of prejudices.

Tired of high taxes and spending huge sums of money on people too lazy to work? Tired of paying black teenagers to stay home all day and have babies while you work your butt off? Tired of providing an incentive for Mexicans to skip over the border in the middle of the night? Welfare reform is for you!

The legislation is a real political winner for the Republicans, and has caused a dramatic and fundamental change in the philosophical underpinnings of the Democratic Party.

The legislation approved by the House and Senate is monumental because, after sixty years, it withdraws federal protection from the weakest and most vulnerable members of our society. The United States of America will no longer guarantee minimal support for hungry and disabled children or for the poor. Instead, there will be a massive cut in funds and responsibility will be transferred to the states.

Here is what "reform" will actually accomplish:

- Benefits will be limited to a lifetime maximum of five years. All recipients must find work within two years or lose their benefits. These regulations take effect regardless of economic conditions in a community or the availability of jobs.
- Seventy percent of recipients of Aid to Families with Dependent Children (AFDC) are children, including, at any given moment, about a third of all black children. At a time when 20 percent of all kids in the United States live in poverty, "reform" will push one million more children over the edge.
- Three hundred thousand children with disabilities will be denied Supplemental Security Income (SSI). The

bill substantially narrows the definition of disability for poor children with tuberculosis, autism, serious mental illness, head injuries, arthritis, and mental retardation.

- Benefits for legal immigrants will be cut by $23 billion over six years. People who play by the rules, come to the United States legally, and work and pay taxes, will be denied Medicaid, SSI, AFDC, and other resources because they were born in another country.

There was a lot of uncertainty in Washington about whether or not Clinton would support this Republican legislation. Some people pointed out that he had vetoed two previous pieces of similar legislation as being too harsh on kids. But I saw a harbinger of his ultimate decision in the administration's rejection of a request to study the actual impact of the provisions on the nation's children. Clearly, they chose not to do the study because it would confirm the fact that large numbers of children would descend into poverty. So my bet all along was that Clinton would acquiesce. A few hours before the vote, Clinton held a press conference to announce that, while he had certain reservations about the bill, he would sign it. The legislation is a step forward, he asserted.

What was especially noteworthy about these past few weeks, especially in terms of so-called welfare reform, was the historic collapse not only of the president, but of much of the Democratic Party in Congress in supporting draconian cuts that five years ago nobody in the party would have seriously discussed, let alone voted for.

That collapse indicates the enormous success that Newt Gingrich, Rush Limbaugh, corporate America, and the far right have had in changing the political and social landscape of America. It also makes clear that there is now *no* major political party that represents the poor and the vulnerable.

There is no question about it. Beating up on the poor is now "good politics." As Rush Limbaugh has told us: "The poor in this country are the biggest piglets at the mother pig and her nipples . . . They're the ones who get all the benefits in this country. They're the ones that are always pandered to." Congress and the president have heard Limbaugh's message, studied the polls, and clambered aboard.

It is astonishing how little fanfare accompanies such an historic event. Here is the Democratic Party, a party which prided itself for sixty years on defending the interests of working people and the poor, making a radical shift to the right, and accepting policy which Richard Nixon would have summarily rejected. If, five years before, someone had suggested that a Democratic president and the vast majority of Democrats in Congress would have supported legislation that cut food stamps by over $20 billion, viciously attacked legal immigrants, and terminated a child's right to minimal economic support, they would have been laughed at. But that's exactly what happened. And where was the great debate in the party? Where were the attacks on the president, the demonstrations, the mass resignations from the administration?

The speed of the collapse is breathtaking. Only two years before, in 1994, the Democrats brought forward a welfare reform bill sponsored by Representative Nathan Deal of Georgia. It was the most conservative welfare bill ever supported by the Democratic leadership. (Mr. Deal, by the way, subsequently left the Democratic Party and became a Republican.)

But compared to the welfare bill that the Democrats supported in 1996, introduced by Representative John Tanner of Tennessee, the Deal legislation was a model of humane concern. Despite its many defects, it was based on the assumption that if the federal government wanted to get people off welfare, it would have to provide the education, job training, and child care necessary for people to make the transition and at the same time protect their children. It actually *increased* funding for food stamps, child care, and other programs. Although I had very serious concerns about the Deal bill, I ultimately voted for it, as did most House Democrats, because it maintained federal support for the rights and needs of poor children and their parents, and was clearly the best welfare bill with a chance of passing.

Two years came and went. Gingrich became Speaker, and Rush Limbaugh's brutal attitude toward the poor had permeated both parties. Now the Democrats have lent their weight to the Tanner bill, a far more punitive "reform" than the Deal proposal, which calls for $20 billion in cuts in food stamps and in most respects is a miniature of Republican proposals. It accepts the brilliant proposition that poverty is caused by the poor, and advances as a solution an end to government support for the most vulnerable people in the country. This bill, which is not quite reactionary enough for the Republicans, wins the support of 159 out of 195 Democrats. Eventually, 98 Democrats support the Republican bill, which is passed by a vote of 328 to 101. Significantly, relatively few *white* Democrats vote against the Tanner bill—only ten. Most of the opposition comes from minority members.

In passing this legislation, the Republicans have been successful not only in playing on people's fears but also in exploiting voters' lack of knowledge. The degree to which the American people are alienated and uninformed about the political process is hard to appreciate. In January 1996, a poll conducted by the *Washington Post* revealed that only 40 percent of Americans were able to name the vice president of the United States, 66 percent did not know the name of their member of Congress, and 75 percent could not name their two U.S. senators. Further, 40 percent of the respondents believed that either welfare or foreign aid constituted the largest single expenditure of the federal government. This, at a time when the budget for AFDC was $14 billion—one percent of the federal budget—and foreign aid was slightly less.

So here we have millions of Americans who believe that cuts in welfare are necessary to move the country toward a balanced budget, while they are unaware of the fact that at exactly the same time the Republican leadership is increasing military spending by about $60 billion over a six-year period, an increase *larger* than the savings produced by cuts in welfare.

The Republicans have succeeded in convincing Americans that poor people are responsible for the federal deficit, rather than a series of policies over the last twenty years that have given huge tax breaks to the rich and thrown billions of dollars at defense contractors. Not only that. They have also successfully propagated the view that compassion and human sympathy are not the province of government. For the federal government to reach out and provide assistance to those in need is bad and harmful.

And what is the right thing to do? Cut welfare. Cut food stamps and nutrition programs. Cut affordable housing. Cut health care. Cut education. Cut fuel assistance. Are these things not harmful acts? Is this not selfish, cruel, and immoral? No. Increasing hunger, homelessness, and human misery is how we *help* the poor.

The Republicans get away with this absurd argument, the Democrats collapse before it, and the American people swallow it because there is virtually no organized opposition. The Children's Defense Fund, the National Council of Catholic Bishops, and a few other organizations stand up for kids and the poor. But overall, the silence is deafening.

A further reason that the Republicans can mount this assault on the poor is because they understand an obvious social fact: the vast majority of poor people do not make campaign contributions, do not vote, and do not participate in the political process. In fact, the poor are almost totally irrelevant to contemporary politics, except when being using as scapegoats.

Poor people are a good target for the Republicans. Exhausted by an increasingly difficult struggle for survival, they are not organized and can't fight back. Seventy percent of welfare recipients are children, a constituency that cannot vote and has few civil rights. What a target. It's like shooting fish in a barrel. You can't miss.

Here is the great catch-22 of American politics: as long as low-income people do not vote or participate politically, they will be scapegoated. But as long as both major parties continue to ignore the problems of low-income citizens, the poor will see politics as irrelevant and won't vote or join the political process. The politicians who get elected will continue to ignore their needs.

How many times have I knocked on doors at low-income housing projects and heard people say, with pride in their voice, "I don't vote. What difference does it make? Nobody's going to represent my interests."

Let me digress here to share a few observations.

When I was mayor of Burlington, we came close to *doubling* voter turnout. Why? Because we made it clear that we would stand up and fight for low- and moderate-income people—and we did. Many low-income people understood that and, as a result, they supported us. If poor people believe that voting will make a difference, they will vote.

The ruling class of this country knows perfectly well how important it is for them to keep voter turnout *down*. The United States has, by far, the lowest rate of electoral participation in the industrialized world. In 1994, when Gingrich and friends took power, only 38 percent of Americans voted. The vast majority of poor people stayed away from the polls. For the Republicans it was a great election. Almost nobody voted, and rich people contributed huge amounts of money. This is the kind of "democracy" the ruling class likes.

In Third World countries, when political organizations want to protest against what they consider an illegitimate government, they organize voter boycotts. In this country, it would be impossible to *organize* a voter boycott, because we already have an *unorganized* one. In the 1994 elections, 62 percent of the people boycotted.

In 1993, President Clinton signed the Motor Voter bill, which makes voter registration easier for low-income people. Registration forms can be filled out when applying for a driver's license, at the welfare office, at the unemployment office, at the public library, at various government office buildings. It's a good bill, but only a tiny step forward in terms of where we ought to go in improving people's access to the voting booth. Nonetheless, the Republicans went berserk at the passage of the bill, and a number of Republican governors flatly refused to implement the law. How terrible! Imagine that. Poor people are registering to vote. What next?

Yet, when the next war comes, who will be returning home in body bags, or without legs or arms? Who, as a result of their wartime experience, will be unemployed and end up sleeping in the streets? It will be the sons and daughters of the people who don't vote, and who the Republicans don't want to vote ever.

If voter turnout in this country reached the levels of Canada or Europe—70 to 80 percent—American society would change substantially. Most importantly, if poor people would utilize their leverage at the polls, they would realize the great principle that in a democratic society they, as much as anyone else, have the right to determine the future of this country and shape its social contract. That sense of empowerment, in itself, would transform the lives of millions of people and, ultimately, the entire nation.

If poor people voted, the government would pay far more attention to economic injustice, health care, education, and other issues largely ignored today. At the very least, legislation like the recently passed welfare "reform" bill would never be enacted, would just be a dim dream of the far right fringe. The Republicans agree with me on this point. They fully understand the implications of expanded participation by low-income citizens in the electoral and political process. That is why they work so hard, in so many ways, to prevent it from happening.

Welfare, gay and immigrant bashing, increasing military expenditures, and cuts in Medicaid and education are scarcely all I have to deal with. Back in Vermont I have to juggle these painful realities with trying to figure out what to do with the campaign. On that front, I'm not sure where things are heading.

It's May 21, and I'm in Washington. Jane gives me the bad news that Susan Sweetser has begun her television advertising. This is an unexpected development that catches us completely by surprise. By Vermont standards, going on television in May is almost unprecedented. In the last three elections, we began our TV advertising in October. Her ad is a high-quality thirty-second spot. In the trade, it's called an "intro piece," designed to familiarize viewers with her life and her views. The ad has been produced by Dresner and Wickers, a big-time Republican media company.

While we try to figure out how we should respond to this major campaign development, one thing is clear—if Sweetser is already putting substantial sums into TV, she must be confident of raising a very significant amount of money. Could she raise a million dollars? Is corporate America that anxious to get rid of me? And what about the additional help that she will almost certainly get via "independent expenditures" from the NRA and other organizations? My first thought concerning Sweetser's TV ads is that we'd better accelerate our own fundraising efforts. We're in for a tough and expensive race, and we'd better get moving.

Should we go on television early ourselves or just wait? It's a big question. In the 1994 campaign, my Republican opponent, John Carroll, went on TV in late August, which we considered "early," and we made a mistake by not responding. We gave him a full month to get his message out without any reply from our side. I don't intend to make that mistake again, but it's strange to think about going on TV with the election five months away. Not only did we have no intention of going on the air this early, but we are not financially prepared to do so.

The question of how we should respond to Sweetser's TV campaign is largely answered by a "baseline" poll that we have commissioned. This year, for the first time in my life, and with great reluctance, we hired a professional Washington polling firm, Bennett, Petts & Blumenthal, to conduct an in-depth survey of my strengths and weaknesses among Vermont voters. For most politicians, this is pretty standard fare, but although we have done lots of polling within our progressive movement, we have never done anything this thorough before. The poll costs us $15,000, which seems to me a staggering amount.

We work with the pollster in helping to design questions for a thirty-minute interview with respondents. You are supposed to throw out all of the arguments your opponent will use against you, and see how people respond. In that way you learn where you're vulnerable and what your strengths are. We also include a "horse race" in the poll, to see how we are doing against Sweetser.

To make a long story short, the results of the baseline poll are very reassuring to us. In fact, the consultants who analyze the results with Dave Petts say they have never seen anything quite like it—and they have been looking at polls for many years. The bottom line is that Vermonters know me very well. Some of them agree with my views, and some do not, but they all know where I stand. The pollsters are surprised at the enormous numbers of respondents who believe that I am honest and straightforward with voters, and who see me as someone who fights for what I believe to be right. Few Vermonters, it turns out, regard me as a typical politician.

What most interested me was that the poll indicated that very few of the arguments and attacks that we anticipate Sweetser using against me will have a major impact on changing the views of voters. In the head-to-head "horse race," we are ahead by 27 points. Although her feel-good television ads have been on the air for two months, Sweetser's negatives are unexpectedly high.

Frankly, I think the poll is too good to be true, even if these pollsters are professionals and come highly recommended. But it does convince me of one thing. We don't have to spend money putting ads on television yet. We'll husband our resources, and save them for the end of the campaign when we'll really need them.

At around this time the Becker Poll comes out, a major statewide poll commissioned by the business community and Vermont's largest television station. This poll has us up by 20 points, and also finds Sweetser's negatives to be high. No one quite knows why Sweetser seems not to be doing well. Even though she is pouring $80,000 into television ads, my lead remains wide and her negatives continue to go up. It's very strange, but we're not complaining.

Our immediate strategy is to keep things reasonably quiet, try not to make too many stupid mistakes, and then sprint hard toward the end of the campaign. It's likely that Sweetser will receive a huge amount of money from her wealthy supporters and buy up the airwaves, but there's not a lot that we can do about that. Everything being equal, I am now feeling more confident than I expected to be two or three months ago.

At the outset of the campaign I identified three areas in which we had to improve over past efforts. The first grew out of my dream of seeing a thousand politically knowledgeable people, part of our movement, canvassing all over Vermont. If a thousand people each knocked on two hundred doors, we would knock on every door in the state. Frankly, that ain't gonna happen now—and I know it. But it's a dream worth having.

Many people don't pay much attention to TV news, don't read the papers or listen to the radio. They are not actively

Congress of Racial Equality (CORE) meeting (1962). I was a steering committee member, and here I'm standing beside George Beadle, University of Chicago president.

Congress of Racial Equality sit-in (1962). I spoke to protestors on the first day of action. At the time, CORE was working to end segregation in Chicago public schools.

With my son, Levi, then two and a half, at a Liberty Union Party meeting in the fall of 1971.

The Sanders clan. I'm happily sandwiched between my wife, Jane, and youngest grandson, Dylan.

The Burlington mayoral campaign (1981). Jane and I watch the returns on television amid a crowd of supporters.

The victory party. My political career was launched with the defeat of Gordon Paquette in the race to become Burlington mayor.

In uniform with the People's Republic of Burlington softball team.

A portrait from the early '80s from Burlington weekly the *Vermont Vanguard Press*.

On the roof of the old Hotel Vermont building, overlooking Burlington City Hall. After four successful terms as mayor, I decided not to run for reelection in 1989 and set my sights elsewhere.

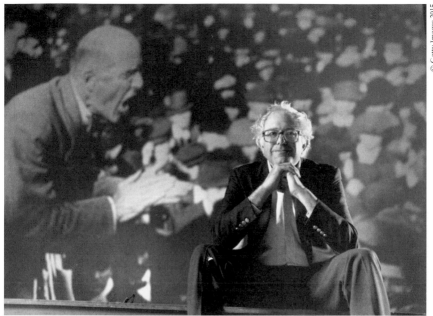

Running for Congress in 1990. Featured in the backdrop is the labor organizer and presidential candidate Eugene Debs.

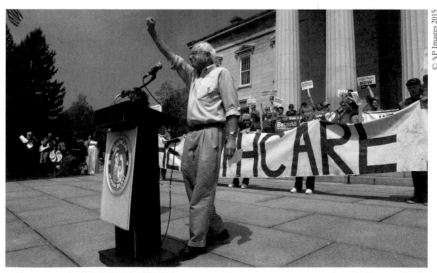

Addressing a crowd gathered outside the Vermont statehouse to express support for a single-payer health care system (May 1, 2010).

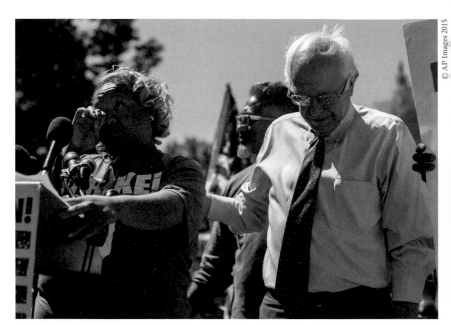

At a rally pushing to raise the minimum wage to $15 an hour, I stood beside Sontice Bailey as she spoke movingly to the crowd. Her low pay meant Bailey was unable to take time off work from her two jobs during her pregnancy, which ended in miscarriage (July 22, 2015).

With Jane during my presidential primary campaign, at the Los Angeles Memorial Sports Arena (Aug. 10, 2015).

Greeting presidential candidate Jesse Jackson, Montpelier City Hall (Dec. 31, 1988). That night I endorsed Jackson in front of a thousand-strong crowd.

Heading for the Senate floor where I spoke for eight and a half hours against renewing Bush-era tax cuts for high earners (Dec. 9, 2010). The marathon speech made national headlines and kick-started a movement to get me to run for president.

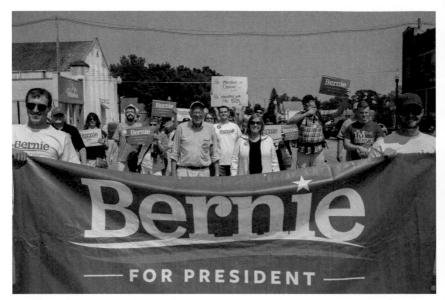

Marching with Jane as part of a July 4th parade on an early leg of my campaign to win the Democratic presidential primary (Denison, Iowa).

Members of National Nurses United on the day the union publically endorsed my candidacy in the presidential primary, Oakland, Calif. (Aug. 10, 2015).

involved in the political process—especially in trailer parks and low-income areas. The goal of a canvassing effort is to bring political ideas right to the front doors and, if possible, into the living rooms of thousands of Vermonters through face-to-face contact. In my view, all the TV ads in the world are not as effective as an intelligent and personable canvasser who is able to discuss the issues and listen to voters' concerns. I refuse to give up on the idea that a campaign in a democratic society should include a significant educational dimension.

A few months ago two young people, Peter Baker and Ashley Moore, walked into our campaign office looking for jobs. Both of them had extensive canvassing experience working for environmental organizations in Oregon. They were bright and energetic—just the sort of people I wanted. In the beginning, the two of them would just go to a town that we had selected and knock on doors by themselves. But after a while, Phil Fiermonte and Tom Smith were able to organize local volunteers in the various towns to go out with Peter and Ashley.

The canvassers take campaign material to every door in a community. If no one is home, they leave a leaflet. When they come across a supporter, they give him or her a "Bernie 96" bumper sticker—these are beginning to show up in large numbers on cars all over the state. They take addresses for lawn signs—we have over a thousand people who have indicated they want to put these up, a remarkable achievement for a campaign many months from election day. They are also signing up supporters to volunteer and are registering people to vote as well as bringing back questions from constituents to which we try to respond.

The canvassers have also asked supporters to write to newspapers, resulting in more letters supporting me on editorial pages than ever before. Occasionally, they even manage to sell a "Bernie for Congress" T-shirt. An added bonus is that some of our supporters are making campaign contributions. Five dollars here, twenty dollars there. It all adds up. Further, and very importantly, by knocking on doors every evening we are getting firsthand impressions of how people are feeling about the campaign and the issues.

In St. Albans last night, four local volunteers who know the community well went with Peter and Ashley and another staff person: that meant there were seven people canvassing for the evening in a small city. That gives you a real presence. The people of St. Albans will know that the Sanders campaign was in their town—and that's great. Tonight, five or six people will be going to the suburban community of Williston. Every day the effort continues in another city or town. In some of the smaller towns, three or four people can knock on every door in one night.

Canvassing gives people a chance to interact with the Sanders campaign in new ways. Even though I return from Washington each week to spend three or four days in the state and I make a concerted effort to visit every area of Vermont, tens of thousands of people have never met me personally. So while we are handing out literature, registering voters, giving out bumper stickers, obtaining signatures to get on the ballot, raising money, we are doing what is most important of all: talking directly with people. If you are serious about building a movement, you have to go out and talk politics. We haven't done enough of that in the past, but we are doing better now. The canvassing effort is something I am very excited about.

Perhaps the high point of the campaign for me so far has been the meeting Phil Fiermonte put together a few weeks ago in Montpelier, the state capital. The goal was to bring volunteers together to discuss the role they could play in the campaign. Seventy-five people turned out to learn how they could be effective campaign workers—a great turnout.

One of the challenges that any serious campaign faces is how to deal effectively with volunteers. If you give them "make work" that is not useful or challenging, they're not going to come back. Nobody wants to waste their time. If you ask people who hate making phone calls to use the phone, they're gone. A good campaign is successful when it matches volunteers with the work they enjoy and are interested in. We need people to canvass and to maintain booths at the state fairs and on street corners. We need volunteers to hand out literature and to make phone calls, to work in the office in Burlington, to get out the mailings, and to run our computers. In the fall, we'll need supporters to help out in our regional offices. We have a lot of work to do, and this meeting is to get volunteers to do it.

I was surprised and gratified by the number of low-income people who attended. For these folks, Gingrich's policies are not issues for intellectual debate. They are life-and-death matters of food on the table, health care, education, and Medicare premiums. When Phil first suggested the idea of the meeting, I had my doubts, because it took a lot of work to organize it. But I was wrong. We were bringing some great people into the campaign.

While we seem to be attracting more working-class and low-income volunteers, we're not generating quite as much enthusiasm and support as we have in the past among progressives, who, historically, have been the backbone of our movement. I'm not complaining. The new volunteers are hard workers and know their communities very well.

The second goal I set was to do better with direct mail in Vermont. While this is an area where being an Independent places me at a real disadvantage compared to the Democrats and Republicans, there is no question that we should be able to improve greatly on our past performance.

Direct mail is an expensive proposition when you're talking about 250,000 voters. In the last campaign we sent out about 35,000 pieces targeted mostly to hunters, to deal with the gun issue and to counter the NRA's vehement opposition to my candidacy. Historically, the Republicans mail to every household in the state, and the Democrats are not far behind. They usually push their entire ticket, so the state or national parties can pick up the cost. For us, everything has to be paid for out of my campaign funds.

This year we got smart and started early. We took advantage of resources that have always been there. Many professional and occupational groups in Vermont must register with the state, and these lists are available to the public for free, often on computer disks. Using them has enabled us by mid-August to send mail to 95,000 Vermonters.

Our plan of action is not complicated. We get people who are well known within the various professions to write letters of support, we enclose our standard literature and a return envelope with a contribution form, and we mail out bulk rate—about eighteen cents a letter. And we are making an exciting discovery: these mailings have almost paid for themselves; in fact, some of them have actually made money. In other words, we're able to do mass mailings to Vermonters at no cost to the campaign. So far, we have sent out letters to doctors, lawyers, and every teacher, nurse, physical therapist, chiropractor, farmer, and university professor in the state. Now we are buying lists of senior citizens and environmentalists.

Our success with bulk mailing encouraged us to come up with an even bolder plan. What would happen, we brainstormed, if we picked a district in which we did well in the last election, and sent a mailing to every single household? Well, the results of the first few tries are in, and we did well, getting the one percent response necessary to cover our costs. An advantage of this kind of mailing is we can use a "postal patron" address (which means mail goes to *every* residential address, instead of to a named addressee), which is the cheapest form of mail. The disadvantage is that a number of the people you are sending mail to don't vote. But frankly, for us, this is not so much of a problem. We want to communicate with those folks, too.

In general, then, our mailing efforts are going far better than ever before. We're communicating with more people, we're raising more money, and we're drawing more supporters into the campaign. I'm very excited about this aspect of our work.

When you run a campaign you have to become an expert in all kinds of things: mail solicitation, direct mail, postal rates, buying drive-time slots for radio advertising, writing campaign brochures and laying them out, estimating printing costs, purchasing buttons and bumper stickers, scripting radio ads, and editing television slots. Believe me, a campaign is more than just giving speeches and turning up at debates.

Our third goal was to do a better job using the telephone. Yes. I apologize. We also engage in that activity hostile to human sentiment, telephone canvassing. Generally, most congressional candidates and political parties hire professional telemarketing organizations that are located in South Dakota or some other faraway place. I think that the geographical location of the company is dependent upon the callers being "accent free"—Vermonters would not appreciate callers with an Alabama accent—and the cost of labor being cheap. These companies have hundreds of workers who do nothing else but dial phones automatically, give the same spiel over and over again, and type the results into a computer. "Yes. I intend to vote for Congressman Jones no matter what happens." Strong supporter. "No. I haven't a clue as to who is running for office. Is there an election coming up this year?" Undecided.

For years, we have argued among ourselves about the advantages and disadvantages of making calls in-state or out of state. The clear advantage of making the calls through a professional telemarketing company is that they'll get made. You put down your money, and they can make fifty or one hundred thousand calls—whatever you want to pay for. And you'll get voter ID responses back nice and clean, done by professionals. It's expensive, but it's simple.

The disadvantage of this approach is that the people who are making the calls couldn't care less about what they're doing. They don't know Vermont, they don't know Bernie Sanders, and some of that will surely come through. Also, when it works well, telephoning is an excellent activity for our volunteers. It is very effective for a supporter in Hinesburg, Vermont, to call a neighbor and talk about the campaign. You can't beat that. But it's very hard to get the number of volunteers that you need to make any sizeable number of calls. A lot of folks, quite understandably, do not like calling up strangers. Also, given the fact that our callers are not professionals, and that they're not working on computers, some of the results come back a bit jumbled.

Once again, after a lot of discussion, we decided to do our telephoning in-state. We have to get lists of registered voters and phone numbers to our volunteers, order a bunch of telephones for our office—and do the best we can. Although Tom Smith is doing an excellent job in coordinating this, and we're doing better than in the last campaign, we're still struggling. On any given night we only have three or four people on the phones. People say they'll come in, and don't. I have my doubts as to how successful our overall telephone campaign will be. It will be better than last campaign, but still won't be very good.

You don't have to be a political genius to know that if you function alone, there are real limits to what you can accomplish. The Democrats have their party, the Republicans have theirs. As an Independent, functioning outside the two-party system, I have worked hard throughout my political career to bring people together into the progressive movement in the fight for social justice.

When I was first elected mayor of Burlington, I knew that a progressive agenda could never be implemented without the efforts of a strong and successful political movement. Working with other progressives in Burlington, we created the Burlington Progressive Coalition, which, in the city, has been a de facto political party for the last fifteen years. During that time, the Progressive Coalition has elected two mayors, dozens of city councilors and school board members, and four representatives to the state legislature.

Statewide, we have not developed a formal third party. I have, however, been active with many others in creating a strong Vermont progressive movement, which over the years has, among other activities, run a number of candidates for state legislature.

Obviously, when I took office in Congress in 1991, the dynamics were very different than those in Vermont. I was the only Independent in Congress, the only person outside the two-party system. There was no way that was going to change in the next two years. In Congress, there were Republicans, Democrats, and me—and that was that. Given that reality, I thought hard about the political role I could play.

After a short time in Congress, I decided to try to bring together the most progressive members so that we could more effectively fight for economic justice. There were already a number of caucuses in Congress, some of them doing excellent work, but there was no group explicitly fighting for a progressive agenda to address the needs of America's working people.

I was aware that, over the years, the most progressive positions in Congress had been articulated by the Black Caucus. For decades it had done an excellent job in fighting not only for the needs of the black community, but for the needs of low- and moderate-income people of all races.

When I was mayor, I became aware of the "alternative budget" introduced by the Black Caucus every year. In this document, they showed how we could increase funding for affordable housing, community and urban development, health care, education, and the general needs of low- and moderate-income Americans by shifting the funding priorities of Congress. In a very simple and effective manner, their "alternative budget" exposed the moral bankruptcy of congressional priorities. It was a terrific initiative and was widely used by political activists all over the country. For years the Black Caucus had been, in effect, *the* progressive caucus in Congress.

But not every progressive in Congress is black, and so it seemed to me an important step forward to develop a caucus which brought *all* progressives together—white, black, Hispanic, Asian, male, and female—so that we could stand together in fighting for rational priorities.

Obviously, the Black Caucus will always focus its attention on the particular needs of the black community, the Hispanic Caucus on the particular needs of Hispanics, the

Women's Caucus on the particular needs of women. A Progressive Caucus, however, would try, on an ideological and class basis, to represent *all* Americans who were struggling to obtain a decent standard of living. I bounced the idea of a progressive caucus off some of my friends.

One of the first members I talked to was Ron Dellums of California. Ron is one of the great heroes in the United States Congress. For twenty years he has been a leading voice in the struggle for a world of peace and social justice. He entered Congress from the Berkeley area and was already well known for his opposition to the war in Vietnam, and for his struggles against racism. He has continued to fight for justice, year after year.

I also talked to Peter DeFazio of Oregon, who was one of two members of Congress to endorse me when I ran in 1990. (Barney Frank was the other.) I didn't know Peter well then, but he has since become a very close friend. He represents a rural district in Oregon that, in many ways, is similar to Vermont. We end up approaching many issues with a similar outlook. Peter has been especially strong in the fight against corporate welfare, and on trade and the environment.

Then there was Lane Evans, a Vietnam-era veteran from Illinois who had one of the strongest anti-Reagan voting records in Congress. Lane received national recognition for leading the effort to expose the Pentagon's cover-up of the Agent Orange fiasco, and has been a leading voice for veterans throughout his tenure. (He is also a good landlord. I live in the basement apartment of his house.)

Finally, I approached Maxine Waters of California, who came into Congress the same time as I did and sits next to me on the Banking Committee. Maxine was well known as a powerful progressive voice in the California State Assembly, and firebrand advocate for low-income people. She was born in a low-income housing development, and did not forget where she came from.

We five got together and formed the Progressive Caucus. Over the years the group grew slowly and steadily, so that by the time our largest battle took place—against Newt Gingrich and his reactionary "Contract with America"— we were fifty-two members strong. I was elected chairman of the Caucus in 1991 and have held that position since.

In addition to the founders, other members of Congress who have been active in the Progressive Caucus include Major Owens, Maurice Hinchey, Cynthia McKinney, Nydia Valazques, Lynn Woolsey, Bob Filner, Jerry Nadler, Eleanor Holmes Norton, Barney Frank, Marcy Kaptur, and Jesse Jackson, Jr.

In October 1992 I got my first major piece of legislation through the Congress when the National Cancer Registries Act was signed into law by President Bush. Every so often, Congress actually works the way it is supposed to: ordinary citizens see the need for new legislation to tackle a problem, approach their elected representatives, and their proposal gets translated into law. This was the genesis of the National Cancer Registries Act.

In 1991, a number of Vermont women became concerned that the mortality rate for breast cancer in Vermont was extremely high, and significantly higher than in the rest of the country. Why was this and what could be done about it? Led by three breast cancer survivors—Joann Rathgeb, who eventually died after a courageous battle with cancer, Patricia Barr, and Virginia Soffa—these Vermont women mounted a strong educational campaign in the state and a petition drive that secured thousands of names. Their demand was the establishment of a national cancer registry.

I learned from these women that the United States was far behind most major countries in keeping uniform statistics on who was contracting cancer, their place of residence, their occupation, the types of treatment they were receiving, and the effectiveness of the treatment. Clearly, if researchers are going to get a better handle on the causes of cancer, and the most effective ways of dealing with it, we need more information.

What does it mean that certain types of cancer are more prevalent in Vermont than in California? What is the relationship between environmental degradation and cancer? Are people working at certain types of jobs more likely to come down with particular types of cancer than people working at other jobs? Are people living near landfills or incinerators more likely to develop cancer?

If we had uniform national statistics, would we learn more about the connection between diet and cancer, and lifestyle and cancer? Would we discover more geographical "clusters" of certain types of cancer? Are there reliable national statistics about the rate of cure for one type of procedure as opposed to another?

Given the fact that one American in three is expected to develop some type of cancer in his or her lifetime, these issues are of enormous consequence. I learned about the problem not only from women in Vermont, but from trade unionists in the Oil, Chemical and Atomic Workers Union. The people in their union do work that exposes them to a lot of unhealthy substances, and they have great difficulty in getting information from their employers about the rate and kinds of cancer workers in their union are developing. Workers all over the country face similar obstacles.

This issue is especially important to me because I have long been interested in preventive health care measures. This country spends $1 trillion a year on health care, and almost all of it goes into treatment. We spend relatively little trying to prevent disease—whether it is cancer, heart disease, or the common cold. In the long run we can eliminate much human suffering, and great cost, if we better understand the *causation* of disease.

After undertaking some research, we found that only ten states in the country had effective cancer registries. And while some national statistics were being tabulated by the National Cancer Institute, they ignored 90 percent of the population. In early 1992, I introduced the Cancer Registries Amendment Act. The bill was later introduced in the Senate by my Vermont colleague Senator Patrick Leahy. As a result of some excellent work by my staff member Katie Clarke, we picked up strong support from physicians and health care organizations all across the country. Then we had a stroke of good fortune.

In their June 1992 issue, *Reader's Digest* ran a lead article by Dr. John H. Healey, of the Sloan-Kettering Cancer Center, titled "The Cancer Weapon America Needs Most." And what was that weapon? The passage of the Cancer

Registries Amendment Act of 1992. The *Reader's Digest* also ran full-page ads in the *New York Times* and other papers discussing that article. We could not have asked for better publicity. Soon, letters of support for the legislation began flooding the Capitol.

The legislation wound its way through the committee process, winning support as it proceeded. Unfortunately, we were heading into the very end of the session, and it was likely that time would run out before we got a vote on the floor of the House. If that were the case, I would have to start all over again—assuming I was reelected.

There we were on the very last night of the session, with Congress rushing toward adjournment. At this point in the legislative process, the only legislation passed is through "unanimous consent." There is no time for debate or vote taking. The only bills that pass have got to win support from the floor leaders of both parties, with no opposition from any member, even one who only wants to see the bill debated. If there is any objection to "unanimous consent," the bill is dead.

At four o'clock in the morning, I was desperately trying to figure out how I could get my bill on the floor and secure unanimous consent. The Democrats were amenable to bringing it up, but the Republican floor leader was William Dannemeyer of California, one of the most right-wing members of the Congress. He only had to say "I object," and it was all over for the session. Frankly, I thought I would do the bill more harm than good if I approached Dannemeyer alone. He and I did not see eye to eye on most things.

My heroine of the hour, the person who saved the day (or rather the night), was Representative Mary Rose Oakar of Ohio. Mary Rose, who served with me on the Banking Committee, literally took me by the hand and led me to the Republican offices off the floor, where we discussed the issue with the Republican staff. She personally intervened with Dannemeyer and other Republicans and, I believe, even tried to call Dannemeyer's wife. (I don't remember if she ever got through.) In any case, on the morning of the last day of the session, the legislation was approved by voice vote with no objections. I was a sleepy but happy congressman. I believe that the National Cancer Registries Amendment was the second-to-last piece of legislation passed in the House in the 102nd Congress. Today, as a result of that legislation, and some $50 million in appropriations, almost every state in America now has an effective cancer registry and researchers are gaining valuable information from the data.

In 1992, two Republicans were vying for the right to oppose me in the general election: Tim Philbin, a right-wing Christian Coalition type, and Jeff Wennberg, the conservative mayor of Rutland, the state's second largest city. No strong Democrat entered the race. A relatively unknown candidate from Brattleboro, Lew Young, put his name into the Democratic primary.

Both Philbin and Wennberg had their strengths. Philbin was a dynamic speaker and had strong, conservative grass-roots support. Wennberg, on the other hand, was an experienced politician and, as the Establishment candidate, would receive substantial funding from the monied interests.

Philbin won the Republican primary. Consistent with his ideology, he opposed a woman's right to abortion, even in the case of incest and rape. In Vermont, every statewide officeholder was pro-choice. It was very definitely the prevailing opinion in the state. Moreover, on a variety of issues Philbin was out of touch with the Vermont Republican Establishment, and he got little support from them.

On November 3, I was reelected as Vermont's congress-man. The results were Sanders 58 percent, Philbin 31 percent, and Young 8 percent.

6

Getting Around Vermont

Last month, the *Rutland Herald* ran a detailed article by Diane Derby contrasting my views on abortion with Sweetser's. My position is that a woman's decision whether to have an abortion is a private one, and that this principle must hold true for all women, regardless of income. Susan Sweetser is a "moderate" Republican and describes herself as pro-choice. On the surface, our positions appear similar. But there is one significant difference: Sweetser opposes the use of Medicaid funds for abortion. She supports a woman's right to an abortion, but only if that woman can afford to pay for one. So, while our positions seem similar, there is a very real difference between us. The *Herald* article made that clear.

Unfortunately, serious articles that explore, in detail, the difference in positions between the candidates are few and far between. We need more of that kind of writing, and less emphasis on campaign gossip.

On the subject of women's issues, one of the more gratifying aspects of the campaign so far is that we are winning very strong support from women and women's organizations—despite my running against a female candidate who has been active in victim's rights activities. Poll after poll shows the "gender gap" to be enormous. We're ahead with women by as much as two to one, while we're barely winning among men. We have also been endorsed by the National Organization of Women (NOW), the National Abortion Rights Action League (NARAL), and the Business and Professional Women's Association. Sweetser has won the backing of the National Women's Political Caucus, which only endorses women candidates.

Over the years my office has played a very strong role in the fight for women's rights. I not only have a 100 percent voting record on women's issues, but have worked hard and successfully on women's health matters and against domestic violence. The women of Vermont know that. Furthermore, most women understand that it is hard for a candidate to be "pro-woman" while supporting a political party that wants a constitutional amendment to ban abortion and is waging war against low-income workers and Medicare recipients, who are mostly women, as well as single mothers and their kids.

Yipes. I'm the subject of a major editorial in the *Wall Street Journal*. I'm pissed. Not only is the content absurd, but the picture they run of me stinks. Now why is the *Wall Street Journal*, the voice of corporate America, worried about the congressional race in little old Vermont? Don't they have bigger things to worry about? Well, in truth, they're really not too concerned about me, they *are* on to bigger things.

In an editorial which refers to me as "the nation's highest-ranking socialist elected official," the *Journal* is despondent over the fact that the national Democratic Party and President Clinton are not supporting Jack Long—the Democratic candidate for Congress. See, we told you all along, suggest these perceptive editorial writers. That Clinton, those Democrats, they say they're "moderates," but when given a choice between a moderate Democrat and a socialist, whom do they choose?

Yup. The Democrats are backing an incumbent, favored to win, who helped lead the opposition to Gingrich rather than a candidate nobody's ever heard of who is running 6 percent in the polls. Big surprise. Clinton and his friends may not be too progressive, but they ain't dumb. Interestingly, this was the exact theme used in an editorial in the extreme right-wing Moonie newspaper, the *Washington Times*, a few weeks earlier. I wonder. Is this the prelude to a national Republican redbaiting ad campaign? Are we going to see thirty-second TV ads all over America on how Clinton is supporting a socialist?

Of course, I have been winning the support of Vermont progressive Democrats for years, and have worked on a number of important issues with Democrats in the legislature like Cheryl Rivers, Liz Ready, and Dick McCormick. We have our differences, but we've found it mutually advantageous, and in the best interests of Vermont, to work together when we can.

Generally speaking, what appears in the *Wall Street Journal* is of no concern to me. I'd estimate that over 98 percent of the people in Vermont do not read the

Journal—and most of those who do aren't going to vote for me in any case. So the editorial by itself doesn't mean much. But what happens is that this sort of attention from the national press can become a focus for political gossip in Vermont. The very fact of the *Wall Street Journal* carrying a story on a Vermont issue may well become news in the state.

Shortly after its appearance, the *Journal*'s analysis gets picked up by the Vermont media, and my office receives umpteen calls on the now-famous "Jack Long story": "How come Sanders has the support of many leading Democrats in Vermont while Jack Long, a Democrat, doesn't?" (To the best of my knowledge, Governor Dean is the only major Democrat to come out for him.) The fact that I won widespread support from Democrats in 1988, 1990, 1992, and 1994 is now forgotten, and we're starting this discussion all over again.

And what a strange discussion it is. Here is a man who has yet to hold a press conference explaining his position on any issue since he announced his candidacy, a man who has raised almost no money, a man who is between 4 and 8 percent in the polls—and yet the great unexplained point of interest turns out to be—remarkably—why Democrats will not support him. The recirculation of superficial punditry never stops. Story after story appears in the *Burlington Free Press* and elsewhere, and the issue attracts the attention of the largest television station in the state.

WCAX-TV calls for a comment on the *Journal*. I'm not particularly interested in discussing political gossip. What do I have to say that hasn't been said ten times before? But

I'm ready to deal. I'll give them a response if I'm also allowed to say a few words about something substantive—something that might actually be of interest to someone. "If you allow me to discuss a recent press release I just sent out," I say, "I'll talk about the editorial." My press release was critical of a Pentagon policy that is farming out billions in Defense Department contract work to countries abroad, work that should be done in this country by American workers. At a time when the defense industry is laying off tens of thousands of American workers, it's an issue of real concern—especially in a state with several defense plants. The reporter calls back and we have a deal. They get their comment on the absurd *Wall Street Journal* editorial and I get a decent story about something relevant.

Not only did we make the *Journal* last week, but we also made the *New York Times*. The *Times*, covering "all the news that's fit to print" got the scoop. As careful as they are perceptive, the paper calls me to confirm the story. Their details are accurate. "Yes, it was me. I did it. I really was the back half of the tiger in the Bread and Puppet Circus that took place in Glover, Vermont, a week ago." I had been asked, not for the first time, to participate in the huge outdoor drama/celebration, and had been cast in the role of the hind end of a large tiger puppet. (It's better than being a horse's ass.) I told the writer the whole story, and he wrote a few lines about it in the Chronicle column. He also quoted me accurately: "As for the conventions, Mr. Sanders said: 'I'm the luckiest man in the U.S. Congress. I'm not in Chicago, and I didn't go to San Diego.'"

There was a story here, but it is not about me. The Bread and Puppet Domestic Resurrection Circus, an annual two-day gathering in August, is put on by a radical theatrical troupe that, traveling from its base in Vermont, performs street theater all over the globe. On this occasion it brought out between twenty and thirty thousand people to Glover—a beautiful town in the north of the state. The Bread and Puppet theater—founded by Peter Schumann—is a political company whose accomplished theatrical productions are truly radical. They are especially well known for their huge masks and the performers who wear them while walking on stilts. Bread and Puppet does a tremendous job, and we in Vermont are very proud of them.

While there are many out-of-staters at the festival, the number of Vermonters who attend the Bread and Puppet Circus always amazes me. In the week since my appearance as the back end of a tiger I have been stopped a dozen times by people who told me that they saw me there. I'm not sure how many of them actually heard my fourteen-second speech about the dangers of Newt Gingrich, given when I stepped out of my tiger costume. (The Bread and Puppet Circus is performed without electricity or microphones.) Still, it was great to be there.

My son Levi was with me at the event. Levi works full time for the Chittenden County Emergency Food Shelf, but whenever he can get a free weekend, he travels with me around the state. I enjoy his company a lot, and he helps me by doing most of the driving and by working the crowds: handing out buttons and bumper stickers while I shake hands. With the enormous crowd in Glover, we had four other campaign workers there. It's a great place to campaign.

One of the fun aspects of being a congressman is the different kinds of people that I meet. After we left Glover, Levi and I took a beautiful drive across the width of the state to Swanton, which is located in northwest Vermont, just south of the Canadian border. I often think how lucky I am not only to live in Vermont, but to campaign there. Driving along beautiful Vermont country roads in August, as the sun goes down, just ain't hard work. It's exactly the kind of thing I would do if I never ran for office. In the back of the car I always have a bathing suit, and it's not uncommon for us to stop midday on the campaign trail and jump into a nearby lake or river.

My business in Swanton that Saturday night was to address members of the Missisquoi Valley Emergency Rescue Service. The contrast between the huge crowd of the afternoon and the dinner event of the evening, attended by forty or so members of the rescue service, was striking, from radical theatrics to community-based service. (Interestingly, the differences strike me as more superficial than deep: both the rescue workers and the drama troupe are focused on giving, on giving of themselves to build community.) The rescue workers are all volunteers. Their work is difficult and emotionally traumatic. Since Interstate 89 passes right through Swanton, serious highway accidents are not uncommon. These men and women are often the first people to arrive at the scene of an accident. They deal with life and death in the course of their work. At the dinner, person after person talked about the trauma of seeing people die and the joy of saving people's lives.

They were an impressive group of working people—young and old, men and women, with a strong pride and attachment to their community. Being among these people reminds me, once again, of why Vermont is such a good place to live: here is an organization whose members are not paid a nickel but serve the community because they care. There are hundreds of organizations like this one in the state.

While I have been going to county fairs, parades, "circuses," banquets, picnics, and shopping centers all over Vermont, on the national scene something far more visible—and scripted—has been taking place. The last couple of weeks have witnessed both the Republican and Democratic conventions.

What was most noticeable about the Republican convention—I held a press conference on this—was the degree to which the Republicans were running away from who they are. They spent almost a week on prime-time TV erasing recent history and substituting image for actuality. The Republican Party established a record in the Congress over the last two years. Newt Gingrich and Dick Armey led what I believe is the most reactionary Congress in the modern history of the United States. Yet, when it came to the convention, these people, and the issues they advocated, disappeared entirely. I couldn't find them on CBS, NBC, ABC, or PBS. Puff. They were gone.

Two years previously, the Republicans were pushing large photos of hundreds of their candidates signing the

"Contract with America." Now, that term was never mentioned. Newt Gingrich was sidelined. Dick Armey was barely noticeable. Everything the two of them had fought for with the almost unanimous support of the Republican House was pushed into the hinterlands. It was as if two years of Republican legislative activity never existed. Even the Republican Party platform, which a majority of the delegates had just approved, was ignored. Golly. Bob Dole just didn't get around to reading it.

Instead, on center stage were people like Colin Powell—a black, pro-choice, pro–gun control, pro–affirmative action, moderate Republican. His views are not shared by more than 5 percent of the Republicans in Congress, but it was he and not the "revolutionary" Speaker of the House Newt Gingrich who gave the major speech. The keynote speaker was a pro-choice woman, Susan Molinari of New York.

As the selection of speakers and the entire tone of the GOP convention revealed, when the Republicans have to go beyond the narrow confines of congressional committees and $1,000-a-plate fundraisers and speak to tens of millions of ordinary Americans, they choose to hide who they are. In a five-day period, on prime-time TV, the Republicans went from a party of right-wing extremists to the center of the political spectrum.

The convention also showcased my opponent. In her ninety seconds on national TV, Sweetser said, "This will be an historic election. Why? Because we have the opportunity to replace the most liberal, most out-of-touch member of Congress. Bernie Sanders." According to the

Associated Press, "after mentioning his name, the crowd erupted in boos." I must be doing something right. Sweetser got a lot of Vermont media coverage from her appearance in San Diego.

It was deeply depressing to see the Republican ticket go up fifteen points in the polls in the course of the convention—for no other reason than that the American people happened to see them on their television sets every night. It does make one think: What could happen, what would happen, in this country if progressives were allowed to have four or five nights of prime-time television and front-page newspaper coverage? What would happen if we could present a point of view that most Americans are unfamiliar with? Would we suddenly become the dominant political force in America? No. Would millions of Americans develop a much more sympathetic attitude toward democratic socialism? Yes.

Predictably, the rise of Dole and Kemp in the polls was ephemeral. Two weeks later, when the Democrats got their four or five days in the limelight, the Dole-Kemp surge evaporated. Clinton is now back to where he was before the conventions—fifteen points ahead.

At both conventions there was a general acknowledgment on the part of the Republican and Democratic leaders alike that it was not in their best interests to allow serious discussion on the most important issues facing the American people. Both parties put on well-produced TV shows. Each had a different focus, but both were in complete agreement that debate on the problems facing America was not something they were going to get into.

The Democratic convention was heavily scripted and entirely poll-driven. They made emotional appeals on several issues where the polls showed they had significant support. Seventy-five percent of the people support the ban on assault weapons. So they focused on the tragedy of Jim Brady, and support for gun control.

Christopher Reeves is a very popular actor, handsome and articulate, so his accident and paralysis became a major focus of their convention. So, too, did the issue of cigarette smoking, especially among the young. This is a serious health concern, and Clinton and Gore deserve credit for addressing it—although how far they will really go in taking on the tobacco industry remains to be seen. But it is only one small part of the health care crisis in America. The fact that it is a relatively easy one politically—you lose the votes of a few thousand tobacco farmers in return for those of millions of parents—made it *the* central health care issue the Democrats addressed.

Perhaps more remarkable were the issues *not* talked about. There was virtually no discussion of class, despite the fact that we have the most unequal distribution of wealth and income in the industrialized world, and real wages of workers continue to fall. There was no discussion of our huge trade deficit, nor of corporate investment in China, Mexico, and other Third World countries, which is causing the loss of millions of decent-paying jobs. There was no mention of the fragility of a democracy in which half the people no longer vote and have given up on the political process.

And what about health care? Three years before, Clinton and the Democrats had raised the banner high for a universal health care system that covers all Americans. At the time, I disagreed with the details of their proposal, but the Democrats deserved credit for at least addressing this issue of critical importance to tens of millions of Americans. The health care crisis is now *worse* than it was three years ago. More people are uninsured or underinsured. More people have less choice of providers as medicine becomes more and more corporatized. During the convention the best the Democrats were willing to allow was that at some undetermined time, in some undetermined way, we should try to provide coverage for children. That was the sum total of their commitment.

In a convention that focused on gun control, smoking, and the personal tragedy of a popular actor, most of the important issues facing the American people were ignored. The vast majority of Americans reject the right-wing extremism of the Republican Party. The Democrats held a convention that refused to address the most important issues facing the middle class and working families of the country. Is it any wonder that most people don't vote and have lost interest in politics? Is it any wonder that the United States faces a major crisis regarding the viability of our democracy?

Watching the convention coverage, it was hard to decide which was worse—the speeches on the floor or the "analysis" by the media pundits. David Brinkley, for instance, complained that President Clinton's acceptance speech dragged on too long, lasting more than an hour. Imagine— at a time when the average American watches forty hours of television a week, fifty-two weeks a year, Brinkley's main concern was that the president of the United States, and candidate for reelection, spoke for more than an hour on the future of the nation. What a profound analysis. And they pay him for saying things like that.

Although I agree with his critique of American trade policy and his opposition to NAFTA, I am no great fan of Ross Perot. There's no way he would be a major political leader if he weren't a billionaire. But I think that he is getting a bum rap from the media when they refer to his half-hour speeches as "infomercials" and make fun of his use of charts. Instead of putting thirty-second attack ads on the air, he is trying to seriously discuss some of the most important issues facing the country. You may not agree with his analysis or his conclusions, but at least he's treating the American people with some respect. What's wrong with that?

During the summer and fall, there are a large number of parades in Vermont—from one end of the state to the other. Fortunately for me, I love parades—I always have, even as a kid. I try to participate in as many as possible. Not only is it good politics, because you get to see and talk to a lot of people, but it's a helluva lot of fun. Parents and their kids lining the streets. The high school and military bands. The fife-and-drum corps. The Scottish bagpipes. The country-music dancers. The Girl Scouts and the Little Leagues. The fire trucks. The antique cars. People dressed in Civil War outfits. The Shriners driving around in their tiny go-carts.

From the town of Brattleboro, to Middlebury, to Vergennes, to Essex Junction, to Lyndonville, to St.

Johnsbury, to Windsor, to Burlington, to Rutland, to Swanton, to Waitsfield, to Barre, to Montpelier, to Bellows Falls, to Bradford, to Irasburg, to Springfield, to Woodstock, to Newport, to Brandon, to Enosburg Falls, to White River Junction, to St. Albans—I've marched in all their parades, and dozens more. And I enjoy it every time.

Yesterday was Labor Day. I went, as I almost always do, to the Labor Day Parade in Northfield, Vermont. It is one of the larger parades in the state, and certainly the largest on this holiday commemorating workers and their labor. Some 10,000 people are there, either participating in the parade or lining the streets to watch.

Over the past few years, progressives and union activists have made a concerted effort to involve workers and labor unions in the Labor Day parade. Just a few years ago there was virtually no union involvement. But yesterday several hundred workers from Vermont's unions joined in. That may not seem like a large number, but Vermont isn't a major union state, and for us it was a terrific presence.

It was nice to see a whole lot of kids and spouses there. That's how you construct a movement, build a political presence: one step at a time, adding person to person until you have involved enough people to make a difference on the political landscape.

It gave me a strong feeling of solidarity, that most important of all political emotions, as I marched together with them. After the parade, the Vermont Association of Letter Carriers sponsored a roast beef dinner on the green. We ate, played some football with the kids, and had a great time.

There was very strong support for my candidacy among the thousands who lined the sidewalk. Our campaign supporters were getting rid of buttons and bumper stickers as fast as they could get them into their hands. Parades are a pretty good indicator of what's happening politically. And the response at Northheld was strong and positive—with almost no negativity.

Labor Day weekend is not only a time for parades, it is a time for the largest fair in Vermont. Throughout August I have been attending county fairs all over the state, and talking to thousands of Vermonters. In addition to my presence, "Sanders for Congress" has booths manned by volunteers at almost all the fairs—and we are giving away large amounts of literature and campaign paraphernalia. Fairs are probably the best places to make contact with Vermonters.

County fairs have been going on in Vermont for well over a hundred years. Originally, they were large agricultural exhibitions, an opportunity for farmers to learn about new products and techniques. Today, obviously, they are much changed and more commercialized and entertainment-oriented, but the agriculture component remains strong in a number of them. At the Barton Fair, at the Rutland Fair, and at most other fairs, boys and girls still exhibit their prize cows. The 4-H clubs are out in full strength. New tractors and other farm equipment are on display. At the Champlain Valley Fair, Huck Gutman has won a number of blue ribbons for his outstanding tomatoes.

Depending on the fair, there are also ox-pulling contests, balloon rides, demolition derbies, horse racing, pig races, spitting contests, professional wrestling, parades, exhibition halls, bingo and other games of chance.

The most "notorious" fair in the state, and the last major fair of the season, is the "Tunbridge World's Fair." Well, what can I say about the Tunbridge World's Fair? Let's just mention that, among other exciting activities, they have a beer hall. I believe that I'm one of the few politicians in the state to campaign *inside* that beer hall. Or at least who lived to talk about it.

This year the Tunbridge World's Fair celebrated its now famous hometown movie star, Fred Tuttle. Fred, now seventy-eight, milked cows in Tunbridge for most of his life before being discovered by his neighbor, filmmaker John O'Brien. (John's dad, Bob O'Brien, was a friend of mine who was a state senator from Orange County in the 1970s.) John made a hysterically funny (fictional) film about Fred and his run for Congress called *Man with a Plan*. It played for months in Vermont's movie theaters and is being shown around the country. Now that Fred has been featured on the front page of the *New York Times*, appeared on the *Late Night with Conan O'Brien* TV show, and was fêted by the congressional delegation in Washington, the local folks don't know what to do with him anymore. In fact, Fred was at the first congressional debate of the campaign between Sweetser, Long, and me. Guess who got all the attention?

The largest fair in the state is the Champlain Valley Fair, in Essex Junction, which in a little over a week draws close to 300,000 people (although obviously some of these are repeat visitors) in this state of less than 600,000. It is far and away the largest single attraction for Vermonters each year.

During several nights at the fair, some of the best known names in country music perform—before huge crowds. There are also all kinds of rides and games for the kids.

At the fair, which is in my home county and only five miles from Burlington, I walk around, shake hands, and talk to people who freely offer opinions on every conceivable issue. Interestingly, much of what I hear about has nothing to do with Congress, but concerns over high property taxes, a state issue.

Our booth is fully staffed with volunteers—senior citizens and long-haired young people, veterans and peace activists, trade unionists and women's advocates—reflecting the diversity of our coalition. The heart of our campaign is in that booth, and they do a terrific job.

Perhaps the most active volunteer at the fair is Ed Walton, a disabled Vietnam veteran. I met Ed last year at a conference for veterans organized by my congressional office. Ed lives in Bristol, about an hour away from Essex Junction, and stays with relatives in Essex during the fair. Every day, first thing in the morning, he helps set up the booth, and makes certain that it is covered throughout the day. When no one else can take a shift, Ed does. It makes me extremely proud that people like Ed are supporting my candidacy.

As I walk around the fair, I can sense that our support is strong. While this is a different part of the state, it reinforces the feeling I got from the Labor Day parade in Northfield—there is a lot of good feeling out there, and things appear to be going well.

Any good politician develops that extra sense. You can look into people's eyes, shake hands, say hello, and after a few hours, develop a real feeling about how things are going politically. At a fair, or other public place, when people bump into you unexpectedly, their feelings are transparent—right on their sleeves. There you are, right in front of them, and they don't have time to hide their emotions. If they like you and what you're doing, they smile and are happy to meet you. If they're not feeling good about you, their eyes don't meet yours, and they look away. Sometimes people are rude and overtly hostile. But that's very rare in Vermont. Most people in Vermont are very civil, even when they don't agree with you.

And let me tell you. The feelings out there this time are much different than they were two years ago, in 1994— when I only won by three points in the midst of the Republican tidal wave. Why is that? I don't know. The economy is better. The anti-Clinton hysteria has died down. The NRA is quieter. Most importantly, I think, people are concerned about the Gingrich agenda and the right-wing extremism he represents. I believe that they appreciate my willingness to stand up for them, and against the savage cuts that the Republicans are proposing.

My sense that things are going well is borne out by a more "objective" measure. Recently, a new poll appeared in the *Burlington Free Press*, the largest paper in the state. It had us at 47 percent, Sweetser 24 percent, Long 8 percent. (The rest are undecided or are supporting another candidate. There are a total of seven candidates in the race.) That's a very good poll for us because it suggests not only that we have a large lead, but that we're going up and Sweetser is going nowhere. While 47 percent is not necessarily a great number for a well-known incumbent like me, 24 percent is a poor number for an establishment Republican at this time of the campaign—especially one who has spent big bucks on TV ads.

For whatever reason, the Sweetser campaign is not clicking. Peter Freyne, not an infrequent critic of mine, is an astute and long-time observer of the Vermont political scene. He offered a few observations in the September 11 issue of *Seven Days*:

> The GOP's best political minds were absolutely certain a woman like Susie Creamcheese would be Ol' Bernardo's worst nightmare. After all, none of the three Republican notches on Congressman Bernie's gun belt (Peter Smith, Tim Philbin and John Carroll) were female. Aha! they thought—the key is to match him up against a woman! "Bernie can't handle a strong woman," they crowed. Susan Sweetser had all the necessary credentials and then some.
>
> Sweetser signed up one of the top political consulting firms going: Dresner & Wickers. Dick Dresner worked for Jim Jeffords for years . . . and just upped his fee by pulling off the upset of the century in getting Russia's Boris Yeltsin reelected. Knocking off the only political aberration on Capitol Hill surely would be child's play for these political heavyweights, right?
>
> The plan was simple. Hit the airwaves early to build up statewide name recognition, and with it garner a bump in the polls. Take that bump to the bank and close in for the kill. Keep Sanders on the defensive. Attack his contributors. Portray him as out of touch, a fringe-type who consorts with out-of-state left-wing extremists.

But in life, things don't always go the way you plan. Susie's TV blitz in June did build up her name recognition statewide. Unfortunately, a whole lot of Vermonters who began to recognize her also began to get a bad taste in their mouth. Her commercials were too slick, too New York. A clear gender gap developed. Women didn't like her. Too brassy, too bitchy, too loud-mouthed. The bump in the polls never came. Instead, her unfavorable rating doubled. Oops. Iceberg, dead ahead!

The campaign is going well. But the last thing in the world that we need now is to become overconfident. It's still two months to polling day and in a political campaign that can be a lifetime. Anything can, and probably will, happen.

In early August 1993, seven months after Bill Clinton became president, I voted for the Clinton budget. It passed by two votes, 218 to 216. As the only non-Democrat to vote for it, you could say my vote was the decisive one for the passage of that important piece of legislation. (On the other hand you could also say that *anyone* who voted for it cast the winning vote.) No Republicans supported it, and forty-one Democrats voted against it. In the Senate it won by one vote.

As the vote on the budget approached, the president and his cabinet scrambled for support. There was an enormous amount of jockeying for votes. The conservatives in the Democratic Party wanted more cuts in social spending, and a smaller tax increase. The Progressive Caucus worked hard to make certain that the legislation remained as responsive to low- and moderate-income people as possible. We expressed our concerns to Leon Panetta, who was then head of the Office of Management and Budget (OMB). We met with Speaker Tom Foley, and told him not to count on our support if the Democratic leadership caved in to the conservatives and cut back on children's programs, health care, and other needs. And we eventually met with the president.

While the bill contained some regressive elements, it was the most progressive budget that Congress had voted on for many years. It increased funding for children's programs, lowered taxes on the working poor by expanding the earned income tax credit, and raised taxes on the rich and corporate America.

For as far back as I can remember, I have always been a proponent of a national health care system. It just seemed eminently fair and right. How can we call this a civilized society when some Americans have access to the best medical care in the world and others are unable to walk into a doctor's office because they lack money? How can we tolerate a situation where the children or parents of the rich get the medical attention they need in order to stay alive, while members of working-class families, who lack health insurance, have to die or needlessly suffer—or go hopelessly into debt to get the care they need? This is an outrageous injustice and it cannot be rationally defended.

Wherever I go in Vermont, people talk to me about health care. Old people tell me about the difficulty they have paying for their expensive prescription drugs. Young people tell me that the jobs they have do not provide health insurance. Union workers tell me that their bosses are attempting, at every contract negotiation, to cut back on the health insurance benefits they provide. And people of all income levels tell me that various kinds of alternative treatments they want to use are not covered by their insurance plans.

People from almost all income levels are growing increasingly concerned about the depersonalization of medicine and the quality of care they are receiving. They often no longer have a personal physician and believe that the care they receive is dictated more by the financial needs of their HMO or managed care provider than by their illness.

The fight for a national health care system today is not basically different than the struggle for universal public education that took place in this country over a hundred years ago. At that time, children of the well-to-do received an education, and a tremendous advantage in life. Most of the children of working people and the poor did not. Finally, after enormous struggle, our society concluded that all children, regardless of income, were entitled to at least a high school education. Some day we will also accept that all people, regardless of income, are entitled to health care.

The fact that the United States continues to be the only major nation in the industrialized world without a national health care system should be a source of national shame. Canada, Great Britain, France, Germany, and Scandinavia all have one. Alone, among the great nations of the earth, we do not guarantee health care for all people.

Despite the fact that 40 million Americans lack any health insurance, and many more are underinsured, we spend a far greater amount per capita on health care than any other nation. Increasingly, the function of the health care industry in this country is not to make sick people well, or to prevent disease, but to make huge profits for insurance and pharmaceutical companies and some well-paid professionals.

In my first year in Congress in 1991, I worked with Doctors David Himmelstein and Steffie Woolhandler on legislation to create a state-administered, single-payer national health care system. A husband-and-wife team, David and Steffie are two of the most knowledgeable and effective proponents of national health care in the country. They have produced an enormous amount of writing on the subject, both technical and popular, and have appeared often in the mass media.

Steffie received a grant to intern in my office and drafted legislation for me, HR 2530, which set out the creation of a national health care system. Simply put, this bill created a single-payer, comprehensive, universal health care delivery system, to be administered by the states. It had many advantages over the system in place then, and over the strange hybrid—corporate-run managed care—which emerged in the period following the collapse of Clinton's health care reform initiative.

The legislation would have created a health care delivery system that covered *every* American. It was a "single-payer" plan—which means there would have been only one state-administered insurance agency paying the bills, creating a far more efficient delivery system. About one-quarter of American health care costs go to cover bureaucracy, billing, and administrative overhead. Canadians spend half that much on administration; the British, one-quarter!

Under this proposed single-payer plan, any American, upon presentation of a health care card much like a credit card, would have been able to get *all* the health care he or she needed, from the doctor of his or her choice. The coverage would have been portable—not connected to a particular job or employer. And, because it would have been administered by the states, citizens would have had more control over their own plan. No distant Washington bureaucracy would have been responsible for health care. While the major single-payer bill that session was introduced by Representative Marty Russo of Illinois, my bill won support from those who preferred to see the program administered by the states, rather than from Washington. In that sense, my bill was closer to the Canadian health care system than Russo's.

Two years later, Bill and Hillary Clinton raised the health care debate to the highest level that it had ever reached in this country. They deserve credit for that. They also deserve credit for proclaiming that all Americans are entitled to health care. Unfortunately, the complicated and compromised bill they brought forth was not something I could support.

Throughout that congressional debate—a debate ultimately decided by the millions of dollars that the insurance companies put into "Harry and Louise" ads and a massive lobbying effort—a number of us, led by Representative

Jim McDermott of Washington, worked hard for the single-payer system in Congress.

At the same time, as an adherent of addressing health care concerns on the state level, I also fought to implement health care reform in Vermont. It seemed to me then, and now, that a small state like Vermont could become a model for the rest of the country in health care. I was also mindful that national health care did not come to Canada until it had first been implemented in one of the provinces. Vermont has two major tertiary hospitals in the area, eleven regional hospitals, a medical school, and very competent physicians and health care workers. If there is any state in this country where a single-payer system could be implemented quickly and successfully, it is Vermont.

In 1993, a number of health care reform advocates began working together to gather political support for a single-payer system in Vermont. My office was an active part of that coalition. Among other activities, I appointed a task force to develop a single-payer model for Vermont. It was easy to talk about the benefits of a single-payer system in general, it was harder to be specific as to how it would work in Vermont.

How much would it cost to provide comprehensive health care to all of our people? What would be the mechanics of the delivery system? How could we finance it? Bob Brand, a former health care analyst for the Service Employees International Union, and John Franco, a long-time associate who had worked with me when I was mayor and in my first year in Congress, did an extremely thorough job in leading the task force, and their work generated much discussion. Their conclusion was that, under a single-payer system, we could provide health care to every man, woman, and child in Vermont—without spending any more than we were currently spending.

As part of our health care educational campaign, we held well-attended town meetings all over the state. Sometimes these meetings included state representatives like Cheryl Rivers and Dean Corren who were active in the fight for a single-payer plan in the legislature. Sometimes they included Vermont physicians like Dr. Jason Kelley and Dr. Leigh LoPresti, advocates of the single-payer system.

Needless to say, our efforts were not successful in Vermont or in Congress. The insurance companies and the medical establishment poured tens of millions of dollars into massive and effective lobbying and advertising campaigns against any kind of real health care reform. And they won.

Let's be clear. The debate over health care in this country is *not* a debate about medical treatment or the best way to prevent disease. It is a debate about economics and class politics. Either we maintain a profit-driven health care system whose main function is to enrich certain individuals and institutions, or we develop a nonprofit, cost-effective system that provides quality health care for all people as a right of citizenship.

Health care reform in America will not come without radical political change and the growth of a strong progressive movement.

While I strongly disagreed with Clinton's health care proposal, I respected his willingness to raise the issue and fight for the right of all Americans to have some form of health insurance. But at the very same time as health care was on the congressional agenda, Clinton pushed another issue to the forefront. And on this major initiative, Clinton was just plain wrong—very wrong. His support for the North American Free Trade Agreement (NAFTA) was a sellout to corporate America. Pure and simple, it was a disaster for the working people of this country.

Consider the following: The United States has a federal deficit problem and the Republicans, President Clinton and many Democrats, and the corporate media have made it the focus of their attention. Over and over again we hear about the federal deficit and its implication for the future of this country. Their way of dealing with this has been to come down heavy on low- and moderate-income people and cut programs that currently benefit tens of millions of Americans.

Now, the United States has a major trade deficit problem. In fact, the deficit is at record-breaking levels. For most Republicans, President Clinton and many Democrats, and the corporate media the trade deficit is no cause for alarm. We hear very little about proposals to eliminate *that* deficit. No one suggests that we hold corporate America responsible or demand that they rebuild the manufacturing base in this country rather than invest tens of billions of dollars in China, Mexico, or other impoverished Third World countries.

The United States currently has a trade deficit of $114 billion. Economists tell us that $1 billion of investment equates to about 18,000 (often decent-paying) jobs. Connect the dots. Our current trade deficit is causing the loss of over 2 million jobs. Over the last twenty years, while the United States has run up over a trillion dollars in trade deficits, millions of American workers have been thrown into the streets. During that period our industrial base has declined and real wages for American workers have plummeted. While corporate America shuts down factories in the United States and invests in low-wage countries abroad, young Americans can expect to earn the minimum wage flipping hamburgers at McDonald's, with no benefits or opportunities to advance.

The function of trade agreements like NAFTA is to make it easier for American companies to move abroad, and to force our workers to compete against desperate people in the Third World. But our workers cannot compete, and should not be asked to do so, against people who are forced to work for incredibly low wages, as they do in Mexico.

It is absurd to merge the economy of a modern industrial nation like the United States with a Third World economy like Mexico's. It is absurd to merge the economy of a democratic society with a country whose president at the time of the passage of NAFTA, Carlos Salinas, was elected through massive electoral fraud. It is absurd to merge the economy of the United States with a country where workers are unable to join free trade unions. The result of such a merger will only make the wealthy in both countries richer, cause massive dislocation, and hurt both Mexican and American workers. That's precisely what's happening.

In 1993, I traveled through Mexico with a congressional delegation led by my friend Representative John Conyers of Michigan. It was an eye-opening experience. In one maquiladora area I toured a modern factory owned by Delco Battery. The workers, almost all women, were earning a dollar an hour. Later, a few of us walked a half-mile up the road to the homes of some of these workers: wooden shacks, without electricity or running water. Not so long ago workers in the United States were earning a living wage producing the same product.

At a meeting with Mexican workers we heard firsthand about their atrocious working conditions. One woman described the chemical vapors that permeated the workspace. A number of the workers had experienced miscarriages.

We also went to an agricultural region. There, we heard from small farmers who believed that they would lose their farms and be forced into the cities if they had to compete with American agribusiness. They predicted massive dislocation if NAFTA passed.

During the course of the NAFTA debate, various congressional members expounded on the need for American workers to become more competitive in the global economy. I was so impressed by their arguments that I introduced legislation that would make the president and members of Congress competitive with their Mexican counterparts. My office discovered that members of the Mexican Congress earned about $35,410 a year. If American workers were going to have to compete against Mexicans who were forced to live on $1.00 an hour, I thought that members of Congress should lead by example and lower their $133,644 salaries to the Mexican level. I didn't get many cosponsors for this legislation.

In late October, my office organized a large meeting in Montpelier in opposition to NAFTA. About 300 Vermonters showed up, mostly workers, farmers, and environmentalists, to protest the agreement. Dave Bonior of Michigan, the Democratic Whip in the House, who, along with Marcy Kaptur of Ohio, was helping to lead the anti-NAFTA effort in Congress, gave the major speech.

During the NAFTA debate, every editorial page in the state of Vermont opposed my position—over and over and over again. As the only statewide official who opposed NAFTA I was called a "protectionist," an "anachronism," a "tool of big labor." Some of my political opponents even suggested that I was a racist and anti-Mexican.

But the media support for NAFTA went far beyond Vermont. In fact, in a nation which polls said was divided pretty evenly on this legislation, *every* major newspaper in America supported NAFTA. Every one. It was an incredible display of the power and unity of corporate America defending its interests. The *Washington Post* was running editorial after editorial, column after column, in support of NAFTA—and printing virtually nothing in opposition. Toward the end of the debate, the paper ran a huge story that showed how much in campaign contributions members of Congress who opposed NAFTA received from trade unions. Somehow, they forgot to run the story about the money that pro-NAFTA members were getting from corporate America.

The class divisions in the NAFTA debate were very apparent. Virtually every major corporation in America supported it, while opposition came from unions, many environmental groups, family farm organizations, and working people throughout the country. The political divisions created some strange alliances. On the pro-NAFTA side were the corporatist elements of both the Democratic and Republican parties, including liberals, moderates, and conservatives. Bill Clinton, George Bush, Jimmy Carter, Ronald Reagan, and Jerry Ford stood together with moderate Speaker of the House Tom Foley and the arch right-winger Newt Gingrich.

In opposition to NAFTA were progressives like Jesse Jackson and Ralph Nader, centrists like Ross Perot, and right wingers like Pat Buchanan. In the House, the most vocal opposition came from a left-right coalition. On November 17, 1993, NAFTA won approval in the House by a vote of 234 to 200. One hundred fifty-six Democrats, 43 Republicans, and I voted against it. It is one of the great political ironies of the NAFTA debate that if George Bush had been reelected in 1992, NAFTA would not have passed. A number of Democrats who voted for NAFTA did so because they wanted to support a Democratic president.

Three years have come and gone since NAFTA was passed and the results are clear: a soaring trade deficit with Mexico and the loss of over 260,000 jobs. Polls now show a sizeable majority of Americans are opposed to NAFTA, as are an increasing number of congressional members.

In 1993 I spent a great deal of time fighting the carpet industry. What? The carpet industry? Let me explain: In 1992 a woman from Montpelier, Mrs. Linda Sands, called my office. She had an unusual story to tell. Seven years earlier a new carpet had been installed in her house. After the installation, the air in her home became heavy with a strong chemical smell. A short time later, she and several of her children became ill with body tremors, chronic headaches, dizziness, and respiratory problems. They went through hell.

Frankly, I had real doubts about this story. A congressman receives a lot of strange phone calls. But a member of my staff, Anthony Pollina, who had been talking with Mrs. Sands, urged me to take this seriously, and so I paid her a visit. This was my introduction to the very serious problem of indoor air pollution, and a disorder called "multiple chemical sensitivity." Mrs. Sands, it turned out, was not alone in having been made ill by certain carpets. During one stretch, over 6,000 people telephoned the Consumer Product Safety Commission wanting information about the problem, and twenty-six state attorneys general across the country had petitioned this agency to have the carpet industry issue warning labels on their products. Both the industry and the agency were stonewalling the attorneys general.

In the course of my investigation I met a researcher in Massachusetts, Dr. Rosalind Anderson, who had developed a test with mice to measure the toxicity of carpets. A lot of her mice were dying.

I met with three workers in northern Georgia who had worked in a factory that produced carpets, and they told me about the serious health problems experienced by the employees.

I heard from physicians around the country who were treating people who had been made ill from certain carpets. For instance, Dr. Doris Rapp recounted her experience with school children: "Over the years I have treated a large number of children from all over the United States, many of whom could no longer attend school after new carpets were placed in their school." Dr. William J. Rea wrote, "My colleagues and I have seen over 20,000 chemically sensitive patients over the last 20 years. Many of these patients have been made ill by the fumes emanating from new carpet." And Dr. Aubrey Worrell, Jr., wrote, "I have seen many patients who have become chemically sensitive and completely disabled because of exposure to toxic carpet in their home or their workplace. It is my feeling that the chemicals coming from carpets, in many instances, cause severe illness."

I discovered that, irony of ironies, the Environmental Protection Agency itself had removed over 20,000 feet of new carpet from its *own* headquarters in Washington after several hundred workers there suffered health problems caused by toxic carpets.

At my request, Representative Mike Synar, chairman of the Subcommittee on Environment, Energy, and Natural Resources of the Government Operation's Committee, held a very well-attended hearing on the health problems associated with carpets. The media picked up on the issue and it received wide coverage in newspapers and magazines, and on national television.

And my phone was bopping off the hook from people all across the country who had been made sick by carpets.

Throughout this entire process, we had been pleading with the people at the Consumer Safety Products Commission and the Environmental Protection Agency to do something. There's a problem here. Address it. Meeting followed meeting. Letter followed letter. Nothing happened. They were worse than pathetic.

Finally, after extensive negotiations with the Carpet and Rug Institute, the attorneys general, Mike Synar, and I reached an agreement with the industry. The manufacturers agreed to put a warning label on all carpets, place a counter display of the label in the stores, and commit substantial sums to researching the problem in order to produce a safer product.

In 1994, I faced my toughest campaign since winning political office in 1981. I barely survived.

I knew we were in for an interesting race when my conservative Republican opponent, State Senator John Carroll, opened his campaign by expressing concern about the growing gap between the rich and the poor. How come I always run against the only Republicans in the country who want to tax the rich and are worried about income inequality?

Carroll ran a very smart race. Overnight he went from a conservative to a moderate, and spent most of his campaign appealing to Democrats. He also benefited from the strong anti-incumbent, anti-Washington sentiment that was blowing across America, which gave the Republicans their first majority in the House in forty years.

I assisted his efforts by running a very stupid campaign— the worst of my political career. I allowed Carroll to define me, and didn't at all go on the offensive. He had been the leader of the state senate during a disastrous, unproductive, and unpopular session, but I barely discussed his record.

When he put some slick ads on television and attacked me and my record, I allowed them to go unanswered for a whole month. In addition, my voice failed me over the final several weeks—making me sound tired and sick. My whole campaign was overly cautious and poorly executed.

At 11 p.m. on election night, political pundits thought Carroll would win. But overcoming historical trends, we did better than expected in small, rural towns that usually vote Republican. At 1 a.m. the Associated Press declared me the winner, and at 10 a.m. the next morning, Carroll called me to concede.

Susan Sweetser has hired a private investigator to dig up dirt on me. Cathy Riggs is the wife of right-wing California congressman Frank Riggs, a former police officer, a lawyer, and a well-known GOP operative. She has been listed on two consecutive Sweetser Federal Election Commission (FEC) financial reports as a consultant.

We first learned about Riggs when we were formally contacted by the official House of Representatives bureaucracy that she was examining all of the bulk mailings that my office sent out. There was nothing improper or surprising about that. If a member of Congress sends a mailing to hundreds or thousands of constituents, an opponent has every right to research those mailings. They are a matter of public record, an expression of the candidate's position on the issues, and worthy of political scrutiny.

Riggs, however, went a lot further than that. She contacted my ex-wife, Deborah Messing, from whom I've been divorced for over twenty-five years. Deborah contacted her friend and neighbor, Anthony Pollina, who used to work with me, and Anthony contacted me. Deborah and I then talked.

Clearly, Riggs was hoping to find a disgruntled ex-wife who would spill the beans on her former husband. But that was not going to happen with Deborah, who has been remarried for over twenty years. While we don't see each other very often, we remain good friends, so Deborah told Riggs where to get off. Her sentiments were reflected all over Vermont. Christopher Graff, the long-time bureau chief for the Vermont Associated Press, captured the feeling in the state in a September 19 article under the headline "Vermonters Hold Their Own View on Fair Play in Politics":

> Vermonters, grasping sometimes desperately to the belief and hope their state is different, have a unique criteria to judge people, places, and proposals. "That's just not Vermont," is the oft-heard refrain, with the variation "That's so un-Vermont-like."
>
> Things and ways that fit well elsewhere just seem inappropriate for Vermont. It may be as concrete as a Wal-Mart or as ambiguous as a neighbor's airs. The judgment is very subjective, but the verdict always deeply felt.
>
> This is especially true in politics. What may be considered fair and proper in other states leaves Vermonters apoplectic. Campaign ads that even hint of criticism of an opponent are harshly condemned as mudslinging in Vermont, while they would be considered upliftingly positive in most other states.
>
> It is against this background that Vermonters viewed Susan Sweetser's hiring of a private eye to probe Sanders' background.

Such a hiring would not even gain a passing mention in most states these days. It is accepted practice. Cathy Riggs is a rising star in the ranks of Republican "opposition researchers."

She says her background as an ex-cop, a law school graduate and wife of a congressman gives her an edge in political probing. And she said in a newspaper interview this past week that she checks everything. "I'm very thorough. I do a total, complete package," she said. "Contacting an ex-wife is just something on my checklist."

But clearly it is not on the checklist of Vermonters. Riggs' call to Sanders' ex-wife was viewed in Vermont as crossing the line. It's not fair play. It's not Vermont-like.

And what was especially un-Vermont-like was the reaction of the Sweetser campaign. Instead of talking to their own investigator to find out whether she had called Sanders' ex-wife, the campaign officials put the burden of proof on the ex-wife, a woman who had worked for 25 years to maintain her privacy.

The story of the hiring of Riggs came out on Wednesday. The Sweetser campaign spent most of Wednesday night and all day Thursday denouncing the story, calling it a fabrication and saying it was merely hearsay.

The campaign kept insisting that since the only source of the fact Riggs had called Sanders' ex-wife was Sanders, the story was suspect. The campaign spokeswoman spent Thursday saying, "All of this is innuendo and hearsay. We would like Bernie's ex-wife to come forward."

Deborah Messing of Middlesex, who was divorced from Sanders more than 25 years ago, was reluctant to talk to the media on Wednesday, but when contacted again on Thursday, as the Sweetser campaign was casting doubt on the story, she agreed to be interviewed and have her name used.

It was a few hours later that Sweetser finally talked to Riggs and found out the telephone call had been made. Sweetser said she could not condone such a call. But by then, Deborah Messing had been dragged into the spotlight.

My campaign always does research on our opponent's public record. Needless to say, however, we have never hired a private detective to dig up dirt. It is a sad comment on the tenor of national politics that Cathy Riggs, responding to a piece about our refusal to probe my opponent's private life, "scoffed at Sanders' claim. 'Everyone does research,' she said. 'He's full of it.' "

The second Tuesday in September is primary day in Vermont. Voters select the Democratic and Republican representatives they want to represent their parties. This year, except for the Republican nomination for lieutenant governor, there's not a whole lot of excitement. Sweetser is unopposed for the Republican nomination. Long is unopposed for the Democrats.

Some Democrats are urging a write-in vote for me. They are strongly anti-Gingrich and are afraid that Long's presence on the ballot could take away enough votes from me to elect Sweetser. As in the past when this same situation arose, I announce that if, by chance, I win the Democratic nomination I will respectfully decline. I am an Independent, and proud of it. On September 10, Long wins the Democratic nomination. With his name on the ballot he receives 9,291 votes. I receive 4,037 write-ins.

Two years before, when the Democrats had no name on their primary ballot for U.S. Congress, the primary turned

out to be very serious business. I announced that I would
not accept the Democratic nomination and would certainly
not campaign for it. John Carroll, the Republican candidate, waged a last-minute stealth write-in campaign to
become the Democratic candidate. Fortunately, with no
activity on our part, we managed to get a few more votes
than he received. If we hadn't, he would have been on the
ballot as both the Republican and Democratic candidate.
As a result of my victory, there was no Democratic name
on the ballot in 1994. That was just as well—in an election
which I won by three points, a bipartisan designation could
have resulted in a Carroll victory.

In letters to Vermont newspapers, and even in the left-
wing national press, I am sometimes criticized as not being
a true Independent because I almost always vote with
the Democrats. Some reporters view me as a "quasi-
Democrat." People who believe this miss the point. I am
not an Independent because my views fall somewhere
between the Democrats and Republicans. It's not my goal
to vote with the Democrats half the time, and the
Republicans half the time. I am an Independent because
neither of the two major parties represents the interests of
the middle class and working people of this country.

In Congress, you're given three choices on a vote—yes,
no, present. I almost always vote with the Democrats
because, of the choices available to me, their position is
usually better than the Republicans'. That's the reality I
live with in Congress.

I read with amusement how some of my congressional
colleagues engage in two or three debates during a

campaign—sometimes even fewer. That Rose Garden strategy wouldn't work in Vermont and it shouldn't work anywhere else. If you want people to reelect you, you should be prepared to debate your opponents. In a typical campaign, I participate in between ten and fifteen debates all over the state.

Obviously, the most important debates are those that are televised and are broadcast on statewide radio. In the past, all five of the state's major television stations, WCAX, WPTZ, WVNY, WNNE, and VT.ETV, have held debates. Surprisingly, this time around, Vermont Public Television (VT.ETV) is the only major station sponsoring debates— two of them (although Vermont public access TV stations are also holding one). The first is on September 29, at the Statehouse in Montpelier. The second will be held at the very end of the campaign.

The debate at the Statehouse turned out to be controversial—but not because of anything the candidates said. VT.ETV decided to invite only three candidates—the Republican, the Democrat, and myself. They did not invite those running for the Libertarian, Grass Roots, Liberty Union, or Natural Law parties. When the format of the debate was explained to me, I urged VT.ETV to invite everyone who was running. As someone who ran on four occasions on the Liberty Union slate, I knew what it was like to be left out—and I didn't like it. VT.ETV's response was that everybody would be invited to the second debate, but, because this event was part of a national public television event, it could only feature the "major" candidates.

I was in a no-win position. If I refused to attend the event on the grounds that all candidates should have been invited, I would have been criticized for running away from the most watched debate of the campaign. If I attended, I would be criticized for participating in an unfair, undemocratic event. In the end I chose to participate. Mr. Diamondstone of the Liberty Union Party staged a nonviolent attempt to enter the hall, and was arrested. His arrest generated more media coverage than the debate.

I was not overly impressed with my performance that night, in any case. I did alright, but was not in top form. Sweetser, I thought, gave an articulate presentation of her views. She is bright—and got her positions across. Perhaps the big surprise of the night was Jack Long, who demonstrated a keen sense of humor and effectively played the role of the moderate against the "extremists" of the right and left.

One of the key components of Sweetser's campaign is to show that she is a serious candidate who has the full support of the national Republican Party. The clear implication is that, if elected, she will have clout with the powers that be, especially if the Republicans continue to control Congress. On the other hand, Bernie Sanders, as an Independent, will always be out of the loop and unable to deliver anything for the state.

To prove how well connected she is, Sweetser brings a long and impressive list of Republican heavyweights to campaign for her in Vermont: Representative Dick Armey, majority leader of the House; Representative Bill Paxon, chairman of the Republican National Congressional

Campaign Committee; Steve Forbes, former Republican presidential candidate; Haley Barbour, national chairman of the Republican Party; Representative John Kasich, chairman of the House Budget Committee; Representative Susan Molinari, keynote speaker at the Republican convention; and Representative Deborah Pryce. There is a Republican invasion of the state.

The goal of these visits is not only to show Sweetser's clout within the party, but to raise money at big-dollar fundraising events and to generate news coverage. Armey raises $30,000, Paxon $40,000, and Kasich $25,000. The others raise lesser amounts. Representative Bill Paxon, on his visit, tells the party faithful that the national GOP will kick in the maximum amount allowed by law—$123,600. He expresses the sentiments of his national party when he states, "We're going to pull out all the stops" to defeat "that god-awful Bernie Sanders."

Will all of these endorsements by big-name Republicans have an impact on the campaign? I have my doubts. While they generate a great deal of publicity for Sweetser, I don't think endorsements mean a whole lot in Vermont, where people know more about the candidates than in most other states. (I speak here from experience. In the past I've endorsed candidates who've ended up doing terribly.) Also, I think Vermonters may resent all of this heavy hitting coming from Washington. I note with interest that when John Kasich endorses Sweetser he doesn't criticize me. John and I have worked together on some issues regarding corporate welfare.

One Republican endorsement does bother me, however. I'm not surprised that Jim Jeffords, Vermont's Republican junior senator, came out in support of Sweetser. He had signed a fundraising letter for her early in the campaign and, as the leading Republican in the state, it would have been odd if he had not endorsed her. What disturbs me, however, is the tone of some of his comments. Frankly, I had knocked my brains out to see that the Northeast Dairy Compact, legislation vital for Vermont farmers, was passed. And Jeffords knew that. Our staffs frequently communicated on the issue. While almost all of the action took place in the Senate, and Leahy and Jeffords did an excellent job there, I did all that I could in the House to see the Compact pass, and helped lead the effort there. I really do not appreciate Jeffords's assertion that I am claiming credit for something I didn't do. It is a cheap shot.

7

The Final Push

One month remains before the election. According to various statewide polls and our own polling, we are now ahead by fifteen to twenty points. Further, Sweetser's negative ratings are quite high. As they say in the trade, this is our election to lose.

At this point in the campaign, the most important thing we can do is go back to the basics—and try to avoid any stupid mistakes. We have our game plan and must play it out effectively: focus on our issues, respond strongly to inaccurate statements about my positions in either the free or paid media, get around the state as much as we can, motivate our volunteers, be well prepared for the debates, keep raising money, and make certain that our advertising campaign—TV, radio, newspaper, and tabloid—is effective. All this is a lot easier said than done.

We are operating now with a major gap in our campaign staff. In August, my wife, Jane, left the campaign to become provost of Goddard College in Plainfield, Vermont. The president of the college had resigned amid a great deal of on-campus controversy. Jane, who had been chair of the Goddard board of trustees for the past five years, had been asked to replace him.

Before making a decision about this, Jane and I talked at great length. She had been the nonpaid chief of staff at the congressional office, and had then moved over to a key position in the campaign. She has a very good sense of practical politics, is excellent with details, and does a much better job than me in communicating with the media. But it was clear that this was an opportunity of a lifetime for her. In 1980, she had graduated from Goddard as a single mother with three kids and no money, and the college had always remained an important part of her life. She is great with young people, enthusiastic about education. It is an offer we cannot refuse, but the job will be more than full time. While Jane can still play some role in the campaign, Phil Fiermonte and Tom Smith will have to pick up a lot of the responsibilities she is leaving. I will have to spend more time on the administrative end of things.

I have no intention of trying to compete with Sweetser in bringing "big names" to Vermont for the campaign. But we do bring some people up. In August, Representative Barney Frank of Massachusetts joins me in Burlington and Brattleboro. In Washington, Barney serves with me on the Banking Committee. While we have some political differences, he is a good friend and one of the smartest members of Congress. He is also very funny—his acid wit has sent many a Republican running for cover during debates on the House floor.

Barney is here not only to campaign for me but also for Ed Flanagan, Vermont's auditor of accounts. Ed has recently announced that he is gay, and he is now the only openly gay statewide-elected official in the country. Barney, who is also gay, is one of the leading gay rights advocates in Congress and has acted very courageously in forcing some of our colleagues to act with a modicum of decency in this area. The turnout for the Frank event was terrific in Burlington, but not good in Brattleboro. The media coverage in both areas was excellent. I am also talking to Representative Pete DeFazio about coming up. If his schedule allows he will make the visit, but it's a long way from Oregon to Vermont.

Bad news. What we had feared and anticipated has now begun. Sweetser is running negative TV commercials—big time. In politics, media consultants have a tried-and-true formula. It's ugly, but sometimes it works. When your candidate is behind with high negative ratings and is going nowhere in a hurry, your best chance of success is to try to destroy the credibility of your opponent. That way, you leave voters with what is perceived as two bad choices, and you have a shot at winning in a lesser-of-two-evils contest. That's what they're trying to do now.

The ad that they're running is a blatant lie. In the past, I would probably have shrugged my shoulders, assumed nobody would believe it, and left it at that. Not now. Early in this campaign I decided that I would respond vigorously when people distorted my record. Sweetser and I have strong philosophical differences. There is more than enough room for her to distinguish her views from mine without distorting my record.

The ad states: "After raising our taxes . . . on gasoline . . . small businesses . . . and on farm families . . . In 1993 Sanders cast the deciding vote for the largest tax increase in history." An accompanying chart suggests that every Vermonter now pays $5,178 in federal taxes, compared to $4,209 in 1993. The ad continues: "The result: a higher per capita tax burden of almost $1,000 for every Vermonter. Thanks a lot, Bernie."

Well, if I had raised taxes for "every Vermonter" by almost $1,000, as the ad implies, I wouldn't vote for me either. But what are they talking about?

Obviously, they are referring to the Clinton budget of 1993, which passed the House by a vote of 218 to 216. Of course, they don't mention Clinton's name in the ad because he is now twenty-five points ahead of Dole in the last Vermont poll.

The big lie that the Republicans are peddling here, and all over the country, is that Clinton's 1993 budget resulted in a large tax increase for *all* Americans. What they have done is simply added up the total increase in taxes in the 1993 budget, and divided it by the population. Mr. Jones pays $1 million in taxes. Ms. Smith pays zero in taxes. On average, per capita, they are paying a half million in taxes, say the Republicans. But, clearly, the *impact* of the tax burden is a little bit different.

The truth is that Clinton's 1993 budget included a largely *progressive* tax proposal which fell disproportionately on the wealthiest people in the country. Ninety percent of the total tax increase fell on the *upper* 4 percent, those people then earning $100,000 a year or more. Only the top 1.2

percent saw an increase in income taxes. In fact, as a result of a substantial increase in the earned income tax credit included in that budget, 20 million low-income families, including 26,000 families in Vermont, saw a *decrease* in their federal income taxes. For the middle class, and the vast majority of Vermonters, there was almost no tax increase at all, certainly not $1,000 a head as the ad implies.

Unfortunately, there *were* elements of regressive taxation in that proposal, including a 4.3 cent increase in the gas tax. That's about $30 a year for the average Vermonter, not much but still regressive in that it hits the average working stiff who travels a hundred miles a day to and from work. Clinton also increased the amount of taxable Social Security income. That hike affected the upper 13 percent of Social Security recipients, many of whom live on only $44,000 a year. I opposed these aspects of the legislation when it was debated because I have always been a strong proponent of fair taxation. I also knew that the opponents of that budget would sooner or later exploit the issue, which is precisely what they are doing now.

There is a lesson here: if you raise taxes on the rich, raise taxes on the rich. Keep it simple. And if your opponents want to oppose taxes on the rich, let them do it. But don't include *any* taxes on working people, even if it's only a tiny amount, because your opponents will distort the reality of the situation.

When I met with Clinton in the Oval Office in the summer of 1993, I told him about an experience I had the day before at the Washington County Fair in central Vermont. The media in Vermont and nationally was then playing right into the Republican Party's hands. They were talking over and over again about the aggregate sum of the tax increase that Clinton was proposing, the so-called "largest tax increase in history," but no one was talking about *who* would be paying the increase in taxes. I asked person after person at that fair if they understood what was in the tax proposal, and only one out of twenty people did.

Clinton acknowledged to me that he was having a very difficult time getting the information out. Shortly afterwards, he organized what I thought was a successful press conference with low-income workers who would be getting a *reduction* in their taxes. Meanwhile, I had to actually raise my voice to a reporter in Vermont just to get him to identify in his story who would actually foot the bill for the tax increase.

This is an issue of enormous consequence, well beyond the ad that is currently being thrown at me. If the media refuses to differentiate between a progressive tax proposal that hits the wealthy and a regressive tax increase that hits working people, and simply defines the proposal as a "tax increase," no president is ever going to raise taxes—no matter how appropriate that may be. No member of Congress is ever going to support a tax increase. In order to balance a budget it will always be easier for elected officials to cut back on Medicare, Medicaid, education, the environment, and other important social programs.

But the truth of the matter is that the vast majority of the people do not stay up nights worrying about tax increases on the rich. By and large, given the unfair distribution of income and wealth in this country, and the fact that tax rates for the wealthy have declined dramatically over the last twenty years, most people think it's quite reasonable to ask upper-income people to pay their fair share of taxes. Several years ago, my campaign did a poll and we asked Vermonters if they would prefer Congress to increase taxes on the rich or cut Medicare. Eighty percent replied, TAX THE RICH.

In any case, one day after Sweetser's negative ad was aired, I hold a press conference refuting its bogus allegations and demanding that she take it off. "Susan Sweetser is a tax lawyer," I say, "and she knows full well that 90 percent of the tax increase fell on the upper 4 percent of income recipients, those people in 1993 who were earning $100,000 or more." Sweetser responds, "I'm not going to take off ads that I believe are truthful, that I believe are comparative, that I believe are depictions of his record. The fact is, Bernie raised taxes on Vermonters." She then issues a long press release attacking the TV ad that *I* had just put on the air as "misleading and unsubstantiated," containing a "disingenuous" statement that is "not accurate."

Now, for all of you readers who are interested in seeking political office and don't want to pay media consultants huge sums of money for advice on how to do it, let me explain how you proceed. The first thing is that before you go negative, attack your opponent for running a negative campaign—then, after your ads are on the air, and your opponent responds in righteous indignation, you can expect that much of the media will describe how both sides are attacking each other for negative campaigning. That's Sleazy Politics 101. And it works quite often because the media wants to be "evenhanded." For example, after my press conference, the large headline in the *Burlington Free Press* reads, "Sanders, Sweetser attack TV ads." Needless to say, the issue is far too involved and complicated for the thirty-second TV coverage it receives.

Fortunately, however, this approach isn't working for Sweetser, because reporters at the Vermont Press Bureau (who write for the second and third largest papers in the state, the *Rutland Herald* and the *Montpelier Times-Argus*) actually checked the facts, concluded that Sweetser's ads were dishonest and misleading, and wrote intelligent articles on the subject. Diane Derby of the Press Bureau wrote, "Smulson [Sweetser's press secretary] conceded that Sanders' vote on the deficit reduction bill did not result in a $1,000 tax increase for every Vermonter, as the ad's chart says. But he said the ad's narrative use of the words 'per capita' was intended to *clarify* for viewers that the figure represented only an average." Clarify? Right!

Jack Hoffman, wrote a long Sunday column for the *Herald* entitled, "Sweetser's New Ad Doesn't Let Facts Get in the Way," dissecting the ads contents: "The $1,000 figure is absurd on its face, and the ad is another example of how far political candidates are willing to distort the truth to try to make an opponent look bad." The *Rutland Herald* also ran a front-page story titled "GOP's Figures On Tax Off Base," which noted, "The Vermont Republican Party and congressional candidate Susan Sweetser are using incorrect figures to describe the effects of 1993 tax law changes on Vermonters, according to a spokesman for the organization that prepared the information being used by the Republicans."

I won't let up either. In virtually every public appearance I hammer away at the dishonest ads saturating the airwaves. Even at a speech before 500 people at a conference on mental health, I talk about the ads. This is something I never would have done in the past. Obviously, there is self-interest in my actions, but I honestly believe that if candidates can get away with blatant lies in TV ads, then the political process in America is in very deep trouble.

In January 1994, the Republican Party took control of the House of Representatives for the first time in forty years. Newt Gingrich, a brilliant, articulate political strategist and right-wing ideologue, was elected Speaker of the House and, in a very bitter moment for the Democrats, Dick Gephardt handed the Speaker's gavel over to him. I disagree with everything that Gingrich stands for, but I was impressed by the scope of his vision. He thinks big.

The Democratic loss in 1994 was devastating. In an election in which 38 percent of the people voted, thirty-five incumbent Democrats lost their seats in the House. Not one Republican incumbent was defeated. The Republicans went from a minority of 176 members in 1992 to a majority of 230 members in 1994. Seventy-four new Republicans were sworn in, a huge freshman class. Gingrich became the darling of the media, on the front pages every day. As the leader of the new American revolution, he proclaimed, as had Franklin Delano Roosevelt sixty-two years before, a period of "one hundred days" in which Congress would enact landmark legislation on its way toward fulfilling his "Contract with America."

The Democrats were in a tailspin. Early in the session they held their first caucus. Although I am welcome to attend these meetings, I usually go only when the president is speaking. But I went to this meeting, and the shock and confusion were palpable. There did not appear to be a clear analysis of why the Democrats were beaten so badly, nor agreement as to how they should go forward. They were angry and demoralized by their new status as the minor party, symbolically represented by their "banishment" to the House Ways and Means Committee room. From now on, Republicans would meet on the House floor.

Veteran Democrats who had chaired powerful committees, sometimes for years, were now consigned to the position of ranking members, that is, leaders of the opposition. Many of them had to lay off large numbers of loyal staff who had worked for them for years. It was not a happy time for Democrats.

While most Democrats responded with confusion and paralysis to the Republican victory, the members of the Progressive Caucus immediately mobilized to fight back—both in Congress and back home at the grassroots level. We were not confused or hesitant. We knew exactly what we had to do. Intellectually, we had to expose the Contract with America for exactly what it was: a vicious assault on working people and the poor, orchestrated at the behest of the most affluent and powerful people in America. Politically, we had to rally public opinion in opposition to the Gingrich agenda, and bring our constituent groups together into an effective counterforce.

Moreover, if the stated purpose of the Contract was balancing the budget in six years, we decided we would accept that challenge. While there was some disagreement among us as to how much emphasis we should give to the importance of a balanced budget in a specified time frame, most of us agreed that we could expose the bankrupt vision behind the Contract by demonstrating that the budget could be balanced in a way that was fair and did not wreak havoc on the lives of millions of low- and moderate-income Americans.

There was an enormous amount of work to be done, and Bill Goold, Elizabeth Mundinger, and Eric Olson in my office, along with the staff in other progressive offices, undertook the responsibility of providing the members with the information they needed. It was an example of the vital role that staff play in the United States Congress, where there are so many issues and so many functions that no congressperson can get a handle on them without back-up.

We launched our anti-Contract campaign with a press conference in the House Radio-Television Gallery. We notified the media and waited. That day, the room was so mobbed with reporters and TV cameras, we had to fight our way in. They had come to hear some of the first voices of opposition against the Republican agenda in the Capitol.

Yes. We had all heard that the Gingrich vision was supposed to be sweeping America, and that Americans were no longer concerned about the needs of the elderly, children, and the poor. Yes. We had been told for months that what we believed in was "old-fashioned," "outdated,"

"1930s-style" government, and that social justice and human dignity should no longer be issues of concern for Congress.

But we disagreed—strongly, and began the long, hard fight against the legislation that Gingrich and his corporate sponsors were beginning to introduce. We used every tool at our disposal to educate Americans on the content of the Contract, from press conferences to "special orders" at the end of each legislative day that enabled us to communicate with C-Span's growing audience. We introduced "one-minutes" before legislative business began in the morning and we vigorously debated the specific pieces of legislation as they came to the floor. Clearly, we didn't have the votes to defeat the Republicans, but we fought them tooth and nail and in the process helped to illuminate the dirty business behind the high-flying rhetoric.

What we soon realized was that most Americans didn't have a clue as to what was in the Contract. It *sounded* good, but the more they learned about it, the less they liked it.

Do you want to see Congress move the country toward a balanced budget? "Yes," the American people responded overwhelmingly. Do you want to cut Medicare by $270 billion and increase Medicare premiums by $500 a year while providing lower quality service to senior citizens? "Hell, no," the American people shouted back. And it turned out that the American people really did not want to cut health insurance for millions of low-income children or eliminate the guarantee that low-income senior citizens would have access to nursing homes. They didn't want to cut loans and grants for college students. They didn't want to eviscerate environmental legislation. They didn't want a constitutional amendment to ban abortions. They didn't want to cut back on school lunch programs and increase funding for B-2 bombers.

In the midst of all of this, the American people surely didn't want to give huge tax breaks to the rich and the largest corporations in America, while cutting back on the earned income tax credit—which would have resulted in higher taxes for the working poor. The more that people learned about the Contract with America, the stronger the opposition became.

Members of the Progressive Caucus were not the only people in Congress in opposition to the Contract. As the new session progressed, Dick Gephardt, Dave Bonior, John Lewis, and the other Democratic leaders became stronger, more focused, and more confident. After forty years in the majority, they were beginning to learn how to function effectively as the minority opposition. Gephardt's office did an excellent job in sending out clearly written, digestible information about various aspects of the Contract.

I was especially impressed by my friend Rosa DeLauro of Connecticut, who is not a member of the Progressive Caucus. Rosa never stopped. It seemed that every day, morning, noon, or late at night, she was on the floor talking about the devastating impact that the Republican cuts in Medicare would have on senior citizens. She was relentless.

Gradually, as people learned more about the Gingrich agenda, the fight against it spread all across America. Trade unionists began to respond as they learned about the impact of pending legislation on workers' rights; senior citizens were getting organized as they began to realize how devastating the cuts in Medicare, Medicaid, and other senior programs would be; women were fighting back against the horrendous attacks on abortion rights; and students began organizing on college campuses against the cuts in student loans and grants.

And then Gingrich and the Republicans shut down the government in the winter of 1995. They showed the American people that not only were they prepared to make savage cuts in desperately needed programs, but they were unwilling to respect basic constitutional divisions of power. These right-wing extremists lacked the votes to override President Clinton's vetoes, so they just stopped appropriating money and brought government to a halt.

And support for Gingrich and the Contract with America eroded even further.

In early 1995, I decided that the major effort my office would make in Vermont over the next two years was to help lead the opposition to the Gingrich agenda. In that regard we held twenty-five town meetings throughout the state— in our larger cities and our smallest towns. Sometimes hundreds of people showed up and sometimes a few dozen. In general, the turnouts were excellent.

Meanwhile, grassroots organizations throughout the state organized a demonstration against the Contract, timed to coincide with the National Governor's Conference in July 1995 in Burlington. The turnout for the demonstration was huge. Progressives also distributed 50,000 copies of a well-produced newspaper that showed the Contract's impact on Vermonters.

During the 1995–96 session we held six major conferences in Vermont, involving thousands of people. Some of them dealt specifically with aspects of the Contract with America, and some did not. All of them were based, however, on the belief that in a democratic society the government has a major role to play in protecting the rights and economic well-being of ordinary people. It has long been my view that one of the important roles of a congressional office is citizen education—bringing in some of the most knowledgeable people in the country to discuss issues that they are concerned with. All of these conferences were free and open to the public, and almost all were held on Saturdays—when working people could attend. They were also videotaped and broadcast on public access television throughout the state.

In March 1995 we held a conference for senior citizens, and 400 seniors from all over the state turned out. Our keynote speakers were Eugene Lehrmann, national president of the American Association of Retired Persons, and Max Richtman, vice president of the National Committee to Preserve Social Security and Medicare. In my helter-skelter life as a congressman, I sometimes forget how important education is as part of human life. At the senior citizen conference, which was held at Montpelier High School, I was very moved to see seniors, in workshop after workshop, taking careful notes and intelligently discussing issues of concern to them. They wanted to know not only about what was going on in Washington but also about health and nutrition and how they could play a more active role in their communities.

We held an excellent conference on economic and social justice in conjunction with many of the antipoverty groups in the state. Frances Fox Piven, one of the outstanding experts in the country on social welfare policy, explained the implications of right-wing "welfare reform" to a large audience.

Then there was the conference we held on veterans' affairs—an area of growing importance to my office. This event was organized with the help of the Veterans' Council, which advises my office on veterans' matters. I am an antiwar congressman, but I am strongly pro-veteran, as all antiwar activists should be.

The young working-class men and women who fight our wars, who lose their limbs in our wars, who come home sick or traumatized by our wars—*do not make the wars they fight in*. Wars are made by politicians. It is an outrage that these men and women, who put their lives on the line for their government, often find that this same government turns its back on them in their times of need. This conference brought to Vermont Jesse Brown, the former head of Disabled American Veterans (DAV) and Clinton's secretary of veterans' affairs. The many veterans who attended the conference were especially pleased to see Brown's staff sympathetically and immediately responding to their personal concerns.

Another conference that brought out a surprisingly large crowd, despite a snowy January day, was an all-day event on alternative health. Wow! Is there interest in that issue.

I am a fierce proponent of a national health care system that guarantees health care for all people. I am also a firm proponent of a much stronger approach toward disease prevention. We spend huge sums of money treating disease, and relatively little trying to prevent it. Further, in the midst of the explosion of modern medical technology, we too often ignore traditional, low-tech medical treatments that have cured diseases for thousands of years in different cultures throughout the world.

The conference, held in conjunction with alternative health care providers throughout the state, included fifteen workshops dealing with topics ranging from diet to acupuncture to massage. Dr. Wayne Jonas, director of the National Institute of Health's Office of Alternative Medicine, and Dr. Herbert Benson, of Harvard University's Mind/Body Medical Institute, contributed their expertise.

The last major conference was a labor conference, which featured Richard Trumka, the secretary-treasurer of the AFL-CIO. It was organized by the Vermont AFL-CIO, the Vermont National Education Association, the Vermont State Employees Association, the United Electrical Workers, and other unions, and was the most successful labor meeting in the state in many years. Trumka, the former president of the United Mine Workers and now part of the AFL-CIO's progressive new leadership, is a very forceful speaker. When working people come together and stand up for their rights, it is amazing how politicians suddenly become interested in labor issues. The governor of Vermont, Howard Dean, and the junior senator from Vermont, Jim Jeffords, both asked for time to address the conference.

In late spring of 1996 we held our last conference, on women's health. Dr. Susan J. Blumenthal, the deputy assistant secretary for women's health, outlined women's health care needs and her department's efforts to address this long-neglected area in a very effective speech. That conference was held in conjunction with many of the women's health organizations in the state, who provided a number of workshops.

Meanwhile, back in Washington, members of the Progressive Caucus were expending a great deal of energy focusing on corporate welfare—the massive government tax breaks and subsidies that are given to some of the largest corporations in the country. We focused on this issue for two reasons. First, it is absurd that working people should provide handouts to multinational corporations that are earning billions in profits and paying their CEOs astronomical salaries. Second, we were able to use the corporate welfare issue to contrast our priorities with those of the Gingrich agenda. Newt and his friends proposed to balance the budget on the backs of the poor and working class, slashing Medicare, Medicaid, education, environmental protection, veterans' benefits, school lunches, and other programs. Meanwhile, they were leaving untouched approximately $125 billion a year in corporate welfare. This exposed not only the vulgarity of the Gingrich agenda, but also its hypocrisy. If Gingrich's supporters were serious about balancing the budget, they could do it without savaging programs essential to the most vulnerable members of our society. Of course, this would require them to stand up to their corporate sponsors—something they were not likely to do.

But could we, the progressives in Congress, balance the budget in seven years in a way that was fair and would not hurt the kids, the elderly, the sick, or the poor? Damn right we could! In an article I wrote for the *Burlington Free Press*, I showed how we could save more than $800 billion over seven years by dealing with *some* of the giveaways in corporate welfare and tax breaks for the rich. This illustrative list gives some details:

Loopholes

- Change how income of multinational corporations is allocated between nations: increased income—$143.5 billion.
- Eliminate foreign tax credit for multinational corporations and subsidiary income exemption: increased income—$82.5 billion.
- End U.S. firms' delay of tax on income of foreign subsidiaries: increased income—$5.7 billion.
- Close loopholes for foreign-owned firms in the United States, including bond-interest exemptions: increased income—$1.9 billion.
- Repeal housing and wage exemptions for U.S. citizens working abroad: increased income—$7.2 billion.
- Eliminate the Overseas Private Investment Corporation (OPIC): increased income—$.560 billion.
- Subject major foreign stockholders in U.S. companies to capital gains tax: increased income—$7 billion.
- Reduce Export-Import Bank subsidies to foreign purchases of U.S. products, increase fees based on credit risk and direct loans to worthy firms in growing countries: increased income—$1.4 billion.

- Tax capital gains at regular rate: increased income—$49 billion.
- Repeal exemption on income earned by U.S. firms in Puerto Rico and other U.S. possessions: increased income—$19.7 billion.

Subsidies

- Cap the home mortgage interest deduction at $300,000: increased income—$34.8 billion.
- Reform standards allowing corporations to deduct equipment faster than it wears out: increased income—$160 billion.
- Cap deductions for CEO pay, counting excess salary/stock options/perks as taxable profit: increased income—$50 billion.
- End deduction of advertising costs, instead depreciating 20 percent as a capital cost to build recognition: increased income—$18.3 billion.
- End nuclear weapons production and test site costs: increased income—$3.06 billion.
- Terminate the Advanced Neutron Source Project, Tokomak experiment and Gas Cooled Reactor: increased income—$9.1 billion.
- Phase out grants for fossil and nuclear energy development: increased income—$2.3 billion.
- Suspend purchases for Naval Petroleum, Oil Shale Reserve, Strategic Petroleum Reserve: increased income—$1.4 billion.

- End funding for Clean Coal Technology research: increased income—$.330 billion.
- End 1872 Mining Act's patent provision and set an 8 percent royalty on minerals recovered from public lands: increased income—$.300 billion.
- Phase out Senatech and Technology Reinvestment Project subsidies: increased income—$1.5 billion.
- End NASA's subsidy of U.S. aerospace firms: increased income—$1.8 billion.
- Discontinue subsidies to foreign purchasers of U.S. defense products: increased income—$2.5 billion.
- Raise fees to cover Securities and Exchange Commission and commodity market operation costs: increased income—$.400 billion.
- Reduce subsidy of wealthy farmers by limiting payments to $50,000 per person: increased income—$.760 billion.
- End subsidy of produce purchased by foreign consumers: increased income—$4.2 billion.
- End subsidy of overseas advertising campaigns and trade shows for U.S. firms: increased income—$.5 billion.
- End tobacco subsidies: increased income—$287 million.
- Raise fees for grazing on public lands: increased income—$.280 billion.
- Rescind new funding for highway projects that do not qualify under state transportation plans or highway grant programs: increased income—$2.6 billion.
- Conduct competitive bidding for operating concessions at National Parks: increased income—$.280 billion.

Defense

- Stop funding for 20 additional B-2 bombers: increased income—$30 billion.
- Stop funding for Star Wars and space stations: increased income—$35 billion.

The total seven-year savings for such a budget deficit program is over $800 billion—enough to balance the budget in the year 2002. And these are only *some* of the savings that I, and other members of the Progressive Caucus, came up with. There was no question that we could move this country forward to a balanced budget without decimating the safety net on which tens of millions of Americans depend.

In October 1995, I introduced HR 2534, the Corporate Responsibility Act, which contained many of these provisions. While the fight against corporate welfare has been led by progressives in Congress, we've also had support from honest conservatives who are rightfully appalled at this waste of taxpayer dollars. As a result, the concept of corporate welfare is now filtering into the mainstream, and some legislation has been passed which is beginning to chip away at this outrageous waste of money.

I may not have the majority leader of the U.S. House campaigning for me, but I do have some of the funniest people in America lending a hand. In Washington, Al Franken, a star of *Saturday Night Live*, and author of *Rush Limbaugh Is a Big Fat Idiot and Other Observations*, does a fundraiser for us at the Eastern Marketplace and about 100 people show up, including a number of long-lost Vermonters. I had met Al during our joint appearance on the show *Politically Incorrect* with Bill Maher. (Although why I went on that show I will never know.) Al Franken is one of the funniest people in America, and he does not like Newt Gingrich and right-wing Republicans. He gives a hilarious performance.

Back in Burlington, Michael Moore, the filmmaker, television producer, and writer, is here to help the campaign, and I'm proud to have his support. His film *Roger and Me* is one of my favorites, and one of the most successful documentaries in American history. Moore is one of the very few media people in America with serious politics, a great sense of humor, and an ability to utilize the media effectively.

We only charge seven dollars for admission, so this is not going to raise a lot of money, but that's not the purpose. We want to bring out and politically energize a lot of young people who might have been familiar with Moore through his program *TV Nation*. Three hundred people turn out to see Moore in his now legendary baseball cap. There is no front to this man—he is exactly what he appears to be. Whether he's up on the stage, writing inscriptions in his bestselling book, *Downsize This! Random Threats of an Unarmed American*, or having dinner with Jane and me, he *is* unassuming, down to earth, and very funny. Moore is a big hit in Burlington. Unfortunately, there is almost no interest in his presence on the part of the local media.

But despite all of the lively fundraisers that we're having, I'm getting nervous. Sweetser now has not one but two negative ads on the air attacking me. How should we respond? (On a personal level, it is the damnedest thing to be lying in bed, watching TV, and out of nowhere comes an ad attacking you. If I live to be 500, I will never get used to that.)

In my view, and in the view of people who talked to me, the ads we're running are very good. Produced by Shrum, Devine and Donilon, they are straightforward and positive—addressing themes that I have long been associated with. I'm not sure how they did it, but they've even managed to make me look cheerful, optimistic, and friendly.

They show me with Vermont workers, senior citizens, and young people. They talk of my opposition to the Gingrich agenda. The ads speak to my concerns and effectiveness. One of them is sixty seconds, the rest thirty seconds. The *Burlington Free Press* conducted a focus group comparing Sweetser's ads to mine. The almost unanimous opinion of the group was that our ads were much better. But that was before the recent bombardment of Sweetser's negative spots. What impact are they having?

I have never run a negative TV ad in my life. I have never run a TV ad for the express purpose of attacking an opponent. I don't believe that Vermonters want to be subjected to a mudslinging campaign nor do I want to participate in one. But how do we respond to all of the dishonest ads that are now flooding the airwaves? Can we afford to ignore them? Should we respond? If so, how?

Our consultants tell us that their general rule is that you don't allow a deceptive ad to go unanswered; in one way or another you must respond. I discuss the options with my campaign advisers. Should we go negative on Sweetser? Nobody thinks we should. We decide to respond by exposing her inaccurate premises, and we ask our media people to produce an ad that corrects the record but does not attack Sweetser personally.

On October 22, we have a great event at the University of Vermont. Gloria Steinem is here to campaign for me, and over 500 students and community people overflow a large auditorium to hear her. I'm stunned and delighted by the size of the crowd, which is our largest of the campaign. Over and over we are being told that college students and Generation X are politically apathetic and concerned only about themselves. Well, not today. It's a beautiful sight.

Gloria is introduced by some of the most active people in the Vermont women's movement, Sally Conrad, Martha Abbott, and Judy Murphy. Her message is both analytic and deeply radical. She tells the students that it is no accident that there is a feeling of discouragement and disillusionment in America today. The Republicans, the right wing, the press with its insistence on sensationalism are all powerful forces that are changing the nature of politics.

The strategy of corporate America, Steinem tells the young people, is no longer to convince people to vote Republican or conservative. The new strategy is to convince them that there is no reason to vote at all, that everyone is crooked, nothing works right, that politics is corrupt and inefficient. But don't get discouraged, she tells them: progressives must fight *for* democracy or democracy will be eroded from under our feet. It is self-destructive for progressives to allow themselves to become disillusioned by the current political process. If the left does not participate, the right wing will only grow stronger.

The young audience listens intently and is very responsive to her message. Gloria makes me an "honorary woman," and congratulates me "for having survived the 104th Congress." It is one of the nicest moments of the campaign.

Sally Conrad, a popular former state senator from Chittenden County, is also very supportive. She says, "As we know, to be a feminist a person does not have to be a woman. A feminist is a person who challenges the power structure of our country. Bernie Sanders is that kind of feminist."

Susan Sweetser, on the other hand, is not quite so kind regarding Steinem's visit: "What is really interesting to me is this is somebody who is supposed to be an outspoken advocate for women, and she comes here to campaign against the only woman who is running for statewide office here in Vermont."

The new thirty-second spot responding to Sweetser's ad has come back from Tad Devine, the very talented media consultant with whom we're working. It's not quite what we had in mind. Jane and I talk to Tad on the phone. While the ad is by no means a "negative" ad, we still think it's too hard, and we ask him to soften it.

Now a group calling itself The Coalition: Americans Working for Real Change has started spending tens of thousands of dollars in "independent expenditures" and is flooding the airwaves with more negative TV ads against me. This group was formed by the U.S. Chamber of Commerce, the National Association of Manufacturers, and the National Federation of Independent Businesses, and is part of a coalition of thirty-three big business organizations. These wonderful folks, representing some of the biggest money interests in the country, have opposed raising the minimum wage and the Family and Medical Leave Act. They are down the line in support of the Gingrich right-wing agenda. And now they're spending a fortune trying to defeat me.

I read in a Washington newspaper that I am one of twelve members of Congress—two senators and ten members of the House—to be targeted by this group. Between their ads and Sweetser's there are now *four* different negative spots attacking me. Sweetser is also running positive ads. It is clear that big money is now rolling into her campaign. Her recent FEC report indicates that she has raised $26,000 in large contributions in the last week. Also, we learn that the NRA is making automated phone calls to their members in Vermont and has called for my defeat in its publication. The National Right to Work Organization, the major anti-union group in America, is sending an ugly letter around the state to the owners of small businesses.

Interestingly, WCAX-TV, the most Republican station, is refusing to accept the ads from "The Coalition." WCAX has a longstanding policy against "independent expenditure" advocacy ads. From a civil liberties point of view, I have mixed feelings about this because groups advocating causes and positions are denied access to the airwaves, even when they are prepared to pay the going ad rates. For the moment, however, I must confess that "intellectual consistency" is taking a back seat to political reality. I'm delighted that corporate America cannot flood the largest station in the state with negative ads against me. I do *not* call up WCAX protesting their policy.

We get another version of the response ad back from Tad, our media consultant. It's more appropriate than their first try, and we discuss among ourselves whether we should air it. It is delivered to all of the TV stations—and is ready to go.

Meanwhile, we have now begun our radio advertising, which, given the dozens of radio stations in the state, takes an enormous amount of time to coordinate. Angela McDonald, Peter Timponey, and other campaign workers help to drive the ads to those stations where we want them to air immediately. We are running five separate radio ads. One is a soundtrack of our TV ad, another is a very funny ad done by my good friend, the great Vermont storyteller Mac Parker, and one is an ad on the environment featuring Robert Redford, which was arranged for me by the League of Conservation Voters. The others are straightforward statements by me of my views on the major issues of the campaign. I write the ads in the morning and record them in the afternoon.

During the last week or two of the campaign, many of the newspapers release their endorsements. Predictably, the two major Republican papers in the state, the *Catedonia Record* in St. Johnsbury and the *St. Albans Messenger*, endorse Sweetser. The big surprise, however, is that the largest paper in the state, the *Burlington Free Press*, endorses

Jack Long. I had an unpleasant interview with their editorial board, and am not surprised by their endorsement. For many years, and up until the early 1980s, the paper's editorial page was very right wing. In the mid-eighties it became more balanced and moderate, but is now moving back to a position as defender of the state's monied interests.

The good news is that we received very strong endorsements from the *Bennington Banner* and the *Brattleboro Reformer*, as well as editorial support from some weeklies. For the second campaign in a row the *Rutland Herald* refuses to make an endorsement in the congressional race—despite going through the endorsement interview process.

On October 30, a new poll comes out from the *Rutland Herald*. It has us ahead by only 13 points, which is significantly less than other polls had indicated. The poll's results are Sanders 50 percent, Sweetser 37 percent, and Long 4 percent. Are we losing ground? Does Sweetser have some momentum that could carry her over the top? We think not. For whatever reason, throughout the entire campaign, the *Rutland Herald* poll has Sweetser doing much better than the other polls, including our own polls. In fact, this poll shows exactly the same thirteen-point spread as the last poll they did a month before. The *Herald* itself concludes that there does not appear to be much movement in the race.

We have finally decided *not* to use the new ad that Tad has sent us. It is well crafted and balanced, and given the fact that there are now four negative ads on the air attacking me, it would be a very useful antidote. But we have gone this far in the campaign using our TV ads in a strictly positive way—talking about our ideas and our vision. We think that's what Vermonters want. And that's the way we'll end the campaign.

Finally. It is November 5, Election Day. Thank God. The campaign is over. This has been a very, very long campaign.

On Election Day, I follow a pretty established routine. In the morning Jane and I vote at St. Mark's Church. David votes with us. (Levi votes at another polling station, and Heather and Carina have already sent in their absentee ballots.) The media knows what time I will be voting, and I say a few words to the TV cameras. I am surprised at how nervous I am. My remarks are forced.

I then drive around alone to all of the other six polling stations in Burlington, an old habit from when I was mayor. I say hello to the candidates and campaign workers who are assembled outside the stations, check on the voter turnout, and do a little campaigning for the Progressive candidates—four of whom are running for the legislature from Burlington. I then go to the campaign office, where Phil, Tom, Martha, David, and others are coordinating what seems to be a very smooth get-out-the-vote effort.

In the afternoon, Jane and I drive thirty miles up to St. Albans, where John Gallagher, our Franklin County coordinator, tells us that things look good. He feels more optimistic than he did two years ago, when he also coordinated the campaign there. I say hello to some folks, learn about the local races, and shake a few hands.

We return to the house. I rest up, and do some reflecting on the campaign. I think I'm going to win, but I'm not 100 percent sure. I thought I would win the last election easily, and only squeezed home by three points. Could I lose tonight? Absolutely. I don't think I will, but it's certainly possible. Maybe Vermonters will believe that barrage of negative TV advertising and that glossy piece of literature that the corporate interests have sent to what appears to be every household in the state, including a couple to my own home. During the last few days I've told my family and co-workers not to be too disappointed if we lose. We worked hard and ran a damn good campaign. We should win, but we could lose.

I make some phone calls, and then head out again to Burlington's polling stations. I spend some time at the Barnes School, in the heart of Burlington's Old North End. This is a strong working-class area, and has lent more support to me over the years than any other district in Vermont. They gave me overwhelming victories when I was mayor, and have continued to back me strongly in the congressional races. As the campaign comes to an end, win or lose, it's nice to be with friends.

The weather is not good. There's a steady drizzle. And I'm concerned about this. We do best when the voter turn-out is high.

I stay out until the polls close at 7 p.m., and then head home. Our election night gathering is at Mona's restaurant, on the waterfront, but I won't be going there until I know for sure if we've won. I'll get the results at home with family and a few friends. Phil and some other people will be calling them in as soon as they hear from our campaign workers around the state. In the house, we have the TV and a few radios on. People are munching on cold cuts.

8

Where Do We Go From Here?

January 7, 1997. I am sworn in for my fourth term as Vermont's representative. Still the only Independent in Congress. Still an outsider in the House. There is much to do, and for an Independent there is no established trail to follow.

But after three terms in Congress, I know what my job is. Vermont is a small state with only one representative: me. Like every one of my colleagues, I must first represent my state. So I'll be looking out for the particular needs and concerns of Vermont and the Vermonters who elected me. I'm going to fight for everything to which my beautiful state is entitled.

I have a second responsibility. I must continue to defend the rights of all working people when the issues affecting them come before the Congress. I must continue to stand up for the needs of the great majority of Americans: workers, the middle class, the poor, the elderly, the nation's children. All Americans are entitled to live lives of decency and dignity, and I will not abandon that struggle.

The longer I have been in Washington, the more clear a third responsibility has become. As the only Independent, I must do my best to force discussion of matters that the entrenched powers and big money interests do not want discussed. I must insist that we address these issues even though commitment to these concerns is not on the agenda of official Washington. Many of these problems are complicated, and I'm not so smart that I have all the solutions. But I do know this: these difficult questions will not be resolved until millions of Americans, as well as the United States Congress, join in the debate. That's what democracy is supposed to be about.

Honest people have differences of opinion as to what they believe are the most important problems facing this country. Let me tell you straight out the way I see it. Here they are: the unfair distribution of wealth, the decline of decent-paying jobs, the erosion of our democracy, the unchecked power of the corporate media, the insufficiency of our health care system, the inadequacies of American education. Obviously, there are other enormously serious problems facing this nation, but these are the ones at the top of my list. In my view, if we could address these problems forthrightly, our nation would become the great society it has always had the promise of becoming.

Why don't we just roll up our shirtsleeves and start addressing these concerns?

Let me begin by presenting two rather startling facts,

and then posing a few questions. Fact 1: in 1993, Michael Eisner, the president of Walt Disney Corporation, earned $200 million. Fact 2: 20 percent of America's children live in poverty. Now, why is neither of these facts—the outrageous vulgarity of Eisner's salary or the unjust condemnation of almost a quarter of our children to a life of poverty—at the forefront of public dialogue? Why do we hear more about O. J. Simpson or the Superbowl or a plane crash than we do about the fact that in a period of declining wages for working people the average CEO of a major American corporation makes more than $3 million a year? Could there be any relation between what we see on the *ABC Evening News* and the fact that Michael Eisner runs Disney and that Disney in turn owns ABC?

I'm not trying to sell you a conspiracy theory. I doubt that Michael Eisner (or Rupert Murdoch or Ted Turner) decides what specific items will be aired on an evening news broadcast. Still, there *is* a convergence. Big money interests own the media. The media plays an enormous role in shaping our view of reality. Our view of reality too often turns out to be that the nation's problems are insoluble. And because these problems are insoluble, democracy is no longer relevant.

Let's take a hard look at some of America's major problems.

While the Rich Get Richer, Almost Everyone Else Gets Poorer; the Standard of Living of Most Americans Is in Decline; Democracy Is in Crisis, and Oligarchy Looms; What We Know Is Determined by the Corporate Media; Our Health Care System Is in Shambles; Our Educational System Is Facing a Crisis

The picture looks grim. In America we have the most inequitable distribution of wealth in the entire industrialized world. The middle class is shrinking, the working class is scraping by, and the poor are ever more deeply mired in poverty. Our democratic institutions are so endangered that a clear-eyed observer might well conclude that we live not in a democracy but an oligarchy. The media, which informs and shapes our perceptions of social problems, is owned by a very small number of powerful corporations with deeply vested special interests. Millions of Americans are uninsured, while the quality of health care delivery has declined dramatically just in the past few years. Our democratic system of education, once the gateway to economic and political equality, often fails to provide children with even the rudimentary skills and may soon be dismantled.

But in spite of the magnitude of these problems, *each of them can be addressed and solved*. This, and not a vindictive scapegoating campaign like Newt Gingrich's Contract with America, should form the basis of our nation's legislative agenda.

No Industrialized Nation Has as Great a Gap Between Rich and Poor as the United States

The richest one percent of Americans now own 42 percent of the nation's wealth, compared with 19 percent in 1976. That top one percent own more than the bottom *90 percent*. Between 1983 and 1989, 62 percent of the increased wealth of this country went to the top one percent, and 99 percent of the increased wealth went to the top 20 percent. The CEOs of major American corporations now earn 170 times what their workers make, the largest gap between CEO and worker of any major nation. In 1982 there were twelve billionaires in the United States. Today there are 135.

Meanwhile, the past twenty years have seen declining or stagnant income for *80 percent* of all American families. In fact, adjusted for inflation, the average pay of four-fifths of American workers plummeted 16 percent in twenty years. The inflation-adjusted median income for young families with children—headed by persons younger than thirty— plunged 32 percent between 1973 and 1990. Twenty years ago, American workers were the best compensated in the world. Today, American workers rank thirteenth among industrialized nations in terms of compensation and bene- fits. In 1973, the average American worker earned $445 a week; twenty years later, that same worker was making $373 a week. And they are working harder for less money. U.S. workers put in about 200 more hours per year than West European workers, who typically obtain four- to five- week vacations, often legally mandated.

Americans at the lower end of the wage scale are now the lowest paid workers in the industrialized world. Eighteen percent of American workers with full-time jobs are paid so little that their wages do not enable them to live above the poverty level. The majority of new jobs created in America today pay only $6.00 or $7.00 an hour, offer no health or retirement benefits, and no time off for sick leave or vacation. One-third of the nation's work force is now "contingent" labor, without any job security.

But enough statistics. The simple fact is that today's economy, which works very well for the super-rich, is not meeting the needs of ordinary Americans.

Reversing these obscene and terrifying trends is not as hard as the experts make out. The solution involves, among other things, talking about taxes. Have you ever wondered why the first words out of any Republican's mouth are always, "No new taxes"? The reason is that a progressive tax policy is the most efficient and powerful way to ensure that wealth is distributed more fairly. The Republicans and many Democrats are not in favor of an equitable distribution of wealth, though of course they never say outright that they favor inequality. They just repeat their mantra, "No new taxes."

To begin reversing the growing inequality in the distribution of wealth, we can rescind the tax breaks given to the rich over the last twenty years. From 1971 to 1981, the combined Social Security and income tax bills of median-income families shot up 329 percent, while the combined tax bills of individuals and families with income of more than $1 million fell 34 percent. Reagan, with the support of a Democratic Congress, cut the top federal tax rate for the richest Americans from 70 percent to 28 percent. Meanwhile, Carter and Reagan substantially raised the regressive Social Security tax for working Americans. From 1977 to 1990, the social security tax was raised nine times—an increase of 31 percent. In 1953, corporations contributed 33 percent of all tax dollars. Today, they contribute less than 10 percent. During the 1980s, some multibillion-dollar corporations did not pay one penny in taxes.

As Citizens for Tax Justice has indicated, nine out of ten Americans would have paid *less* in federal taxes in 1992 if Congress had done nothing to "reform" the tax system since 1977. Yet, incredibly, the government would have brought in almost $70 billion *more* a year—a substantial portion of the federal deficit.

What is needed today is a reversal of the policy direction of the last twenty years and the development of a truly progressive tax system in the United States. At a time when this country is seeing a proliferation of millionaires and billionaires, the rich must start paying their fair share of taxes. To give President Clinton credit, his first budget in 1993 did precisely that. It raised taxes on the wealthy and lowered taxes for the working poor by increasing the earned income tax credit. But that was only a small step forward— one which he does not seem likely to repeat.

We need to establish a more progressive income tax. The more you earn, the more you pay. Not only is that a fair principle, but greater progressivity would lessen the inequities in income that currently afflict us. There is no reason that those who earn over $200,000 a year should not pay a significantly larger percentage of their income in taxes than they currently do. Of course, the greed of the wealthy knows no bounds. They and many of their conservative mouthpieces are even trying to sell the nation on a flat tax, allowing a billionaire to pay at the same rate as a mother of two earning $5.50 an hour in her service-sector job. That is precisely the *wrong* direction to take. We need to reaffirm the just principle that those who benefit the most economically from our society should pay the most to sustain it.

It is also time, high time, to establish a tax on wealth similar to those that exist in most European countries. Simply stated, a wealth tax would require the very wealthiest Americans, people worth millions of dollars, to pay taxes on their accumulated wealth, rather than enabling them to get ever richer without giving anything back to the society that makes their wealth possible. A tax on wealth could raise tens of billions of dollars a year.

We can also reverse the inequitable distribution of wealth by closing loopholes in corporate taxes. If we eliminated tax breaks for corporations, corporate subsidies, and other forms of corporate welfare, we could save $125 billion a year. Those savings could be applied to health care, education, social services—and to balancing the budget. By slashing special breaks for corporations, we could help working families immensely—and ordinary Americans would not have to pay a cent more in taxes.

Why don't the great majority of Americans elect a government that will look out for their interests and fight for a fairer distribution of wealth? We can only answer that question if we look the unpleasant truth straight in the eye.

And the truth is that the fabric of American democracy is currently extremely fragile, and that the U.S. government as currently constituted does not represent the interests of ordinary citizens.

Although the corporate media doesn't discuss it too often, the facts are quite clear. In the presidential election of 1996, less than half of all eligible voters cast their ballots. Two years earlier, when the Gingrich-dominated Congress was elected, only 38 percent of Americans voted. This compares with over 70 percent participation in most other major industrialized countries. In South Africa, millions of black citizens waited patiently in line, some for as long as three days, to exercise their right to vote for the first time. Overall voter turnout figures tell only part of the story. Voting among the poor is almost nonexistent. Among different age groups, the young vote in lower numbers than any other group. Public cynicism about the democratic process has never been greater, and individual belief in the possibility of democratic change has never been more threatened.

What does this tell us about the health of democracy? Today, America is in danger of becoming an oligarchy.

An oligarchy is a form of government in which a small group of people hold power. It seems clear that a smaller and smaller group of citizens are determining our nation's future. The poor are disenfranchised, not by law, but in fact. The young think that voting has little to do with them or their prospects. Ordinary citizens have decided that the political process is likely to fail them, and so they vote in ever smaller numbers.

In recent elections, the concept of "one person, one vote" has been supplanted by the influence of big money. The more money you have, the more power you have. Some citizens participate by contributing hundreds of thousands of dollars to the politicians and parties of their choice. Most citizens contribute no money and do not vote. To paraphrase Orwell, some citizens are clearly a lot more equal than others.

It is in the interest of those who have great wealth and immense corporate power to weaken democracy. The less power the people have, the fewer checks there are on those who already control the American economy and its resources. The greater the belief that participation in the political process doesn't really make a difference, the more likely it is that people will give up hope that we can ever attain a just society and a decent standard of living.

Make no mistake about it: the wealthy and their political representatives are working hard to keep people away from the voting booths. They have vigorously opposed legislation that would make it easier for people to vote. They have corrupted campaign financing, so that citizens have lost faith in the political process. They have turned negative campaigning into a high art, with the result that huge numbers of voters demonstrate their disgust with gutter politics by refusing to vote on election day. They have begun the process of dismantling social programs so that citizens increasingly feel that government cannot and will not do anything to meet their needs.

What can we do to revitalize democracy? How can we bring tens of millions of Americans back into the political process?

Some Simple Steps to Reinvigorating Democracy

Revitalizing the electoral process is, in some ways, a simple matter. If the goal is to get more people to vote—and that certainly should be one of our goals—then it is high time we establish automatic voter registration for every American who is eighteen or older. Given the growth of technology through the "information highway," a social security card or driver's license should be all that is required for voting. Same-day registration, allowing every American to register up until election day, would substantially increase voter turnout.

Similarly, we must make it more convenient for people to vote. We can open the polls, as is done in other nations, over a two- or three-day period—including at least one weekend day—so that working Americans will have more time to vote. Oregon has shown us another possible route: in that state, voting can be done by mail over a period of up to four weeks, and as a consequence voter turnout has risen.

But we need to do more than just increasing voter turnout. We must do a much better job in educating our citizens about the political process. It is time for our schools to offer young people an education for democracy. If our school curricula took the rights and duties of citizens as seriously as they do varsity football, home economics, and even study hall, young people would be far more likely to participate in the democratic process, and be better informed.

"But what about the damaging effect of money on the nation's elections?" I can hear you saying. And you are absolutely right: we will not reinvigorate democracy until we have thoroughgoing campaign finance reform. Not only do campaign finances currently pervert the political process by buying influence, but the existence of huge donations and the access they buy convinces many Americans—not erroneously—that voting is less important than money in determining national policy.

Given the fact that we have huge states like California and small states like Vermont, campaign finance reform on the national level can get a bit complicated, but some elements of *real* reform are clear. Most importantly, we must limit the amount of money that candidates can spend on an election. If less money were required to run success-fully, the impact of big contributors would be reduced. And if there were reasonable campaign spending limits, it would no longer be possible to "buy" an election. Make no mistake: in the current situation, the candidate with the largest war chest will almost always be the victor.

How can we limit campaign spending? There are several alternatives. What we need, immediately, is a national debate about which path is the best to follow. We could provide public funding for campaigns, thereby setting limits on the amount of money that a candidate can spend. Or, as the Democrats proposed several years ago, we could provide matching public funds for every contribution of under, say, $200 a candidate receives. That way, huge dona-tions that would no longer dominate campaign financing and the impact of ordinary citizens would be doubled. Or we could make free television time available, in sizable quantity, to every candidate. Television advertising is, after all, the largest expense in a campaign and the motor that drives the cost of campaigns higher and higher. We could, and should, restrict bundled contributions, "soft money," enormous individual donations garnered at $10,000-a-plate dinners, and "uncoordinated" independent expenditure advertising—all ways of allowing monied interests to buy influence by circumventing efforts to limit campaign spending.

Whatever course we take, we need to address these key requirements: capping the amount of money that can be spent, providing public funding, limiting private funding, encouraging small donations, and making television time available cheaply or at no cost. Our goal should be to get over 80 percent of our fellow citizens to vote, to ensure that votes and not money determine which direction our leaders take, and to increase dramatically our efforts to ensure that those who vote are well informed.

The Corporate Mass Media: America's Untold Story

A knowledgeable and informed electorate is essential to a working democracy. We fall far short of that ideal. A principal source of the crisis in American democracy is the oligopoly—a handful of megacorporations—controlling the media, which ostensibly informs Americans about what is happening and what our political choices are. To say the least, the media is doing an horrendous job of providing Americans with what they need to know in order to be active participants in a vital democracy.

Americans get about 85 percent of their news from television. Almost all of that comes through six major television networks. NBC is owned by General Electric, CBS by Westinghouse, ABC by Disney, and Fox by Rupert Murdoch, the right-wing billionaire. CNN was recently bought by Time-Warner, the world's largest entertainment conglomerate. "Public" television is also increasingly controlled by a wide variety of corporate interests.

The problem with television is not just what is reported but, more importantly, what is *not* reported. It's no accident that we get thousands of hours of discussion about the O. J. Simpson trial and almost no discussion about the growing gap between rich and poor or our regressive tax system. Why is it that there is massive coverage of airplane crashes, but almost no coverage of corporate disinvestment in the United States?

There are any number of business and Wall Street shows. But despite the fact that 15 million Americans are trade unionists, there isn't one national television program exclusively devoted to discussing the goals and problems of the trade union movement, and the needs of American workers. In fact, most Americans have never seen even one prime-time television show on the positive role that trade unions have played in protecting the lives of working Americans. And while extreme right wingers are regular guests on various talk shows, almost no progressive voices are heard on prime-time TV.

The most important "story" of the last twenty years has been the precipitous decline in the standard of living of America's working families. Television, which provides instantaneous coverage of earthquakes thousands of miles away, seems to have "missed" this issue.

The conflict of interest in corporate ownership of our major television networks is enormous. Let's take a brief look at General Electric, the nation's largest corporation, which owns the NBC television network.

General Electric makes billions of dollars producing weapons. So it is keenly interested in defense spending and questions of foreign policy. Additionally, General Electric has shipped thousands of American jobs overseas to take advantage of cheap labor. So it is keenly interested in NAFTA, GATT, Most Favored Nation status with China, and other issues shaping the trade policy of the United States. In the early 1980s, General Electric got away with paying absolutely nothing in federal taxes—and would like to be in the same position again. So it is keenly interested in federal tax policy. General Electric, with a long reputation as an anti-union corporation, constantly battles with workers. So it is keenly interested in federal labor policy.

General Electric contributed $100,000 to a PAC controlled by presidential candidate Bob Dole. In the past, it has contributed heavily to both political parties. So it is keenly interested in the effort to prevent campaign finance reform. General Electric invests billions of dollars in financial institutions. So it is keenly interested in banking and insurance regulations. General Electric has invested billions of dollars in the electronic media. So it is keenly interested in communications legislation. And these are just a few of the areas in which General Electric has a stake.

Is it possible that the enormous financial interests of the General Electric corporation influence the news and programming of NBC? Frankly, you'd have to be very naive to believe otherwise. But of course, it's not just General Electric. Recently, Disney bought ABC, Westinghouse bought CBS, and Time-Warner bought CNN. The *New York Times* bought the *Boston Globe*. Gannett Corporation buys every newspaper in sight. Rupert Murdoch owns Fox Broadcasting—and *TV Guide*, Twentieth Century Fox, HarperCollins publishers, and 150 newspapers and magazines in various countries.

Today, one of the greatest crises in American society is that the ownership of the media is concentrated in fewer and fewer hands. Those hands are, as a result, more powerful than ever before. Needless to say, there is not a lot of discussion in the corporate media of this issue. Just how concentrated is media ownership? Ben Bagdikian has written a very important book called *The Media Monopoly* in which he relates that:

- Eighty percent of the daily newspapers in this country were independently owned at the close of World War II. Today, 80 percent of daily newspapers are owned by corporate chains. Just eleven companies control more than half the nation's daily newspaper circulation.
- Ninety-eight percent of the daily newspapers in America have a monopoly as the only paper in town.
- Although there are more than 11,000 magazines published in the United States, today just two corporations control more than half of all magazine revenues.

- Although there are 11,000 local cable television systems, only seven companies have a majority of the 60 million cable TV subscribers.
- Three companies own more than half the television business. Four companies own more than half the movie business. Five companies rake in more than half of all book revenues.

Limiting this concentration of power over the media, which allows a few giant corporations to determine much of what we learn, presents a very difficult dilemma—and I do not have all the solutions. While we want to address forthrightly the problem of corporate control of the media, we do not want to tread on two of our most precious freedoms: freedom of speech and freedom of the press. But there are reforms we can make which do not impinge on these freedoms.

Three Positive Steps We Can Take to Develop a Freer and More Responsive Media

The first step we should take is vigorous antitrust prosecution. In the early years of this century, when the railroads had a strangle-hold over the crop sales of midwestern farmers, Congress passed legislation to bust the trusts and limit their monopoly. There is an equally pressing—perhaps even more pressing—reason for us to pass media antitrust legislation today: the current monopoly over thought and expression is clearly a serious danger to our fragile democracy.

A second step would be to provide significantly greater funding for public radio and public television. Greater funding would wean public broadcasting from its dependence on corporate advertising, which it euphemistically calls "underwriting." And greater funding would allow public radio and television stations to proliferate. With more stations, public broadcasting could accommodate an even greater diversity of public needs.

Third, the Federal Communications Commission should reestablish two principles that formerly served this country well: the public service requirement and the fairness doctrine. Every television and radio station should once again be required to devote a meaningful percentage of its programming to public service broadcasting. The public, after all, owns the airwaves through which signals are broadcast, and the rights-of-way in which cables are strung. And every television and radio station should once again have to follow the fairness doctrine: those with opposing views should have the right to respond to viewpoints expressed on the station.

Will these initiatives—antitrust prosecutions, public funding for public broadcasting, and a strong FCC role—reverse the current monopolization of those "industries" that inform us as to what is happening, what the world looks like, and how we can change that world? Unhappily, I doubt it. The mass media is too lucrative and too important in maintaining the dominance of monied interests to be reined in that easily. But these initiatives would be important first steps toward curbing corporate control and moving toward a society in which information flows more freely.

Let's suppose for a moment that we could open up the media to a much greater diversity of opinion and ideas, establish a more vibrant and well-informed democracy, and move toward a fairer distribution of wealth. Would the great work of building the America we dream of be accomplished?

Hell, no. The work would only have begun.

Let me put the progressive agenda as plainly as I can. Not until there is good, decent-paying work for every American can we be satisfied that the nation's promise is being fulfilled.

Downsizing, Job Flight, and the War on Workers: The Race to the Bottom

I am old enough to remember the presidency of Lyndon Johnson, when the government fought a "war on poverty." In recent years that war has been transformed by representatives of both major parties into a war on the poor. More important yet, but less reported, is that in the years since Ronald Reagan was elected president, corporate America has waged war against this nation's workers.

We live in an era of "downsizing." Well-paid workers are laid off in huge numbers, while the executives who axe their jobs earn enormous bonuses. Those workers are often replaced by what is called "contingent" labor. Every day over 35 million Americans go to work as temporary or contract labor. That's one out of every three workers. As an indication of what kind of society we are becoming, two out of every three jobs created in the private sector during the 1980s were temporary, not permanent. In fact, the ranks of contingent workers are growing so rapidly that some estimate they will outstrip permanent full-time workers within the next ten years. Manpower, Inc., is now the largest private sector company in the United States, employing some 600,000 workers.

The consequences of downsizing and hiring temps are devastating for American workers. So is another major strategy used to boost corporate profits: reducing labor costs by shipping American jobs beyond our nation's borders. In today's global economy, the major American export is our jobs. Why pay American workers a living wage when in Mexico workers can be hired for a dollar an hour? In China the hourly wage is as low as twenty cents.

We can see the consequences of this war on workers. As the number of contingent workers has grown and millions of jobs have been shipped overseas, the number of full-time employees at the Fortune 500 companies has plunged dramatically, from 19 percent of all American workers twenty years ago to less than 10 percent today. Between 1979 and 1994, just ten of the most prominent Fortune 500 companies (including Ford, AT&T, General Electric, and ITT) eliminated more than one million decent-paying manufacturing jobs at the very same time that many of them were expanding their investments and creating jobs in China, Mexico, and other low-wage countries.

The greatest job growth has been in the service sector, which pays poorly and often provides no benefits. More than three out of every four jobs created in the 1980s were in the low-paying retail trade and service industries.

People are desperate for jobs, but all too often decent-paying jobs are not available. People work longer hours for less. Many people work two, even three jobs to keep afloat. The bond between employer and worker—do good work and your job will be safe—has eroded. Without economic security, the American dream is crumbling.

Let me be blunt. The government must accept responsibility for helping to create an economy that provides work for and ensures the economic well-being of all its citizens.

What We Need to Rebuild the Middle Class and Reduce Poverty: Decent-Paying Jobs

I know it is not fashionable to speak of what government is supposed to do for people. We live in an era of "tough love," of the survival of the fittest, when each of us is supposed to do everything for ourselves. Today, a national industrial policy is considered an anachronism by the apologists for corporate America, even though those same apologists never have any quarrel with massive government efforts to assist "free-market capitalism" or establish "free trade" as our industrial policy. We don't hear the major corporations hollering about "government intervention" when the Federal Reserve Board makes decisions that lead to increased unemployment. While there is a rush to cut welfare for the poor, corporate welfare is vigorously defended by the wealthiest people in America. We seem to have socialism for the rich and rugged individualism for the poor.

Frankly, much of our economic policy is a disgrace, designed to benefit the wealthy few at the expense of the average worker. We have government "payoffs for layoffs" in the defense industry, tax breaks for downsizing, and trade policies like NAFTA, GATT, and MFN with China which make it easy for corporations to ship jobs overseas.

It is time we developed an economic program that works for ordinary people, and that rebuilds and expands the middle class. There is no reason why, in the richest nation in the world, every American should not have a job that sustains a decent living. There is much that government can do to make this happen.

First, government can once again level the playing field between capital and labor. Trade unions in the United States are the main reason we have an eight-hour day, a five-day work week, employer-provided health benefits and pension plans, and occupational safety and child labor legislation. Unions led the effort for Medicare, Medicaid, affordable housing, and many other programs enjoyed today by millions of Americans. Strong unions were the reason why, twenty years ago, American workers led the world in terms of wages and benefits. And not coincidentally, today American workers rank thirteenth in the world in terms of wages and benefits.

In 1954, almost one of every three employees belonged to a labor union. Today, less than one in six workers is unionized. This stunning drop in union membership is no historical accident. For decades the federal government, through labor legislation and the National Labor Relations Board, acted as an umpire to maintain a level playing field between workers and management. But President Reagan's union-busting posture in the air traffic controllers' strike, and a generation of NLRB members hostile to the rights and needs of working people, have given one advantage after another to management. The possibility of workers "winning" a strike is almost unthinkable today: unions are struggling just to preserve past gains. Almost everywhere, corporations are in control and unions on the defensive, if not in actual retreat.

We need to pass labor legislation that ensures equity in contract negotiations between workers and management. Developing fair labor legislation is not hard to do—legislation to achieve the same purpose was passed during the New Deal. Such legislation would ban the permanent replacement of striking workers. It would allow unions to be certified by simple card check: if a majority of employees in a bargaining unit join a union, the union automatically represents them. It would mandate compulsory arbitration of first contracts if a stalemate between labor and management occurred, since refusing to negotiate in good faith is one of management's main tactics. It would repeal prohibitions against strikes and secondary boycotts.

Real labor law reform would also strengthen and expand the enforcement powers of the National Labor Relations Board. All of these provisions sound technical, but their impact would be enormous. They would once again establish "rules" giving workers the opportunity to fight their own battles—for decent wages, for fringe benefits, for safe working conditions—without being fired or stalemated or isolated.

But providing fair opportunities for the trade union movement is not enough. The government must protect the lowest paid workers, men and women who in most instances are not unionized. For working people, the new global economy is all too often a race to the bottom. The wage in China or Guatemala or Poland is increasingly the wage against which American workers must compete.

In the face of this problem, the least we can do is raise the minimum wage to a *living* wage. Last year, the president and Congress took a step in this direction. But it was not enough. The minimum wage should be set at a rate sufficient to support a family of three above the poverty line. In a country where CEOs earn 170 times what the average factory worker earns—where CEO pay has increased 514 percent in twenty-four years, while workers' pay failed to keep up with inflation—we can do no less.

What about the hemorrhage of jobs abroad? Can we do anything about the disastrous effects of the global economy on American workers? According to the experts, no. But the experts echo the message their employers want us to hear.

We need to address the issue of trade forthrightly and understand that our current trade policy is an unmitigated disaster. Our current record-breaking merchandise trade deficit of $112 billion is costing us over 2 million decent-paying jobs. President Clinton, like Bush and Reagan before him, is supporting a trade policy that protects the interests and profits of multinational corporations, while compromising the interests of American workers. NAFTA, GATT, and MFN with China must be repealed, and a new trade policy developed.

Let's look at some of the components of a sensible trade policy. First, we must recognize that trade is not an end in itself. The function of American trade policy must be to improve the standard of living of the American people. America's trade policy must be radically changed, by committing ourselves to a "fair" rather than "free" trade policy. This means developing and supporting legislation that safeguards American manufacturing jobs and cuts our enormous balance of payments deficit. Companies should be encouraged to invest *here*, in the United States. Currently, this is not the case. There are all sorts of incentives, ranging from direct payments of subsidies to tax breaks to tax loopholes, which encourage corporations to ship American jobs beyond our borders. It is time to tighten our tax laws, eliminate corporate welfare, and penalize corporations that eliminate American workers so that they can replace them with low-paid workers overseas.

It is important that we use our leverage as the world's largest and most lucrative market to protect American jobs. Reagan, Bush, and Clinton have all supported policies that opened our markets wide to foreign products, asking far too little in exchange. At the same time, we must explore new economic models here at home. We need to develop more worker-owned businesses. We must move from agribusiness to sustainable agriculture, not only for the sake of our economy but also for our environment. We must once again insist that it is at least as important for businesses to meet human needs as it is for them to augment their bottom line.

But reforming the private sector is not enough. The government has a very large role to play in rebuilding our physical and social infrastructure, and when it accepts that role, it will create millions of new jobs at the same time.

Let's Rebuild America: Government Has an Important Role to Play

Let's face it, under heavy pressure from Republicans and conservative Democrats, the nation has not paid attention to the things government is *supposed* to do. No private company can safeguard the quality of our drinking water. No multinational corporation can provide us with decent roads and inexpensive mass transportation. No amount of charity will house all the homeless, feed all the hungry, or protect the personal safety of all Americans. The government has a very large role to play in making the world we inhabit livable and safe.

Rebuilding our physical infrastructure means repairing our aging roads and bridges, cleaning up toxic waste dumps, constructing sewage treatment facilities, restoring our schools and libraries and equipping them with computers so that all Americans can enter the information age. It means building affordable housing so millions do not have to pay exorbitant rents to live with peeling lead paint and substandard plumbing in crime-infested areas. It means establishing fast, reasonably priced mass transportation in and between our cities.

Rebuilding our social infrastructure is also necessary. It is high time we put more cops on the beat, had more trained teachers in the schools and more nurses in our health care clinics. High-quality and affordable day care should be available in every community. We need more inspectors to monitor the quality of our meat, the potential dangers of our pharmaceuticals, the safety of our airplanes. We require more affordable nursing homes for the elderly and job training for young men and women, together with retraining for workers who have lost their jobs.

Can We Do All of This and Move Toward a Balanced Budget?

Won't all of this cost money? Yes. Isn't it foolish to spend money rebuilding our infrastructure when we have a huge national debt? No. Because there is one final way to build and expand the middle class: we must make radical changes in our national priorities.

If we cut military spending and corporate welfare, we would have more than enough money to meet America's needs. This nation currently spends $260 billion a year on defense, even though the Cold War is over. (We are spending $100 billion to defend Western Europe and Japan against nonexistent enemies.) And this $260 billion does not count the $30 billion spent annually on intelligence or the $20 billion in defense-related expenditures hidden away in our federal spending on energy.

Combine a sizeable chunk of that $310 billion we spend on defense-related matters with the $125 billion we spend each year on corporate welfare, and there is adequate money to rebuild our infrastructure and meet the pressing needs of Americans. (We can do this and still have the strongest military in the world.) And this is before we increase revenues by instituting a more progressive income tax that requires the wealthy to pay their fair share, and before we establish a wealth tax on millionaires.

We do not have to cut back on nutrition programs for poor children, Medicare, Medicaid, Social Security, and other vitally needed programs to balance the budget. We can move toward a balanced budget and significantly increase funding in a wide range of areas that will improve life for the American people and, in the process, create millions of decent-paying jobs. We can do it if we have the courage to put the people's interests before corporate interests, and to make fundamental changes in our national priorities.

In rebuilding America, we need to concentrate in particular on two issues that both the president and Congress have failed to address adequately: health care and education.

Health Care for All Through a Single-Payer System

The United States is the only industrialized nation, besides South Africa, that does not have a national health care system. In every other developed nation, health care is a right and not a privilege.

After Clinton's failure to reform our health care system, we ended up with a cumbersome, profit-driven, consumer-unfriendly, inefficient health care delivery system dominated by insurance companies. And I mean *dominated*.

Managed care pretends to be efficient. That is because it

cuts back on health care for many of us, and rations it for the rest. It is a sign of how bad things have become that the last Congress had to pass legislation allowing a mother to stay in the hospital for at least twenty-four hours after giving birth. The insurance companies had decided that if drive-by banking worked, then it seemed a reasonable bet that drive-by deliveries would work, too.

But in their well-publicized initiatives to reduce costs, not one single insurance company has proposed reducing their profits from "managing" health care. The solution to our health care crisis—80 million uninsured or under-insured—is not difficult to find. We need a single-payer system administered at the state level. Currently, we spend one-quarter of all medical expenses on paperwork and bureaucracy. By eliminating most of the paperwork involved in health care, single-payer systems produce remarkable savings. In the United States, those savings would be enough to insure every single American. We not only would all be covered, we could go back to having freedom of choice in picking our doctors. And this would cost no more than the nation is currently spending on medical care.

Universal medical care would improve the quality of life for tens of millions of Americans. It would also be a major step toward reaffirming that through the development of a rational, nonprofit, cost-effective health care system, government in a democratic society can meet the basic needs of its people.

The Coming Crisis in Education

Conservatives are smart. They know that all across America there is discontent with our educational system. Rather than improve our schools and expand educational opportunities, however, they plan to exploit that discontent to dismantle democracy still further. The vehicle for this dismantling is known as "the voucher system."

The right wants to provide every parent with a voucher—a sort of publicly funded check, allowing them to purchase the education of their choice. Wealthy parents can use the money to reduce their tuition costs at prep schools. Religious parents can send their children to parochial schools—under this scheme, the separation of church and state will be abandoned. Meanwhile, the public schools will get correspondingly less funding. And the public schools, of course, will be where poor and working-class children will be educated. Their educational horizons will contract and their alienation from the American mainstream will widen.

No longer will society have a stake in seeing that every young person learns about American history, about our traditions of dissent and tolerance. Our most democratic institution—the one place in the nation where rich and poor, white and black, native-born and immigrant came together in a mutual enterprise—will cease to exist.

More ominous yet, once the direct link between government and public education is eliminated, it will be very easy to cut back significantly on support for education. Certainly, if the right wing can push cutbacks in welfare that will add another million children to the poverty rolls and cutbacks in Medicaid that will deny health insurance to millions of low-income kids, there is no reason to believe that major cuts in government support for public education will be far behind.

These are real dangers. But once again, there are things we can do to stop them coming to pass. We need to reaffirm our support for quality public education and the right of all children to get the best education possible. We can increase federal funding to improve the quality of our public schools. At the same time, we would be relieving some of the burden of the regressive property tax from the shoulders of the nation's working people and the middle class. Much of the anger at public education today stems from the fact that it is largely funded through very regressive taxes.

We can insist that it is the right of every young person— and every adult—to pursue an advanced education by ensuring that adequate funding is available for scholarships, college loans, and work study. We can provide new funds to expand Head Start programs. If we provide funding for day care centers, we can guarantee a solid base of early education to every child while at the same time really supporting the hard-pressed American family. We can transform President Clinton's embattled and experimental Teach for America program into a massive domestic Peace Corps that would transform every classroom in the nation.

Toward a Progressive and Democratic Future

What I have outlined here is a basic program for rebuilding American society. But there is much more to be done.

First, we have to rid the country of any vestige of racism, sexism, and homophobia. I am convinced that providing decent jobs for all and a better education for the young will be the linchpins of that effort. Too often liberals believe that being "against" prejudice is all that is required to bring about a more just and equitable society. Not true. Only when every man and woman has a *place* in American society—and this means, I believe, a decent-paying job—will we begin to eradicate the hatreds that are based on jealousy and insecurity. And only when every American is economically secure enough to stand up to insults of any sort will all Americans be free of the power of prejudice to define them.

We must be vigilant about protecting our environment. Economically, it makes no sense to degrade our soil, air, and water in the interest of quick profits, only to spend billions ten years from now to remedy the mess we've made. The enormous cost of cleaning up existing toxic waste sites reveals that pollution is only cost-deferment.

In health terms, environmental degradation makes us far sicker than we would otherwise be, and reduces the quality of everyday life. Effective health care begins with prevention, and preserving a liveable environment is one of the best medical investments we can make.

It is not as if acting as careful stewards of our environment is inefficient, as corporations so often claim. Safeguarding the environment creates new industries, new jobs, and new opportunities for workers to make a decent living. And it ensures that future generations will not have to bear the cost—in money, in illness—of our folly.

There is much more that this country needs. We should have a foreign policy guided by the principles of freedom and justice. We should maintain a firm commitment to a woman's right to equality in all areas of life. We need to face up to the root causes of crime and drug addiction, and the escalating circulation of guns. We should support the arts, rebuild communities, and honor our veterans. We must give our children hope and our elders the respect they have earned.

I am convinced that if we can muster the courage to work together, we can do what needs to be done. Building a progressive future requires building a progressive movement. And that means that in every community in America citizens must stand up and say, "We believe in economic justice for all. We will no longer accept a situation in which the wealthy and powerful have undue influence. We are going to change this nation, and we are going to start by doing what needs to be done from the grassroots on up."

It is time, in other words, for you to begin doing in your community what many of us have begun doing in Vermont: take a stand, organize, and use the political process to build democracy all over again.

If Americans—young and old, black and white, male and female, Hispanic and Asian, straight and gay, veteran and pacifist, worker and student and retiree—join together in a progressive politics at the grassroots level, it will surely spread outward and eventually reshape the United States into the greatest society that has ever existed.

As we move toward a progressive and democratic future, I am sustained by the hope that one day, when millions of

Americans are actively involved in the political process and are standing up for their rights and those of their children, a majority of the members of Congress will then represent the interests of ordinary people, and not the rich. When that day comes, we will no longer be outsiders in the House.

That House, and this country, will then belong to all of us. And that's the way it should be.

Afterword:
Outsider in the Presidential Race
by John Nichols

Bernie Sanders finished *Outsider in the House*, the original 1997 edition of this book, with a chapter titled "Where Do We Go From Here?" He was serious about the "we" part, offering up a movement agenda that anticipated the message he would carry into the U.S. Senate and ultimately into presidential politics: "rid the country of any vestige of racism, sexism, and homophobia"; establish a "progressive tax policy" in order to close the "obscene and terrifying" gap between rich and poor; guarantee "health care for all through a single-payer system"; end "race-to-the-bottom" trade policies and assaults on workers; "rebuild America" with massive investments in communities and schools and job creation; begin "addressing forthrightly the problem of corporate control of the media"; and instigate sweeping reforms "to ensure that votes and not money determined which direction our leaders take." As for himself, however, Sanders simply wrote, "There is much to do, and for an Independent there is no established trail to follow."

Sanders understood he was well positioned to remain in the U.S. House of Representatives. After the 1996 election that he and Huck Gutman chronicled in this book, the congressman would win every ensuing statewide race with more than 60 percent of the vote, and he would eventually surpass 70 percent. But in the House he was one of 435 members of a chamber that tends to swallow up even the most outspoken representatives. Democratic socialists had served in the House before—Socialist Party members such as Victor Berger from Milwaukee and Meyer London from the Lower East Side of New York in the 1910s and 1920s, allies of Democratic Socialists of America such as Californian Ron Dellums in the 1970s and 1980s. But none of them made the leap to the United States Senate, let alone to Democratic presidential primaries and caucuses. Sanders was right: there was no historical precedent for an Independent congressman to rely upon, no established trail to follow.

Bernie Sanders had to blaze that trail himself.

In the summer of 2005, the better part of a decade after *Outsider in the House* was published, the trail led the Independent congressman to a spot just beyond the covered bridge in Warren, Vermont.

American flags were hung from the white colonial houses along the main street of the village center. The color guard, the marching units, and the floats that would participate in the community's fifty-seventh annual Fourth of July parade had lined up beside the Mad River, which winds its way through town. At the appointed hour, the local fife and drum corps played "The Battle Hymn of the Republic," an ancient cannon was fired, and the parade stepped off—fire trucks sounding their sirens and children in bib overalls started dancing. In the thick of it, behind the World War II jeep and ahead of the Rotarians, marched the most prominent democratic socialist in America. Dressed in khaki pants and a button-down shirt, Sanders, who was in the midst of his eighth term in Congress, walked the parade route without a cadre of aides handing out literature, without any signs to draw attention toward him, without so much as a campaign pin or a bumper sticker identifying him as a candidate for the state's open Senate seat in 2006. The "minority of one" member of Congress, who sat in the House as neither a Democrat nor a Republican, did not require any introduction anywhere in Vermont. As he marched through Warren, waving his arm and calling out hellos, spontaneous and sustained applause erupted from Vermonters. Everyone was shouting "Senator Sanders!"

The response confirmed what the outsider had suspected when he decided to give up a safe seat in the House to mount what seemed to many outside Vermont to be an unlikely bid for a seat in the U.S. Senate. There were still plenty of Washington insiders who had trouble comprehending the new political calculus of the Green Mountain state. But prolonged exposure to Bernie Sanders—who won just 2.2 percent of the statewide vote as a third-party candidate in a 1972 special election for the Senate seat he would seek in 2006 as an Independent—had turned the outsider into a frontrunner for a place in "the most exclusive club in the world."

Years later, as Sanders prepared to launch what was being dismissed as an unlikely bid for the 2016 Democratic presidential nomination, he warned reporters, "Don't underestimate me." It was a statement inspired not by bravado but by experience. Two of the breakthrough political races for Sanders were recounted in the original edition of *Outsider in the House*—which told the story of the 1981 campaign that upset Democratic incumbent Gordon Paquette by ten votes in the contest for mayor of Burlington, and of the 1990 campaign that upset Republican congressman Peter Smith. But it was a third race, the 2006 run for the Senate seat vacated by Republican-turned-Independent Jim Jeffords, that secured Sanders a place on the national stage. As a senator, Sanders would grab the spotlight by proposing legislation, engaging in high-profile debates, mounting a headline-grabbing "filibuster" and chairing a key committee on Capitol Hill. He would become a regular on progressive talk-radio shows hosted by Thom Hartman and Ed Schultz, and on MSNBC's cable television; he would be a guest on public television's *Bill Moyers Journal*, and eventually (if infrequently) on programs that rarely hosted progressives, let alone democratic socialists, such as NBC's *Meet the Press* and ABC's *This Week*. The longtime critic of the failures of major media outlets to cover grassroots movements and dissident campaigners understood the dynamics of American politics. He recognized how the microphone gets turned up for senators—and for presidential candidates—and he was not about to turn down the opportunity to amplify the agenda. "There are some great people out there who can say, and are saying, exactly what

I'm saying," explained Sanders. "They're not United States Senators."

Remaking a Republican State

The New York City–born Sanders has become so closely associated in the minds of Americans with Vermont, and the once rock-ribbed Republican state has been so commonly reimagined as a progressive stronghold, that it is hard to imagine Sanders as anything but the Green Mountain State's junior senator. But the linkage between Sanders and Vermont, like the state's progressive reputation, did not just happen. It developed and solidified over time. In 2005, a Senate run by an Independent and democratic socialist for a Vermont U.S. Senate seat required at least a measure of political rethinking and recalculation.

For the first century after the founding of the Grand Old Party in 1854, Republicans dominated the politics of the state of Vermont like no other. For more than 100 years, Vermont Republicans won every major race for every statewide office. Republican presidential candidates from John Fremont in 1856 to George H.W. Bush in 1988—with the single exception of Barry Goldwater in 1964—won the state's electoral votes. While Democratic Patrick Leahy had won one of Vermont's Senate seats in the Watergate year of 1974 by a margin of less than 1,000 votes over his Republican opponent (and by a considerably wider margin over Liberty Union Party candidate Bernie Sanders), Republicans such as Robert Stafford and Jim Jeffords kept winning right into the twenty-first century.

The unbroken Republican winning streak for the seat Sanders would seek in 2006 had extended from before the Civil War through the 2000 election, which saw Jeffords reelected with 66 percent of the vote. Jeffords quit the Senate Republican Caucus in 2001 and served the remainder of his term as an Independent. That made him a good fit with Vermont in 2005—when the state had a Republican governor, a Republican lieutenant governor, a combative legislature and the calm and cerebral Leahy as its senior senator. From afar, and even to the eye of some Vermonters, this looked like a political landscape that invited the candidacy of a genteel moderate Republican or perhaps a similar moderate Democrat. Bernie Sanders was neither genteel nor moderate. He was politically volatile and proud of it. He never backed away from his identity as a democratic socialist, he ripped the compromises of both major parties, and he proudly served as an Independent. While some members of Congress respond to close races, and the threat of more close races, by tempering their politics, Sanders showed no sign of changing course. As a congressman, he earned top ratings from labor, environmental, and civil-rights groups; played a vital role in forming and building out the Congressional Progressive Caucus; voted against free trade deals and Wall Street "reforms" promoted by Democratic and Republican presidents; joined the lonely circle that opposed the Patriot Act; and was one of the loudest voices of opposition to George W. Bush's use of military force in Iraq. Above all, he railed against the concentrated economic and political power of multinational corporations, media monopolies, and plutocratic billionaires.

For those who did not know Sanders and did not know Vermont in 2005, the notion that a radical Independent was going to take the most permanently Republican Senate seat in the country shortly after the reelection of George W. Bush to a second term and the seating of Republican majorities in the U.S. House and Senate was hard to fathom. But Margrete Strand Rangnes, a veteran environmental activist who for many years served as director for the Sierra Club's Labor and Trade Program, who helped form the BlueGreen Alliance partnership of environmental and labor organizations, and who now serves as the executive vice president of Public Citizen, was pretty sure Sanders could do it. She had unique experience with regard to Vermont politics. As a young activist, she had helped run the 2000 campaign of the last Democrat who had tried to unseat Jeffords. On paper, that Democrat, Vermont auditor Ed Flanagan, looked like a strong challenger. A former Carter administration aide who had already won two statewide races, Flanagan had gained national attention as a trailblazing, openly gay elected official and was known in Vermont as a progressive watchdog who had used his position to battle for patient rights and better child-care protections. Yet he got nowhere against Jeffords, winning just 25 percent of the vote. On the same day, Sanders was reelected with 69 percent of the vote. That was when Strand Rangnes came to understand something about Sanders and his approach to politics that most national pundits are still struggling to get. "It's mind-boggling how popular Bernie is," she explained as Sanders was preparing to make the Senate race in 2006. "And it's not just progressives. People who tell you they have no interest in politics, who tell you they don't trust any politicians, are the ones who love Bernie the most."

Sanders was not born with the ability to leap the boundaries of partisanship and ideology, and also of frustration and disenchantment; he is not a natural politician. But he is persistent, and by the time he got to Warren on July 4, 2005, he was seen as the front runner to win one of the few U.S. Senate seats where no incumbent would be running in 2006. Sanders knew he would still face a multimillion-dollar GOP attack campaign, but top Republicans were backing away from the race. Democrats were getting in line behind his candidacy—sometimes grudgingly, sometimes not—and polls showed him running 2-to-1 ahead of likely foes.

So the folks shouting "Senator Sanders" along the parade route were not crazy.

And neither was Sanders.

That did not make what was happening in Vermont any less remarkable, however, nor any less significant.

Even if he were not a socialist, and even if he were not an Independent who eschewed most of the trappings of contemporary partisan politics—including those of a Democratic Party he then saw (and still generally sees) as dramatically too centrist, too cautious, and too unfocused to counter the corporate power that dominates our politics—the enthusiasm Sanders inspired in that 2006 campaign in Vermont would have been striking.

That Sanders attracted the support he did with what pundits portrayed as career-crushing liabilities in American politics delighted activists who—since the death of U.S. senator Paul Wellstone (D-Minn.) in

2002—had been casting about for a senator who could preach the progressive-populist gospel. And the interest in Sanders went further than that. At a point when the question of the moment was drawn from the title of Thomas Frank's groundbreaking book on political disconnection (*What's the Matter with Kansas?*), savvy Democrats wanted to know how Sanders was winning tough races by drawing the enthusiastic support of precisely the sort of rural and working-class voters who most Democrats had a hard time exciting.

Unfortunately for the politicos and pundits, Sanders was not peddling an easy fix. What he had to teach was not a new scheme for organizing a campaign or raising money. There was no Bernie Sanders gimmick. Rather, Sanders provided confirmation of a fundamental reality that too many progressive pols, and almost all Democratic leaders, had forgotten: an ideologically muscular message delivered in a manner that crosses lines of class, race, region, and partisanship has always been—and will always be—politically potent. "Bernie earned people's trust over a long period of time by taking strong stands and sticking to them," Peter Freyne, the longtime columnist for Burlington's weekly newspaper *Seven Days*, explained as the Senate race got started in 2005. "There's a connection between what the politician says and what the politician does. And it's always there. The consistency of where he's coming from and who he's looking out for has been there since I started covering him in 1981."

What Sanders had done was stay on message, from election to election, from decade to decade. Yes, the Vermonter opposed George W. Bush's war in Iraq; yes, he decried Bush's Patriot Act; yes, he supported LGBT rights and women's rights and civil rights. But what animated his campaigning in Vermont was honest fury at the neglect of the poor, frustration with the abandonment of the middle class by corporate CEOs and politicians, and an absolute—if lonely—faith that government really could do a lot of things, like guarantee health care for all, that the private sector could not. There was nothing smooth or prepackaged or focus-group tested about the way Sanders communicated. After decades of close to constant campaigning, first as the gadfly candidate of the Liberty Union Party for senator and governor in the 1970s, then as the radical mayor of "The People's Republic of Burlington" in the 1980s, then as a failed candidate first for governor and then for Congress later in the 1980s, and, from 1990 on, as the only Independent in modern history to repeatedly win a U.S. House seat, Sanders forged relationships with generations of Vermont voters. Many of them echoed the sentiments of Warren attorney Mark Grosby, who said, "I used to be a diehard Republican. Now, I'm a diehard for Bernie."

Spending days with Bernie Sanders in the small towns of Vermont in 2005 was the equivalent of signing up for a walking seminar on the real-life struggles of working Americans—as played out on issues ranging from protecting Social Security, Medicare, and Medicaid, to preserving pensions, to expanding access to health care, to lowering drug prices, to raising the minimum wage, to helping small businesses get started and keeping family farmers on the land. The conversations were a mix of personal anecdotes and broad-sweep policies, always pulled back by the candidate to a discussion of the perils of corporate power and lobbying—and of the absolute necessity that poor people and working people come together to counter money power with people power. To be sure, Sanders took questions about the issues of the moment— such as the ongoing war in Iraq. ("When the president and the vice president were telling us that Iraq had weapons of mass destruction, they didn't make the case to me. That's why I not only voted against the war but helped lead the opposition.") But even then he steered discussions back to economics and to what could be done for America if resources were not squandered on military adventurism. Sanders did not avoid what are often referred to as "hot-button" issues; if anything he was more blunt and more precise than most candidates in his statements of support for a woman's right to choose, LGBT rights, some gun control (more than the NRA wanted but, to the lingering frustration of many liberals, less than what the Brady Campaign to Prevent Gun Violence proposed). The issues he returned to, however, the issues he dwelled on with everyone he met, were the kitchen-table economic concerns of working Vermonters.

At a picnic on the village green in Rochester, a central Vermont community of 1,200, eighty-four-year-old Ethel Kingsbury, who explained that her family had owned the same farm since 1794, responded to a question about whether she liked Sanders by narrowing her eyes and exclaiming, "Like him? I love him! I'm worried about these prescription prices. This drug bit is just out of control. Bernie's the only one on our side in this whole mess." That sense that "Bernie's on our side" on bread-and-butter economic issues provided the Congressman with a following even among Vermonters who might otherwise have been put off by his ardent support of reproductive freedom and marriage equality.

"Democrats are not as engaged as they should be on the economic issues that face tens and tens of millions of people," explained Sanders after he finished up in Rochester that day. "That's what the Republicans have been playing off. The Republicans jump in and say, 'OK, look. Democrats are not talking about your economic issues. We're not either, but at least we're telling you about the Ten Commandments, we're telling you about abortion, we're telling you about gay rights.' The biggest mistake Democrats make is to take economics off the table."

In the House, Sanders kept issues of economics and corporate power on the table by using his Congressional franking privileges to send out newsletters that, rather than featuring self-serving photos and pronouncements, offered tutorials on the damage done to workers, farmers, and the environment by free-trade policies, the threat to democracy posed by media consolidation, and the workings of a single-payer health care system. From the beginning of his congressional tenure, Sanders held single-issue town hall meetings in some of the smallest communities in the state, where he brought in experts on international affairs, military spending and national priorities, poverty, children's health, pay equity for women, education and veterans' affairs for discussions that often ran deep into the evening. He even brought Denmark's ambassador to the United States to Burlington, Brattleboro, and Montpelier for discussions about the Danish social-welfare state. The crowds were always big, often packing the halls. People were invited to probe, to challenge, to complain, to disagree with the experts and with Sanders—and they often did, pressing him from the right and the left. But people also got something else—alternative views on how a fair economy and a civil society might be organized to favor their interests. This long-term, intensive education process really is the closest thing to the "secret" of Sanders's success. Vermonters came over time to associate their congressman, and now their senator, with serious discussions about complicated issues. They recognized where he was coming from—and that allowed Sanders to go places where most politicians fear to tread.

"Sometimes, Bernie's biggest critics are on the left," explained Liz Blum, an activist with the Vermont Progressive Party and a former member of the Select Board of the town of Norwich, during the 2006 campaign. "Some people are uncomfortable when they see a yard where there are signs for the Republicans and for Bernie, but I see that as evidence that he has figured out how to talk to people that the Democrats just have not been able to reach." At his best, Sanders has succeeded in separating policy from politics and getting to those deeper discussions about the role government can and should play in solving real-life problems—discussions that are usually obscured by partisan maneuvering.

As he prepared to seek the presidency in 2016, Sanders made the decision to run as a Democrat—arguing, to the frustration of at least some of his backers, that barriers to an independent or third-party run were simply too great. But as a candidate for the Senate a decade earlier, he made no apologies for refusing to be a party man. Yes, of course, he said he would like to see the Democratic Party be more progressive and, yes, he said he wanted third parties (like the Vermont Progressive Party developed by many of his backers) to develop the capacity to pull the political process to the left. But Sanders was not going to wait for the right political moment to arrive. What Sanders was creating in Vermont in the mid-2000s was a model for how an individual candidate might push beyond the narrow boundaries of contemporary politics and connect with voters in the same sense that Progressives and Populists of a century ago— operating within the shells of the Democratic and Republican parties and sometimes outside them—successfully advanced radical agendas.

During the course of his congressional tenure, Sanders has taken criticism for being too independent. Some progressive Democrats argued he should be working inside the party to move it to the left. Some progressive independents argued he should be doing more to build a third party that could compete consistently with both the Democrats and the Republicans. But Sanders said a determination to eschew party labels worked for him in Washington, where he proved to be a frequently effective coalition builder. Much of his House tenure was during a period of Republican control. It was difficult to pass major pieces of legislation, so the Vermonter focused his attention on writing and advancing amendments. "Since the Republicans took over Congress in 1995, no other lawmaker—not Tom DeLay, not Nancy Pelosi—has passed more roll-call amendments (amendments that actually went to a vote on the floor) than Bernie Sanders," noted *Rolling Stone* writer Matt Taibbi toward the end of the congressman's time in the House. "He accomplishes this on the one hand by being relentlessly active, and on the other by using his status as an Independent to form left-right coalitions." During George W. Bush's presidency, Sanders forged a left-right coalition in the House that dealt the Bush Administration a rare setback on privacy issues—attaching an amendment to a Justice Department appropriations bill that zeroed out funding for the use of the Patriot Act to spy on library and bookstore records. The amendment vote, which saw most Democrats and dozens of conservative Republicans break with the White House, inspired a threat by George W. Bush to veto the entire appropriations bill. Ultimately, Bush prevailed, but to this day Sanders and some of his conservative allies continue to work with the American Library Association and civil liberties groups on the issue. At the height of George W. Bush's political power, conservative Republicans such as North Carolina congressman Walter Jones were regular allies of then-Congressman Sanders on issues as diverse as trade policy, foreign investment, and setting timetables for withdrawing US troops from Iraq. "I suppose some people think it's strange that I work so well with a liberal," Jones said in 2005, wrapping his arm around Sanders's shoulders as the two men shared a seat on the underground train that connects the Rayburn Office Building with the Capitol. (Informed that Sanders identified himself as a socialist, Jones smiled. "I know," he said. "I was trying to be polite.") "You can disagree with someone 98 percent of the time, but if you can find the 2 percent where you agree and get together, that's what matters," Jones explained. "Bernie understands that better than some of the Democrats do."

One of the reasons that Sanders said he wanted to go to the Senate was because he believed that, as an Independent, he could build unlikely alliances. "In the sense that we are trying to develop left-right coalitions, we are also trying to redefine American politics," he explained. "You have the trade issue, which is very, very important to people who are worried about losing their jobs. You have healthcare issues, which are very important. You have war and peace issues, economic priority issues, which are very important when we talk about how this country is going to pay for all our domestic needs. And on those issues you can bring together coalitions that redefine the 'normal' paradigm that a lot of the corporate media create when they talk about liberal and conservative."

That dream has often been deferred. In 2006, however, Sanders succeeded in redefining the paradigm in Vermont. Democrats backed off the Senate; Sanders's old nemesis, former governor Howard Dean, who had recently taken over as Democratic National Committee chair, said, "A victory for Bernie Sanders is a win for Democrats." Prominent players in the state party endorsed Sanders. He entered the Democratic primary, won it, and then declined the nomination. In the November race Sanders faced Republican businessman Richard Tarrant, a millionaire who poured more than $7 million into a highly professional and highly negative campaign against the Independent. Yet Democrats let Sanders run his own race—without negative ads (in fact with little TV at all) and with a heavy emphasis on visiting even the smallest towns in the most remote corners of the state.

There were no gimmicks, no easy answers, no quick fixes—just a stubborn faith that people want to talk about the issues that matter in their lives. And it worked. Sanders was outspent and crudely attacked in the 2006 race—especially for his lonely votes to defend civil liberties. Yet he secured the Senate seat that for a century and a half had been won only by Republicans, taking 65 percent of the vote to just 32 percent for Tarrant. Sanders won every county in the state by a landslide, and carried even conservative communities. All those town hall meetings over all those years, all that talk about kitchen-table economics, had forged a connection that could not be severed by big money and negative ads. "Maybe that's the lesson of Bernie," explained Margrete Strand Rangnes. "He doesn't worry so much about winning one election. He's in it for the long haul, because that's how you build the awareness and the trust that allows you to get beyond the spin and talk to people about the real issues in their lives. I don't know if the Democrats have the patience to do that. But if they want to get through to the people they need to reach, they should be paying attention."

Rejecting the Wall Street Consensus

As it happened, the Democrats did not feel much pressure to pay attention at the time. Sanders arrived in the Senate in January 2007, as Democrats retook control of the House and Senate. In 2008, the party would extend those majorities and elect a president. Democrats were on a roll and, while they accepted Sanders as an independent-but-aligned member of their Senate caucus, party leaders were not inclined to embrace the economic populism at the heart of the Vermonter's appeal. That was obvious in September 2008, when the Wall Street meltdown led to urgent moves to provide bailout funding to the financial institutions that had caused the crisis. Even though the crisis came in the middle of a campaign, Democratic and Republican leaders came together in support of the bailout. In the House, Nancy Pelosi and Paul Ryan found common cause. In the Senate, Democratic presidential nominee Barack Obama voted yes, as did Republican presidential nominee John McCain. So did Democratic leader Harry Reid and Republican leader Mitch McConnell.

But Sanders objected. Loudly.

"If a bailout is needed, if taxpayer money must be placed at risk, if we are going to bail out Wall Street, it should be those people who have caused the problem, those people who have benefited from President Bush's tax breaks for millionaires and billionaires, those people who have taken advantage of deregulation who should pick up the tab, not ordinary working people," roared Sanders, as he announced his plan to vote "no" on the $700 billion bailout plan.

The fiery speech that Sanders delivered on the Senate floor on October 1, 2008, set the tone for his service in the chamber. While others were falling in line, Sanders stepped out, refusing to accept a consensus that he said neglected the real economic issues facing America.

Sounding themes that would become his mantra, Sanders argued that:

In our country today, we have the most unequal distribution of income and wealth of any major country on earth, with the top 1 percent earning more income than the bottom 50 percent and the top 1 percent owning more wealth than the bottom 90 percent. We are living at a time when we have seen a massive transfer of wealth from the middle class to the very wealthiest people in this country, when, among others, CEOs of Wall Street firms received unbelievable amounts in bonuses, including $39 billion in bonuses in the year 2007 alone for just the five major investment houses. We have seen the incredible greed of the financial services industry manifested in the hundreds of millions of dollars they have spent on campaign contributions and lobbyists in order to deregulate their industry so that hedge funds and other unregulated financial institutions could flourish. We have seen them play with trillions and trillions dollars in esoteric financial instruments, in unregulated industries which no more than a handful of people even understand. We have seen the financial services industry charge 30 percent interest rates on credit card loans and tack on outrageous late fees and other costs to unsuspecting customers. We have seen them engaged in despicable predatory lending practices, taking advantage of the vulnerable and the uneducated. We have seen them send out billions of deceptive solicitations to almost every mailbox in America.

Most importantly, we have seen the financial services industry lure people into mortgages they could not afford to pay, which is one of the basic reasons why we are here tonight.

In the midst of all of this, we have a bailout package which says to the middle class that you are being asked to place at risk $700 billion, which is $2,200 for every man, woman, and child in this country. You're being asked to do that in order to undo the damage caused by this excessive Wall Street greed. In other words, the "Masters of the Universe," those brilliant Wall Street insiders who have made more money than the average American can even dream of, have brought our financial system to the brink of collapse. Now, as the American and world financial systems teeter on the edge of a meltdown, these multimillionaires are demanding that the middle class, which has already suffered under Bush's disastrous economic policies, pick up the pieces that they broke. That is wrong, and that is something that I will not support.

It was not just the economic system that was broken, Sanders argued, it was a political system that was broken— corrupted by the absolute refusal of official Washington, even in a moment of crisis, to challenge economic elites.

"Under this bill, the CEOs and the Wall Street insiders will still, with a little bit of imagination, continue to make out like bandits," growled Sanders. "This bill does not deal at all with how we got into this crisis in the first place and the need to undo the deregulatory fervor which created trillions of dollars in complicated and unregulated financial instruments such as credit default swaps and hedge funds," the senator continued. "This bill does not address the issue that has taken us to where we are today, the concept of too big to fail . . . There is not one word about the issue of too big to fail in this legislation at a time when that problem is in fact becoming even more serious."

Then he named names.

"This bill does not deal with the absurdity of having the fox guarding the hen house," said Sanders. "Maybe I'm the only person in America who thinks so, but I have a hard time understanding why we are giving $700 billion to the Secretary of the Treasury, the former CEO of Goldman Sachs, who along with other financial institutions, actually got us into this problem. Now, maybe I'm the only person in America who thinks that's a little bit weird, but that is what I think."

Sanders was not the only person in America who had a hard time understanding the bailout as anything more than an insider deal to protect the privileged at the expense of everyone else. When the crisis developed, Sanders wrote a letter to Treasury Secretary Hank Paulson making an argument that "it should be those people best able to pay for this bailout, those people who have made out like bandits in recent years, they should be asked to pay for this bailout. It should not be the middle class." To Sanders' amazement, almost 50,000 added their names to his on the letter.

If Sanders was frustrated with the compromised and compromising politics of the Senate, he was as excited as a Silicon Valley entrepreneur about the disruptive potential of the Internet. With a young staff that was quick to adopt social media tools that other senators resisted, Sanders began to use his Senate website, Facebook, Twitter, and email to invite Americans into debates about their economic future. By 2015, his Senate Facebook page had 1.6 million followers, far outpacing other senators, most presidential candidates, and more than a few rock stars. Coupled with media appearances and a speaking schedule that took him not only to Vermont but to progressive gatherings across the country, Sanders built a constituency for the arguments he made as a lonely opponent of the bailout.

Sanders was not always in opposition. He backed Barack Obama for president in 2008, and he generally supported the key initiatives of Obama's first years in office. Yet he was rarely an uncritical supporter. The senator from Vermont joined senators Robert Byrd of West Virginia, Russ Feingold of Wisconsin, and Tom Harkin of Iowa in breaking with the rest of the Democratic caucus to oppose Obama's nomination of Tim Geithner to serve as Secretary of the Treasury, arguing, "Mr. Geithner was at the Fed and the Treasury Department when the deregulatory fervor that got us into this mess ran rampant. He was part of the problem."

As a senator in a chamber that might decide whether a major initiative would advance or collapse, Sanders used his position to press the administration to improve measures he thought were too weak. One case in point was the Affordable Care Act. Sanders has been a longtime supporter of a universal single-payer "Medicare for All" system, along the lines of the public health systems that deliver care in Canada and most European countries. He was quick to point out gaps and flaws in the ACA. But he kept talking to the administration and Senate backers of the proposal and succeeded in securing

$12.5 billion in ACA funding to expand community health centers and to recruit more doctors, dentists, nurses, and other primary health providers. He also fought to expand the National Health Service Corps in order to address the shortage of health providers in underserved regions of the country. And he fought to preserve prospects for states such as Vermont to experiment with single-payer initiatives. Enough of what Sanders proposed was incorporated into the ACA to get his vote in 2010, even as the senator continued his advocacy for a more robust national health-care program. Similarly, Sanders backed the 2010 Dodd-Frank Wall Street Reform and Consumer Protection Act, even as he acknowledged that the measure "did not end much of the casino-style gambling" on Wall Street. That vote put the senator from Vermont in the company of Elizabeth Warren, the Harvard Law School professor who led the fight for the creation of the new Consumer Financial Protection Bureau, which was established with the enactment of Dodd-Frank, and who in 2012 would be elected to the Senate from Massachusetts. But the vote put Sanders at odds with a frequent ally in financial reform fights, Wisconsin's Russ Feingold, who opposed Dodd-Frank with an argument that: "My test for the financial regulatory reform bill is whether it will prevent another crisis. [This bill] fails that test." The decision to vote for Dodd-Frank illustrated a characteristic of Sanders that is often missed by casual observers of Congress; the senator is passionate, and he is not afraid to go it alone, but nor is he a purist who enjoys being right when everyone else is wrong. If he can get an amendment he thinks is important, or at least useful, attached to a piece of legislation (as he did with a

Dodd-Frank amendment that directed the Government Accountability Office to conduct the first top-to-bottom audit of the secretive Federal Reserve), Sanders may vote for a measure that he finds insufficient. In this sense he is less of a lone wolf than some imagine.

When Sanders does break with the pack, however, he breaks big.

After the "Republican wave" election of 2010 gave the GOP control of the U.S. House, a stronger position in the Senate, and dominance of statehouses across the country, Sanders argued that the Obama administration and congressional Democrats needed to draw dramatically clearer lines in the sand on economic issues. Instead, President Obama cut a deal with congressional Republicans to extend Bush-era tax breaks for billionaires and create a sweeping estate-tax exemption for millionaires. It was not just bad politics, Sanders said, it was bad economics.

The Vermonter's certainty, on both points, fueled a speech that would redefine him in the eyes of millions of Americans, identifying him not merely as a senator but as a spokesman for a point of view that was profoundly at odds with the cozy consensus in Washington and with the austerity agenda of billionaire-funded "think tanks" and politicians who continued to promote tax breaks for the rich and program cuts for everyone else. That agenda had failed, Sanders said, arguing that it was time for a new agenda of taxing the rich and investing in infrastructure and job creation for the great mass of Americans who never got a bailout.

After promising to do "whatever it takes" to block the deal, Sanders appeared on the Senate floor at 10:24 a.m. on

Friday, December 10, 2010. He adjusted the microphone and began speaking about what was wrong with the tax deal, about what was wrong with how Washington did business, about what was wrong with national priorities, about what was wrong with the economy. "You can call what I am doing today whatever you want, you [can] call it a filibuster, you can call it a very long speech . . ." read a message on the senator's Twitter feed. Very long. Sanders remained at the podium for 8 hours, 35 minutes, and 14 seconds.

The senator's bold gesture grabbed the attention of the nation, as Senate video servers were overwhelmed when tens of thousands of people tried to watch the speech online. MSNBC's Rachel Maddow called the speech "a super-human display of endurance and strength of conviction against the tax deal." But the White House was not impressed. On NBC's *Nightly News*, political director Chuck Todd reported, "For most of the day today, the tax debate had been dominated by Vermont's Independent, self-described socialist senator who has been speaking on the floor of the United States Senate by himself continuously since about 10:30 this morning. Well, about 4 o'clock clearly the White House had had enough so instead of briefing reporters about President Obama's private meeting with President Clinton, President Obama decided to trot out President Clinton himself to brief reporters."

CNN's John King explained that "the calculation, both risky and simple, [was] I'll see your Bernie Sanders and raise you a Bill Clinton."

But the story was not Clinton. It was Sanders. Sanders finished speaking not with a *Mr. Smith Goes to*

Washington–style collapse from exhaustion but with an energetic call to action. "If the American people stand up and say, 'We can do better than this, that we don't need to drive up the national debt by giving tax breaks to millionaires and billionaires,' [if] the American people are prepared to stand—and we're prepared to follow them—I think we can defeat this proposal," he thundered. "I think we can come up with a better proposal which better reflects the needs of the middle class and working families of our country and, to me, most importantly, the children of our country. And with that, Madam President, I would yield the floor."

National Public Radio announced, "The whole world was watching Bernie Sanders today." The *Washington Post*'s Chris Cillizza declared, "Sanders' stand symbolized the anger and resentment liberals felt about the deal and turned the Vermont senator into a progressive hero." Politico agreed, explaining, "The left's been looking for a new hero. Tonight they latched onto one: Sen. Bernie Sanders. The Vermont Independent took progressive fury over President Obama's tax-cut deal with Republicans to the floor of the Senate Friday, bringing the chamber to a standstill for eight hours with a filibuster-style speech that set the liberal Twitterverse ablaze."

Inside/Outside Strategies

In the new and more conservative Congress, Sanders would continue to focus on Senate duties—as the chairman of Veterans' Affairs Committee from 2013 to 2015, for instance, he often worked closely with Arizona senator John McCain, the former prisoner of war and 2008 Republican presidential nominee. With McCain, Sanders co-wrote the sweeping Veterans' Access to Care through Choice, Accountability, and Transparency Act of 2014 in response to reports of scandalous neglect by the Veterans Health Administration. Increasingly, however, Sanders devoted his energies to developing inside-outside strategies that brought public pressure to bear on a Congress that after 2010 was gridlocked both by partisan division and by the influence of big-money campaign contributions and corporate lobbying.

To a greater extent than any senator since Wellstone, Sanders used his position to highlight struggles far from Washington, and in so doing to argue for federal interventions in response to popular uprisings. When newly elected Republican governors attacked labor rights immediately after taking office in 2011, Sanders leapt into the fray, declaring his solidarity with union members who were protesting in Madison, Wisconsin, and Columbus, Ohio, and other state capitals. "This is part of the concerted attack on the middle class and working families of this country by the very wealthiest people in America," Sanders said of the effort by Republican governors such as Wisconsin's Scott Walker and Ohio's John Kasich to eliminate collective bargaining rights for public employee unions. "These guys want to return us to the 1920s when working people had virtually no rights to organize or to earn a decent living . . . Wages are going down in this country for everybody. When you destroy unions there will be no standard at all, nobody left to negotiate decent jobs for the middle class." When the Occupy Wall Street movement began in New York City's Zuccotti Park and quickly went national, Sanders embraced the language and the spirit of the protests. "We have the crooks on Wall Street, and I use that word advisedly—don't misquote me, the word is 'crooks'—whose greed, whose recklessness, whose illegal behavior caused this terrible recession with so much suffering. We believe in this country; we love this country; and we will be damned if we're going to see a handful of robber barons control the future of this country," declared the senator, who added, "I applaud those protesters who are out there, who are focusing attention on Wall Street, but what we've got to do is put meat on that bone," he said. "We've got to make demands on Wall Street [and] break those institutions up." When Cook County commissioner Jesus "Chuy" Garcia, who had spent decades working to forge coalitions of working-class Latinos, African Americans, and white ethnics, in the tradition of former Chicago mayor Harold Washington, challenged centrist Democratic mayor Rahm Emanuel and that city's political establishment, Sanders campaigned for him—as a former mayor and as a senator who announced that he needed allies in the nation's city halls to battle the top-to-bottom influence of corporations and the billionaire Koch brothers.

When eighteen-year-old Michael Brown was shot and killed by a police officer in Ferguson, Missouri, Sanders declared that "the shooting of an unarmed person is unacceptable," endorsed calls for a federal investigation and defended the rights of protesters in Ferguson and across the country. "Police must be seen as part of a community and not an occupying force," said the senator, who argued in the immediate aftermath of the shooting of the young African-American man that: "All of us have a responsibility to make sure that what happened in Ferguson never happens again." To that end, Sanders and Congressman John Conyers, Jr. proposed legislation that would provide $5.5 billion in immediate funding to states and communities to address the crisis of African-American youth unemployment, arguing that "instead of putting military style equipment into police departments in those areas, we [should] start investing in jobs for the young people there who desperately need them."

The best members of Congress, of all ideologies and on both sides of the aisle in the House and Senate, respond to crises, challenges, and opportunities outside Washington by launching inquiries, holding hearings and proposing legislation. But Sanders reimagined the role of the legislator, working all the angles on Capitol Hill and then hitting the road to urge citizens at home in Vermont and across the country to pressure Congress to address climate change, to save the Postal Service, to recognize and respond to the damage done by trade policies that led to dislocation and unemployment—especially for African Americans, Latinos, and the young. "To me," he said, "what politics is about is not just coming up with ideas and a legislative program here in Washington—you need to do those things—but it's about figuring out how you involve people in the political process, how you empower them. It ain't easy, but that is, in fact, what has to be done."

In response to the U.S. Supreme Court's 2010 ruling in the case of Citizens United v. Federal Election Commission, which struck down historic barriers to corporate spending on elections, Sanders proposed a "Saving American Democracy Amendment" to the U.S. Constitution—with the purpose of overturning the Citizens United ruling, restoring a century-old ban on corporate campaign donations to candidates, establishing that corporations are not entitled to the same constitutional rights as people, and making it clear that corporations may be regulated by Congress and state legislatures. But he did not stop there. Sanders launched a petition drive to show support for the amendment, he urged citizens to pass local and state resolutions to demand action, he appeared at rallies across the country to promote the idea, and then he brought activists back to Washington to raise the volume. In a city where the billionaire Koch brothers are increasingly influential— thanks to their massive spending on campaigns and their funding of groups that promote right-wing economic agendas—Sanders did not just call them out. He organized a Capitol Hill screening of a documentary exposing the manipulation of politics by the billionaires, *Citizen Koch*, by Academy Award–nominated filmmakers Carl Deal and Tia Lessin, at which he declared, "The paramount issue is the movement of this country toward what I call an oligarchic form of society—where you have a small number of people owning and controlling not only our economy, not only our media (the means by which people get their information) but increasingly, and especially as a result of Citizens United, our political process."

"That's the bad news, and it is very bad news indeed," said Sanders. "The good news is that all over this country millions and millions of people are understanding, and believe in the bottom of their hearts, that American democracy is not about billionaires being able to spend as much money as they want to elect the people they want. Very few people believe that is what American democracy is about."

Vermonters liked the activist approach. When Sanders sought reelection in 2012, he broke almost all the rules of the Citizens United era. He ran no attack ads. In fact, he ran no TV commercials. Instead, he poured his campaign's resources into a grassroots strategy that had volunteers knock on 20,000 doors and that organized dozens of town hall meetings across the state. The meetings were not rallies. Sanders spoke in full sentences, not sound bites; he invited voters to ask complicated questions on controversial issues—and he answered with big, bold proposals to address climate change by "transforming our energy system away from polluting fossil fuels, and towards energy efficiency and sustainability," to really reform health care with a single-payer Medicare-for-all program, to steer money away from the Pentagon and toward domestic jobs initiatives. Rejecting the empty partisanship of both parties, Sanders ripped the austerity agenda of Republican nominees Mitt Romney and Paul Ryan, while warning that President Obama and too many Democrats were inclining toward an austerity-lite "grand bargain" that would make debt reduction a greater priority than saving Social Security, Medicare, and Medicaid. "Why, in God's name, in a tight race, did Barack Obama have a hard time saying six words: 'I will never cut Social Security'? Why won't these Democrats say: 'We will never cut Social

Security'?" asked Sanders. "If they can't say that, how are they ever going to go after Wall Street?"

When the results began to pour in from across the country on election night, one of the first Senate races to be called was for Bernie Sanders in Vermont. Against an aggressive Republican rival, a businessman and four-term Massachusetts state legislator who made a big deal about the fact that he was running to replace "the only admitted socialist in the U.S. Senate," the senator took 71 percent of the vote, sweeping every county in the state in the best finish of the sixteen statewide races he had run since 1972. Yet Sanders was frustrated. He did not like that pundits who didn't know Vermont were dismissing his approach—and his electoral success—as a regional deviation that might work in what is often portrayed as a quirky liberal state but that couldn't possibly have relevance for the rest of the country. "It wasn't that long ago that Vermont was one of the most Republican states in the country. Until two years ago, the governor was a Republican; the lieutenant governor *is* a Republican. This is a significantly rural state. This is a state with some very conservative regions," said Sanders, who argued that he won those conservative regions not by dumbing down or compromising his message but by turning the volume up.

"I go crazy with all these Democrats saying you have to go conservative to win, you have to go cautious to win. These damned consultants come in and say, 'This is how you have to run,' and it's always the same: raise money, spend it on television, don't say anything that will offend anyone. And the Democrats do it and then they end up in tight races, worried about whether they'll make it," said

Sanders. "For the life of me, I can't figure out why progressives listen to consultants. Building movements, making progress on progressive issues—you have to talk to people, educate people, organize people."

Sanders was offering a roadmap for Democrats. But, for the most part, Democrats weren't listening to the Independent who caucused with them in the Senate but who was often "off-message." Wrangling with the White House and Republican neo-conservatives, Sanders was a forceful critic of proposals to send U.S. troops back into the Middle East. At a point in 2013, when Republicans such as Arizona senator John McCain were pushing for intervention in Syria, and when the White House was sending ominous signals about the project, most Democrats in the House and Senate kept quiet. But Sanders kept recalling the rush to war in Iraq and its consequences, while arguing, "To get involved in a bloody and complicated war in Syria makes no sense at all. We would reap consequences we can't imagine." Explaining that the human cost of war is not just counted on the battlefield but on the home front, the then-chairman of the Veterans Affairs Committee pointed out that the United States was still struggling to care for the veterans of the last wars in which it had engaged. He asked who would pay for another war for another regime change in another country. And he answered, "The top 1 percent? No. Children in Head Start, families on food stamps, seniors on Medicare—that's who will be paying for it . . . At a time when the middle class is literally disappearing, when 46 million people are living in poverty and real unemployment is close to 14 percent, and a generation of kids are graduating from high school and college and can't find any work, and when we have the most unequal distribution of income since the Great Depression, what do you think is going to happen if we go to war with Syria?" said the senator, who warned that human needs at home would "keep getting pushed aside because of war and war and war and war."

"I don't want our country to become the Sparta of the twenty-first century," Sanders declared. The White House did not like that sort of talk, but polls showed that the American people were exceptionally ill at ease with the prospect of perpetual war. For his part, Sanders was more convinced than ever of what he described as an increasingly profound "disconnect" between the great mass of citizens and the political and media elites of Washington. Anticipating a disastrous 2014 election cycle for Democrats—in which they lost control of the Senate, made no progress in the House and suffered setbacks in statehouses across the country—Sanders appeared the weekend before the voting on public television's *Moyers and Company*.

A Political Revolution

Sanders talked about how "big money [can] put an unbelievable amount of TV and radio ads out there to deflect attention from the real issues facing the American people." The notion of deflecting attention caught the ear of Bill Moyers, who has been on both sides of the politics and media equation—as a White House press secretary in the administration of Lyndon Johnson, as a newspaper publisher and as a highly regarded broadcast journalist.

"Well, that's interesting," said Moyers. "Because, you know, I've seen you quite recently on television. It's always the same questions and always the same five headlines. What's the story that the corporate press is not letting you tell?"

"Oh, my God. You see, this is the issue," responded Sanders. "I mean, I've been on a million of these shows. They say, 'Here's the story of the day. What do you think about the Secret Service? What do you think about this? What do you think about Ebola?' All of those issues are important. But the issues that impact ordinary people— they're asking why, despite all of the productivity, people are working longer hours for lower wages. Have we had that discussion, Bill? Have you ever heard anybody talking about it?"

The nation's longest-serving Independent member of Congress was just getting started.

"And this issue of income and wealth inequality, wow: one percent owning 37 percent of the wealth in America. Bottom 60 percent owning 1.7 percent. One family, the Walton family of Walmart, owning more wealth than the bottom 40 percent," he said. "Do you think we should be talking about that issue? You can't get the discussion going on TV."

Then came the vital exchange.

"Why?" asked Moyers.

"Because it's not in the interest of the corporations who own the networks to actually be educating the American people so that we're debating the real issues. It's much better to deflect attention away from those issues and get into the story of the day," explained Sanders. Moyers pressed Sanders with regard to solutions to what he referred to as "this fundamental question facing Bernie Sanders: how do you get your message directly to those who need it most?" Implicit in the question was an acknowledgment that, for all his efforts inside the Capitol and across the country, and for all of his electoral success in Vermont, Sanders had not exactly thwarted the forces of plutocracy. Most of the goals he outlined in the last chapter of *Outsider in the House* remained unrealized, and some of them seemed further from realization than they did in 1997.

"I wish I had the magic answer," replied Sanders. "You're asking exactly the right question . . . The idea that you have these working-class people who are voting for candidates who refuse to raise the minimum wage, who refuse to provide healthcare for their kids, who want to send their jobs to China, who want to give tax breaks to corporations, it blows my mind. And that is the issue that we have to figure out."

What Sanders was also figuring out in the fall of 2014 was whether a campaign for the presidency might be a part of the answer to Moyers' "How do you get your message directly to those who need it most?" question. The previous March, in an extended interview with the *Nation*, Sanders had explained, "I don't wake up every morning, as some people here in Washington do, and say, 'You know, I really have to be president of the United States. I was born to be president of the United States.' What I do wake up every morning feeling is that this country faces more serious problems than at any time since the Great Depression, and there is a horrendous lack of serious political discourse or ideas out there that can address these crises, and that somebody has got to represent the working-class and the middle-class of this country in standing up to the big-money interests who have so much power over the economic and political life of this country. So I am prepared to run for president of the United States. I don't believe that I am the only person out there who can fight this fight, but I am certainly prepared to look seriously at that race."

Sanders recognized that it was an audacious proposal, and a complex one. Would the longest-serving Independent in Congress mount an Independent or third-party bid, or would he run as a Democrat? Would an outspoken critic of money in politics be able to raise enough to get past the starting line of a presidential race? Would he be overshadowed by his frequent ally, Massachusetts senator Elizabeth Warren, who progressive groups talked of drafting into the race? Could anyone upset the trajectory of former secretary of state Hillary Clinton, who would always have more name recognition, more money, and more connections? And there was the matter of whether a democratic socialist could get traction in a country where the "S" word was treated as an offensive epithet by most Republicans and scrupulously avoided by most Democrats?

As it happened, the latter question was settled in Sanders' mind. "No, that's not a factor at all," he said. "In Vermont, people understand exactly what I mean by the word. They don't believe that democratic socialism is akin to North

Korea communism. They understand that when I talk about democratic socialism, what I'm saying is that I do not want to see the United States significantly dominated by a handful of billionaire families controlling the economic and political life of the country. That I do believe that in a democratic, civilized society, all people are entitled to health care as a right, all people are entitled to quality education as a right, all people are entitled to decent jobs and a decent income, and that we need a government which represents ordinary Americans and not just the wealthy and the powerful.

"The people in Vermont know exactly what I mean, which is why I won my last election with 71 percent of the vote and carried some of the most conservative towns in the state," he continued. "If I ran for president, and articulated a vision that speaks to working people, I am confident that voters in every part of this country would understand that." In fact, he seemed to relish the prospect of opening up the discussion. "The truth is that, very sadly, the corporate media ignores some of the huge accomplishments that have taken place in countries like Denmark, Finland, Sweden and Norway," he explained. "These countries, which have a long history of democratic socialist or labor governments, have excellent and universal health care systems, excellent educational systems and they have gone a long way toward eliminating poverty and creating a far more egalitarian society than we have. I think that there are economic and social models out there that we can learn a heck of a lot from, and that's something I would be talking about."

Even with that said, however, the gap between talking about big ideas, great ideas, and actually making them central to the discourse requires a level of focus and organizing that dissident campaigns often imagine but rarely achieve. The challenge of building coalitions that might be rooted in economic common interest but that would need to embrace the broader "rainbow" politics that Jesse Jackson developed in his 1984 and 1988 presidential runs—and that at least to some extent shaped the remarkable campaign that elected Barack Obama to the presidency in 2008—was real for every progressive pondering a 2016 run. Sanders recognized these daunting prospects, and he wrestled with them for more than a year, as he and the activists he met with around the country considered the possibility of what would eventually become a run for the Democratic presidential nomination. The decision to run as a Democrat excited activists with groups such as Progressive Democrats of America, which had urged Sanders to run inside the party and move the debate left from there. At the same time, it frustrated independent progressives who argued that change would only come from a challenge to both major parties. Ultimately, Sanders, the outsider, decided to enter the Democratic fold because of the structural barriers to independent and third-party politics on the national level ("given the nature of the political system, given the nature of media in America, it would be much more difficult to get adequate coverage from the mainstream media running outside of the two-party system") and because, he said, he would not play a "spoiler" role that might "[make] it easier for some right-wing Republican to get elected."

Uncharacteristically, what animated Sanders through

this period and once he announced his candidacy on April 30, 2015, was not a specific game plan, but rather a leap of faith. Yes, of course, the odds against a seventy-something democratic socialist from one of the nation's smallest states winning the nomination of a party he had always refused to join, let alone the presidency, were overwhelming. But so, he suggested, were the odds against working Americans in a globalized economy defined by race-to-the-bottom "free-trade" deals. So, he suggested, were the odds against African-American young people in deindustrialized and abandoned urban neighborhoods where unemployment rates rivaled those of the Great Depression. So, he suggested, were the odds against the planet if immediate action was not taken to address climate change. It was too easy, he argued, to be overwhelmed. What was needed was a sense of what the great organizer and author Michael Harrington used to refer to as "the left wing of the possible." Jettisoning the standard candidate line about what he or she would do, Sanders talked about what everyone would have to do to "bring together the kind of coalition that can win—that can transform politics. We've got to bring together trade unionists and working families, our minority communities, environmentalists, young people, the women's community, the gay community, seniors, veterans, the people who in fact are the vast majority of the American population. We've got to create a progressive agenda and rally people around that agenda."

People who don't know Bernie Sanders may not see him as a "leap of faith" kind of guy. In fact, his entire political

career has been characterized by leaps of faith. He infused
his 2016 campaign with a politics that Antonio Gramsci
anticipated with his ruminations on "pessimism of the
intellect, optimism of the will." I talked with Sanders
dozens of times during the 2016 campaign. He recognized
all the barriers in his way. Yet he persevered, and in so
doing inspired others to do the same. His campaign began
and ended as a movement, with a DIY sensibility that
invited grassroots activists to take ownership of the project. In the first months of his bid, Sanders would show up
in towns where campaign organizers had arrived a few
days—in some cases, just a few hours—before him. By any
reasonable expectation, he should have been greeted by a
few dozen sympathizers. Instead, they came by the
hundreds, then the thousands, then the tens of thousands.

The first real sign that the Sanders campaign would be
more than a footnote to the story of Democratic frontrunner
Hillary Clinton's triumphal march to the nomination came
in Madison, Wisconsin, on July 1, 2015. More than 10,000
people showed up for a Sanders rally. "Tonight we have
made a little bit of history," the candidate told the crowd,
which filled an arena more frequently used for rock concerts
and sports events. "Tonight we have more people at a meeting for a candidate for president of the United States than
any other candidate has had in 2015." Barely a month later,
in Portland, Oregon, a crowd of almost 20,000 packed the
Moda Center sports arena to capacity while another 10,000
waited outside. A few days later, after Sanders attracted tens
of thousands in southern California, the *Los Angeles Times*
headline read: "Why a huge Los Angeles crowd turned out

for Bernie Sanders." Like every report on the early stages of the Sanders campaign by every major media outlet, the story began by dismissing the senator as "a presidential candidate whom pundits give no chance of winning the nomination." Yet it acknowledged that Sanders had "touched a nerve in what has otherwise been a low-key Democratic contest." The reporters turned first to a Democratic strategist, Rose Kapolczynski, for a repeat of the conventional wisdom. "Bernie Sanders is sticking his head out of the window and saying, 'I'm mad as hell and I'm not going to take it anymore.' He's giving voice to the frustration that many progressives feel," explained Kapolczynski. "But I don't believe that translates into winning caucuses or primaries." Then they stumbled across seventeen-year-old Tanith Ledbetter, who said of Sanders: "He has the heart to deal with stuff others won't address." Ledbetter, the paper noted, "will turn eighteen in time to vote in the 2016 presidential election."

The *Times* would have been wise to spend more time with Ledbetter, since the enthusiasm that Sanders inspired among first-time voters would transform the dynamics of the 2016 nomination contest. Instead, the journalists scrambled back to an academic safe space. "Just because people are interested, it does not mean people will give money and actually cast a ballot in support," announced Lynn Vavreck, a UCLA political-science professor, who assured the reporters, "People showing up for these rallies have a strong interest in politics. They're not average voters, who are barely tuned in to the election at this point."

In fact, a lot of average voters were tuning in. They were sending small checks—averaging twenty-seven dollars—in very large numbers to a campaign that proudly declared itself to be "Paid for by Bernie 2016 (Not the Billionaires)." They were volunteering in the first caucus state, Iowa; the first primary state, New Hampshire; and a lot of states that were never at the top of Democratic targeting lists. When I spoke at the Salt Lake City Public Library in September 2015, a crowd of Sanders supporters showed up. They wanted to tell me about *their* campaign—and it really was theirs. The national Sanders headquarters in Burlington struggled that fall to keep up with the burgeoning support. So grassroots activists—democratic socialists, union members, Native Americans, LGBTQ advocates, and, always, young people—took control. In Utah, they pooled their resources and opened a Salt Lake City head-quarters. They linked up on Facebook with lefties in Ogden and Provo and smaller communities. The national office was slow to get campaign materials to them, so they printed their own. And they dreamed that maybe, just maybe, the senator would hold one of those big rallies in Utah. When Sanders finally showed up on a Friday night in March 2016, just four days before the Utah caucuses, the line of cars headed to the rally site was many miles long. More than 14,000 people packed a park in downtown Salt Lake City. Surrounded by hijab-wearing Muslim girls, immigrant workers, trans-gender activists, and longtime Democrats who were astonished by the crowd, Sanders took the stage as Bruce

Springsteen's great song of solidarity, "We Take Care of Our Own," played out. Marveling at the cheering throngs, the candidate joked, "It looks like I got some bad information; somebody told me Utah was a Republican state." Then he reflected, "We began this campaign ten months ago and we were at 3 percent in the polls, seventy points behind. We had no money. We had no political organization. Nobody outside Vermont knew who I was. Other than that, we were in pretty good shape. As of today, we have won nine states, most by double digits; we have received 849 delegates to the Democratic National Convention."

Sanders won a lot more delegates the following Tuesday. The *Salt Lake City Tribune*, which reported that Sanders was on track to secure twenty-seven of the state's thirty-three pledged delegates, featured a banner headline: "Feeling the Bern: Utah Dems Give Sanders Near 80 Percent of Their Votes Against Clinton." In Idaho, which held caucuses on the same day, 78 percent of the votes were cast for Sanders.

But most of the national news coverage was as dismissive as ever.

Media Malpractice

The neglect of the Sanders campaign by major media outlets was so notable that in early April 2016, former secretary of labor Robert Reich penned an article that began: "Wait a minute. Last Tuesday, Sanders won 78 percent of the vote in Idaho and 79 percent in Utah. Three days before

that, he took 82 percent of the vote in Alaska, 73 percent in
Washington, and 70 percent in Hawaii."

"In fact," wrote Reich, a longtime Hillary Clinton friend
and supporter who had switched to Sanders,

> since mid-March, Bernie has won six out of the seven Demo-
> cratic primary contests with an average margin of victory of 40
> points. Those victories have given him roughly 100 additional
> pledged delegates. As of now, Hillary Clinton has 54.9 percent
> of the pledged delegates to Bernie Sanders's 45.1 percent. That's
> still a sizable gap—but it doesn't make Bernie Sanders's candi-
> dacy an impossibility ... Bernie is outpacing Clinton in
> fundraising. In March, he raised $39 million. In February, he
> raised $42 million, compared to Hillary Clinton's $30 million. In
> January he raised $20 million to her $15 million. By any measure,
> the enthusiasm for Bernie is huge and keeps growing. Yet if you
> read the *Washington Post* or the *New York Times*, or watch CNN
> or even MSNBC, or listen to the major pollsters and pundits,
> you'd come to the same conclusion (Sanders has no chance).
> Every success by Bernie is met with a story or column or talking
> head whose message is "but he can't possibly win."

A few days later, Sanders won an overwhelming victory in
the Wisconsin primary, and not long after that he scored an
upset in the Indiana primary—confirming, as had an earlier
upset in Michigan, the appeal of the senator's candidacy to
voters in precisely the Midwestern states that would be critical to Democratic chances in a fall race against the
unexpected Republican frontrunner, Donald Trump. Yet
those Sanders victories were quickly glossed over. Indeed,

after the Indiana win, the cable networks focused more attention on an empty podium where Trump was expected to eventually appear than on the appearance where Sanders claimed his victory.

Sanders supporters lodged frequent complaints during the 2016 race about a Democratic nomination process they saw as rigged to favor Clinton—with its bizarre debate schedules, more than 700 unelected and largely unaccountable superdelegates, and party leadership that openly favored the former secretary of state. Yet there is a strong case to be made that the greatest challenge Sanders faced, from the start of his run, was the media's refusal to treat his bid seriously. An early assessment of the coverage by the *Columbia Journalism Review* was headlined, "Bernie Sanders Can't Win: Why the Press Loves to Hate Underdogs." In it, author Steve Hendricks noted:

> For not going with the flow, and for challenging Hillary Clinton, the big fish many elites have tagged as their own, Sanders's entry into the race was greeted with story after story whose message— stated or understated, depending on the decorum of the messenger—was "This crank can't win."

> The trouble with this consensus is the paucity of evidence to support it. "This crank actually *could* win" is nearer the mark. But having settled on a prophecy, the media went about covering Sanders so as to fulfill it. The print *New York Times*, for example, buried his announcement on page A21, even though every other candidate who had declared before then had been put on the front page, above the fold. Sanders's straight-news story didn't even crack 700 words, compared to

the 1,100 to 1,500 that Marco Rubio, Rand Paul, Ted Cruz, and Hillary Clinton got. As for the content, the *Times* declared high in Sanders's piece that he was a long shot for the Democratic nomination and that Clinton was all but a lock. None of the Republican entrants got the long-shot treatment, even though Paul, Rubio, and Cruz were generally polling fifth, seventh, and eighth among Republicans before they announced.

Other coverage of Sanders ran to caricature, as in Paul Kane and Philip Rucker's personality piece in the *Washington Post*, which opened, "He seems an unlikely presidential candidate—an ex-hippie, septuagenarian socialist from the liberal reaches of Vermont who rails, in his thick Brooklyn accent, rumpled suit and frizzy pile of white hair, against the 'billionaire class' taking over the country." The *Post*'s pieces didn't lead with Clinton's hippie past or her age (she became a septuagenarian in 2017) and didn't say she "rails" when she discusses her more ardently held positions (she has a couple). Even the word *liberal*, which doesn't seem the worst quasi-pejorative to hang on a candidate who calls himself a socialist, sits poorly next to the flattering *populist* that the *Post* permitted Clinton, especially since she is a recent and rhetorical convert to the creed that Sanders has lived for forty years.

Other major news organizations ignored Sanders as nearly as they could a sitting U.S. senator entering a presidential race. ABC's *World News Tonight* gave his announcement all of eighteen seconds, five of which were allotted to Clinton's tweet welcoming him to the race. *CBS Evening News* fit the announcement into a single sentence at the end of a two-minute report about Clinton.

Such dismissive media coverage was a constant challenge for the Sanders campaign. Even as it started winning primaries and caucuses, the media kept writing it off as an impossibility. This created the great "what if" of 2016: What if the media had paid closer attention to the campaign as it gained traction? Didn't the upheaval that Sanders's bid caused within the Democratic Party merit at least as much attention as the upheaval that Donald Trump's bid caused within the Republican Party? It is true that Sanders did not begin his run as a reality-TV star who had been a national "brand" for years, yet he moved quickly into contention— and the media never really caught up.

The speed with which the Sanders campaign gained traction should have been a huge story. The senator started with insufficient name recognition and inadequate funding. Those deficits were compounded by initial miscalculations; the campaign launched with a battle plan that was too limited in its sense of its own potential. For instance, the campaign should from the very beginning have highlighted Sanders's long record of activism on behalf of civil rights, women's rights, and LGBTQ+ rights, and it should have been quicker to push beyond the senator's core focus on economic issues to deliver a broader message on social and racial justice, climate change, and peace. Sanders could have done far more to distinguish his approach to foreign policy from Clinton's: their deep differences might well have framed the debates on the Democratic side. At the same time, strategic missteps— including overemphasizing a South Carolina primary that Sanders was never going to win and underemphasizing

Nevada caucuses that he could have won—hampered the campaign. Yet, despite making many of the mistakes that are common to insurgent bids, this one generally went from strength to strength.

Sanders offered broadcast networks and the 24/7 cable news channels one of the greatest up-from-behind stories of the modern political age, moving in a matter of months from fringe status to serious contention. But, in 2016, the media was not inclined to tell this story. The networks were obsessed with the show Trump was putting on. "It may not be good for America, but it's damn good for CBS," announced CBS CEO Les Moonves in a February 2016 rumination on the wall-to-wall Trump coverage. At the Morgan Stanley Technology, Media & Telecom Conference in San Francisco, Moonves explained, "The money's rolling in . . . This is going to be a very good year for us." Moonves went on to add, "It's a terrible thing to say, but bring it on, Donald. Go ahead. Keep going."

If we understand American media as a hungry beast that thinks only about its next meal, then it's easy to see why Donald Trump's presidential campaign fed the beast. With calculated and constant outrageousness, he dominated news coverage of the entire 2016 presidential competition. As veteran political observer Larry Sabato said in the fall of 2015, "It's Trump, Trump, Trump, Trump, Trump, Trump, and Trump." With old and new media providing constant flows of information in a drive for clicks and ratings, Trump figured out how to get the attention he craved—and that powered his campaign. It got to the point where Amy Goodman of *Democracy Now!* observed that: "Trump doesn't even have to go out on the road—he's piped into everyone's home." Trump sucked the air out of the 2016 race.

An all-Trump-all-the-time media let Trump define the discussion, in his own party and in the Democratic Party. "The media's obsession with Donald Trump has real consequences for our democracy," explained Credo Action's Josh Nelson. "Desperate for ratings, the cable news networks have decided to broadcast nearly continuous coverage of Donald Trump's campaign at the expense of giving real issues the coverage they deserve."

And real candidates, like Bernie Sanders.

At the end of 2015, on the Republican side, the Real Clear Politics (RCP) average of all national polls had insurgent candidate Donald Trump attracting 30.4 percent among voters who might reasonably be expected to participate in Republican primaries and caucuses. Trump was showing particular strength in Iowa and New Hampshire. On the Democratic side, the RCP poll averages had insurgent candidate Bernie Sanders attracting 31 percent support nationally. Trump and Sanders had both attracted passionate followings. It was not unreasonable to expect that they would be afforded reasonably similar levels of coverage. But a study by media analyst Andrew Tyndall of network newscast coverage of all the candidates during 2015 found that a total of 327 minutes was specifically devoted to Trump and his campaign. How much was devoted to Sanders? Twenty minutes. Tyndall, who added up specific coverage of the candidates by the broadcast networks, determined that Trump received more coverage than all of the

Democratic presidential contenders combined. But the under-coverage of Sanders was the most dramatically disproportionate. Consider this fact: From January 1 to the end of November 2015, ABC's *World News Tonight* gave Trump's campaign eighty-one minutes of coverage—compared to roughly twenty *seconds* for Sanders.

Despite the lack of coverage, Sanders was beginning to move poll numbers, not just as a contender for the Democratic nomination but as a November prospect. A Quinnipiac University survey conducted in the fall of 2015 found that the senator was leading Trump by nine points—with the senator at 49 percent and the billionaire at 40. (In the same survey, Clinton led Trump by seven points.) Surveys from a number of battleground states found that Sanders was swamping Trump. In Wisconsin, for instance, a fall 2015 Marquette University Law School poll had Sanders beating Trump 52 to 35—a significantly wider margin than Clinton's 48 to 38 lead over Trump. Sanders's campaign manager, Jeff Weaver, crunched the numbers and observed: "The corporately owned media may not like Bernie's anti-establishment views, but for the sake of American democracy they must allow for a fair debate in this presidential campaign." Yet that never really happened. Sanders garnered more coverage after tying Clinton in the Iowa caucuses and winning more than 60 percent of the vote in New Hampshire, but the attention he got still tended toward the grudging "yes, but" coverage that major media outlets accord to candidates who frustrate their predictions. As winter turned to spring, the political and media elites kept angling for an opening to declare that the race for the

Democratic presidential nomination was finished. But Sanders kept complicating things. By winning.

Movement Politics

Sanders had a theory about why he could break through the mainstream media bias:

> The way we overcame that, to the degree that we did, was through social media. One of the reasons I think we did so well among younger people is that most younger people now do not watch the evening news; they don't read the *Washington Post*. And we did, I think, a very good job in terms of communicating directly with many millions of younger people directly through social media.

More than any campaign in the modern era, the Sanders effort focused on social media as a tool for getting new voters engaged with not just a candidate but a set of issues. Slowly but surely, it became clear that no matter how the media covered his candidacy, Sanders was going to keep securing victories. "We have now won by wide margins in states from New England to the Rocky Mountains and from the Midwest to the Great Plains," the candidate declared after winning a two-to-one victory in the Maine caucuses of early March, for his eighth primary or caucus win since the process began. "The pundits might not like it," Sanders added, "but the people are making history."

The history-making continued through the spring until June 7, the last of 2016's Super Tuesdays. Sanders spoke in

Santa Monica, California, to thousands of supporters who cheered as if he had won the nomination. He had not. The results from the last major contests, in California and New Jersey, gave Clinton an insurmountable advantage. Joking that he was "pretty good in arithmetic," Sanders acknowledged the results.

Sanders and his backers still had plenty to celebrate: they had won more than 13 million votes, twenty-three primaries and caucuses, and more than 1,800 delegates. The Sanders campaign changed the calculus of Democratic Party leaders, who had imagined that the contest for their party's 2016 nomination would be a stately coronation of Clinton. Instead, Clinton and Sanders battled all the way to the end. Even as he outlined the steps that would lead to his endorsing Clinton, Sanders proclaimed, "The struggle continues."

Anyone who knew anything about Bernie Sanders understood why. For him, electoral politics has always been an extension of movement politics. Movement politics organizes people around issues and seeks to bring neglected ideas into the mainstream of the political discourse—a transit that ultimately expands the range of debate and the prospects for change. Sanders says the 2016 campaign confirmed his faith in the appeal of a progressive agenda. "I believed from my heart of hearts that the ideas I was talking about are what most Americans would support if they had the chance to hear these views, which they do not under normal circumstances," he told me after the dust had settled.

> You could watch CNN for the next fourteen years, and you're not going to hear a discussion about the need for a single-payer

health care system. You're not going to see a critique of the drug companies, and you're not going to hear much discussion about income and wealth inequality. My view was that if we could get out to the American people, get the exposure, make the personal contacts, we would do well.

Having indeed done well, Sanders turned his attention in June and July 2016 to the party's platform-drafting process, which he said needed to recognize and advance the essential themes of "the struggle" for economic, social, and racial justice. This was the struggle Sanders had engaged in for decades: the fight for higher wages for workers, account-ability for Wall Street, guaranteed access to health care and higher education, investment in communities that had been left behind by bad trade deals and insufficient investment in infrastructure, criminal justice reform, a climate agenda sufficient to save the planet from environmental devasta-tion, and a peace agenda aimed at dialing down the military-industrial complex and preventing new wars.

Sanders believed that pushing for a progressive platform would help Clinton and the party. And he did want to help. By the summer of 2016, Sanders was deeply unsettled by the prospect that Trump might be elected. He determined that he would do everything in his power to prevent that from happening. "Bernie Sanders Packs Schedule with Campaign Stops for Hillary Clinton," noted the *Wall Street Journal* as the fall campaign took off, while ABC News announced, "Bernie Sanders Goes 'All In' for Hillary Clinton." So ardent was Sanders in his campaigning for Clinton that, on the eve of the November election, Amy Davidson Sorkin reported in the *New Yorker*—in an article headlined "Bernie Sanders's Hard Fight for Hillary Clinton"—that

one of the many things that makes Donald Trump angry is that Bernie Sanders does not seem to hold grudges. In recent speeches, Trump has pointed to the information that has come out, through WikiLeaks' disclosures of John Podesta's emails, about the Clinton team's attitude toward Sanders during the primaries: the slights ("doofus"), the schemes ("where would you stick the knife?"), and the eye-rolling ("socialist math"). Perhaps worst of all—at least from Trump's point of view— was Donna Brazile's passing along of debate questions. "Now, Bernie Sanders should be angry right? Shouldn't he be angry?" Trump asked a crowd in Florida. He sounded a little bit puzzled—he would be so mad.

The truth is that Bernie Sanders is very, very angry—at Donald Trump. He is angry enough to have spent weeks travelling on behalf of Hillary Clinton, speaking for her in union halls and arenas, to students and activists. When he talks, he is entirely Bernie—"We are going to fight for that democracy; we are not going to become an oligarchy"—and he hints strongly that he has done some negotiating with her before getting on the stage, and will continue to do so after, as he hopes, she is elected. When praising her positions, he often says "Secretary Clinton has told me" or "Secretary Clinton has promised," as though he knows that it might not work, with the sort of swing audiences he is dispatched to persuade (students, working-class voters), simply to declare that taking these stands is in her nature. But he knows what he wants: for her to win.

For many Sanders backers, the idea of going "all in" for Clinton was frustrating. For some, it was too much to ask. As Sorkin noted,

> He let his supporters yell at him and deride him as a sellout in bleak delegate breakfasts at the Democratic National Convention, in Philadelphia, as he endorsed Clinton and explained why they needed to do the same. He made getting support for her his priority, putting aside any subtle, undermining gestures that might have better preserved his rebel-rock-star status. He has kept doing so despite other revelations in the Podesta e-mails, ones that are not about him personally but about issues that he believes in—for example, about money in politics, as exemplified by the Clinton team's nurturing of donors. And he has earned the right to negotiate hard on such issues in the future.

For Sanders, earning the right to negotiate on the issues has always been an essential premise of his politics. And it is not limited to the one-on-one negotiations that follow a particular campaign. The senator understands that it is possible to lose an election and still advance a cause. Few prominent political figures have been defeated as many times as Sanders. He is a former mayor and a veteran member of Congress. But he lost races for the U.S. Senate, the U.S. House, and Vermont's governorship before getting to Washington. And, in 2016, he lost a presidential bid. Sanders understands the political process as an ongoing struggle. He is a democratic socialist who calls for "a political revolution," yet he is remarkably realistic about what that entails.

What was striking about the 2016 Sanders campaign was the extent to which the senator built a movement consisting of millions of people committed to the idea of revolution as a long game. When Sanders spoke of the struggle as a "very, very steep fight," his backers knew he was right. Yet they also knew they would continue to wage it. Many were, like Sanders, veterans of past campaigns by the Reverend Jesse Jackson and others to change the politics of the Democratic Party and the nation. Many more were newcomers, especially the young people who were revitalizing groups like the Democratic Socialists of America. They believed, as Sanders did, that the winning politics for Democrats in 2016 and beyond had to be a politics that aimed high. During the primary season, the Sanders insurgency had influenced Clinton and the party to such an extent that the *Wall Street Journal* headlined an analysis of Clinton's evolving positions: "Party Shift Left Pulls Candidate With It." Sanders backers did not want that influence to dissipate.

Because a movement politics that is of consequence must necessarily be about bold policies and agendas, Sanders and his supporters saw the platform-drafting process that played out between the last primaries in June and the convention in late July as vital. The same political and media elites who had once dismissed the Sanders candidacy sought to dismiss the platform as a footnote to the presidential race. But the Sanders camp recognized that the document, as drafted and eventually accepted by the Democratic National Convention, would provide a measure of the extent to which the party had moved in 2016—and the extent to which it might be moved in the years to come. Their mission, said Sanders, was to produce "the strongest progressive agenda that any political party has ever seen."

Fighting for a Progressive Platform

Sanders won a sufficient number of delegates—and a sufficient opening in the debate—to demand a say with regard to the platform. In late May, he named some of the nation's leading thinkers and activists to the committee that was charged with framing the document. Sanders secured a place for author and 350.org cofounder Bill McKibben on the fifteen-person drafting committee—ensuring that the issue of climate change would not be neglected. Sanders's other committee picks included Congressional Progressive Caucus co-chair Keith Ellison, academic and activist Cornel West (the author of the groundbreaking 1994 book *Race Matters* and a leading member of Democratic Socialists of America), Native American activist and former Tulalip Tribes vice-chair Deborah Parker (a key advocate for reauthorization of the Violence Against Women Act), and Arab-American Institute president James Zogby.

One of the first wins for the Sanders representatives was on the issue of capital punishment. Pressed by Ellison, the drafting committee ended the party's support for state-sponsored executions and adopted the position that the death penalty "has proven to be a cruel and unusual form of punishment" and "has no place in the United States of America."

When the full platform committee gathered in Orlando, Florida, shortly before the convention, party stalwarts proved to be open to at least some of the issues raised by the Sanders insurgency—and by the mass movements that had worked for years to move the party to the left. There were votes to include more explicit support of criminal justice reform, to remove marijuana from the list of Schedule I drugs under the Controlled Substances Act, and to crack down on monopolies and to tax the rich in order to "protect the earned pension benefits of Americans in multi-employer pension plans." Former Ohio state senator Nina Turner, a key Sanders supporter (see introduction), and Service Employees International Union president Mary Kay Henry, a key Clinton backer, cooperated on language declaring,

> We should raise the federal minimum wage to $15 an hour over time and index it, give all Americans the ability to join a union regardless of where they work, and create new ways for workers to have power in the economy so every worker can earn at least $15 an hour.

But the cooperation did not extend to the debate over trade policy, an issue that has historically divided Democratic presidents (including Bill Clinton and Barack Obama) and grassroots activists in industrial states. The senator had argued against the Trans-Pacific Partnership (TPP) agreement throughout the primary race, and Sanders backers, especially those from the Great Lakes states, argued that the party needed to oppose it formally. A failure to explicitly reject the TPP, they said, would be used by Trump and his allies in their appeals to working-class voters in states hit hard by deindustrialization and the offshoring of jobs. This was a concern that Sanders and others had raised with an increased sense of urgency after the United Kingdom voted in June 2016 to exit the European Union, following a campaign that saw right-wing forces exploit economic fears to their advantage.

Carli Stevenson, a Sanders supporter from Indiana, put it in stark political terms. "We all have to go home tomorrow and face our neighbors and tell them what we did to protect their jobs," she explained. "The best way to do that, and to leave no doubt, is to say that the Democratic Party opposes the Trans-Pacific Partnership." Key Sanders supporter and former NAACP president Ben Jealous proposed explicit opposition to the TPP in the platform. "We need to leave no doubt that Democrats stand up for working men and women in this country," declared Turner. "Leave no doubt that we are against the TPP." Sanders backers chanted, "Leave no doubt!" But the Jealous amendment lost in a 106-to-74 vote. Texas populist Jim Hightower, a leading Sanders backer, made one last attempt to put the party on record as opposing the TPP, which he decried as "a corporate-empowerment deal." Noting that Trump had made it clear that he would campaign against the TPP and the failed trade agreements of the past in Wisconsin, Michigan, Pennsylvania, and other swing states, Hightower warned, "He is going to hammer Hillary mercilessly on . . . wimpy language in her platform." But Hightower's amendment was defeated, 104 to 71.

The platform fight indicated that, while Sanders and his supporters had made progress in moving the Democratic

Party in a progressive direction, they had not transformed it. Then, on the eve of the convention, WikiLeaks released 19,252 emails and 8,034 attachments from the Democratic National Committee, including emails from seven key DNC staff members who were active in the primary campaign, revealing open favoritism toward Clinton and hostility toward the Sanders campaign. That made it harder to preach unity. Yet, even after the WikiLeaks revelation, the Sanders and Clinton camps did their best to maintain a conciliatory tone. Clinton celebrated Sanders and his supporters in her acceptance address. Sanders responded in kind, telling the convention,

> It is no secret that Hillary Clinton and I disagree on a number of issues. That's what this campaign has been about. That's what democracy is about. But I am happy to tell you that at the Democratic Platform Committee there was a significant coming together between the two campaigns and we produced, by far, the most progressive platform in the history of the Democratic Party. Among many other strong provisions, the Democratic Party now calls for breaking up the major financial institutions on Wall Street and the passage of a twenty-first-century Glass-Steagall Act. It also calls for strong opposition to job-killing free-trade agreements like the Trans-Pacific Partnership.

The last line was an artful turn of phrase that suggested perhaps a bit more progress than had actually occurred on the trade issue. Sanders was trying to help the Clinton camp frame its fall run in a way that would thwart Trump's faux-populist appeals. "This election is about which candidate understands the real problems facing this country and has offered real solutions—not just bombast, fear-mongering, name-calling, and divisiveness," he told the delegates. "The choice is not even close."

Unfortunately, the result of the 2016 presidential election *was* close. Though Clinton won the national popular vote with ease, finishing 2.9 million votes ahead of Trump, the fight for an Electoral College majority came down to a handful of industrial states where Barack Obama had won with relative ease in 2008 and 2012 but where Clinton had struggled. Sanders and his delegates had been right to focus on the trade issues and to warn about the threat a weak stance might pose. Trump campaigned relentlessly against the TPP in particular and free-trade policies in general. Ultimately, he secured narrow victories in Wisconsin, Michigan, and Pennsylvania—and their electoral votes gave the Republican the presidency.

As the shock of Trump's victory wore off and the reality of his presidency settled in, the ideas that Sanders had been promoting for years and popularized during the 2016 campaign steadily gained more serious consideration within the Democratic Party. In part, this was a reaction to Trump's election. But it was also a reaction to the reality that the Sanders campaign had shaken the assumptions of Democratic insiders.

Our Revolution

The campaign Sanders had mounted was the most successful insurgent bid in the annals of the modern Democratic Party.

As veteran political analyst Rhodes Cook noted in a survey prepared for the *Atlantic*, Sanders had exceeded the overall vote totals and percentages of Howard Dean in 2004, Jesse Jackson in 1988, Gary Hart in 1984, and Ted Kennedy in 1980, among others. (While Barack Obama's 2008 challenge to Clinton began with many of the characteristics of an insurgency, the young senator from Illinois eventually campaigned with encouragement and support from key party leaders such as former president Jimmy Carter, endorsements from key senators such as Ted Kennedy and Robert Byrd and the backing of major unions and prominent donors. Obama became the frontrunner and finished as the party's nominee.) At the 2016 convention where he spoke of "the historical accomplishments we have achieved," Sanders arrived with more pledged delegates than any insurgent challenger to the eventual nominee since the party began to democratize its nominating process following the disastrous, boss-dominated convention of 1968.

After the convention, Sanders's lower-case term "our revolution" would quickly be capitalized. *Our Revolution* became the title of a bestselling book by Sanders and the name of an independent nationwide political action group. By law, Sanders could not direct Our Revolution's work, but the group served as a vehicle for his supporters, who focused attention on election campaigns and on a legislative agenda that extended on themes raised during the presidential campaign—Medicare for All, free college, worker rights, women's rights, immigrant rights, voting rights, a meaningful response to climate change, criminal justice reform, and taxing Wall Street.

Like Sanders, Our Revolution adopted an agenda that emphasized economic and social and racial justice. Stung during the early stages of the 2016 campaign by charges that he was too focused on economics and did not sufficiently emphasize the need to challenge systemic racism, sexism, and xenophobia, Sanders honed his message to amplify an understanding of the need for an intersectional response to injustice.

This was not a great leap for the senator, who had begun his political activism as a civil rights campaigner in the early 1960s and has advocated for women's equality and LGBTQ+ rights throughout his career. It was, however, a vital one for a political figure whom critics attempted to dismiss as a one-dimensional economic determinist. Sanders acknowledged that, for him, the 2016 campaign was a learning process. "I talked to a lot of Black Lives activists in various states. What I learned is that the relationship of police departments around the country with the black community is far more severe and awful than I had originally known," he explained to me after the campaign was done.

The intimidation on the part of the police, the shooting of unarmed people, the outrage of people being killed in cold blood, is an issue which prompted us to come up with what I believe was the strongest set of proposals of any candidate in terms of the need for real criminal justice reform. But I also believe what Martin Luther King Jr. believed. You remember what the title of the March on Washington was? "Jobs and Freedom." What King understood is that you have to deal with the economic issues as well as the political issues and the civil rights issues. Throughout this campaign, what we talked about is that, in community after community, there are unemployment rates among young African Americans of 30 to 40 percent. Thirty to 40 percent! Kids have no jobs, they have no future. That is an issue that has got to be dealt with simultaneously as we deal with police brutality, voter suppression, and the other attacks that are taking place on the African American community.

During the 2016 campaign, Sanders began to declare in his stump speeches that "there is no president that will fight harder to end institutional racism." Embracing the concerns of the Black Lives Matter movement, he spoke frequently about African Americans who had died in police custody. In particular, he focused on the story of Sandra Bland, who died after being arrested and jailed in Texas. "There's no doubt in my mind," said Sanders, "that she, like too many African Americans who die in police custody, would be alive today if she were a white woman."

Our Revolution, under the leadership of veteran civil rights and voting rights activists such as Nina Turner, advanced a bold agenda on racial justice issues and championed the candidacies of women and people of color in state and local races where some of these justice issues could be tackled. These campaigns often involved challenging establishment Democrats in primaries, a controversial approach that was not always successful but that often raised the profile of new candidates and new issues.

For his part, Sanders recognized the need to push limits and to take the risk of making primary endorsements. Early in 2019, for instance, when he waded into local races in

Philadelphia on behalf of primary contenders who pledged to address mass incarceration by rejecting discriminatory cash bail. "When our movement defeats Donald Trump in 2020, things are finally going to change," the senator explained in an opinion piece for the *Philadelphia Inquitrer* before that city's May 2019 Democratic primary. "But even before we get to that presidential election, the people of Philadelphia have an opportunity to start making changes right now in 2019. On May 21, you will have a chance to vote for local judicial candidates who pledge to end cash bail."

Our Revolution also focused on opening up the Democratic Party. Its ambitious "Transform the Party" project experienced mixed success. Keith Ellison was narrowly defeated by a Clinton ally, former Secretary of Labor Tom Perez, for DNC chair early in 2017. But party leaders knew they could not completely neglect Sanders or his supporters. They invited the senator into the expanded leadership of the Senate Democratic Caucus with a vague title that nodded to his popularity with Democrats and non-Democrats: "chairman of outreach." In April of 2017 he embarked with Perez on a national "Come Together and Fight Back" tour. That Sanders was now seen as vital to the Democratic Party's image—and messaging—showed the extent to which party insiders recognized the need for a reset.

The party of Franklin Roosevelt had begun veering in the 1970s toward centrist economic approaches. By the 1990s, it was swamped by so-called "Third Way" thinking that embraced free trade, deregulation of banking and Wall Street, and the cruel lie that there can be some sort of "win-win" compromise between crony capitalism and the common good. The 2016 nomination race revealed deep frustration with the extent that the Democratic Party had erred on the side of neoliberalism. Movements had for years been advocating for a $15-an-hour minimum wage, fair trade, single-payer health care, taxes on the rich, necessary regulation of big banks, and profound political reform. The Sanders campaign embraced and amplified these messages, exciting millions of voters—above all, the young voters who would decide whether the Democratic Party had a future. Although Sanders did not win the nomination, he won the debate. The party platform reflected movement values, and Clinton embraced elements of the agenda in her fall campaign.

It was clear, however, that the party needed more than the cosmetic change of a platform rewrite and election-season speechifying. Progressives argued that the era of the so-called New Democrats—as exemplified by the Democratic Leadership Council, whose initials Jesse Jackson once suggested might actually stand for "Democrats for the Leisure Class"—had to end. Changing the direction of a party is always hard. But the Sanders–Perez tour of early 2017 seemed to be headed in the right direction. The senator and the party chair announced that their tour would

> speak out for raising the minimum wage to $15 an hour, pay equity for women, rebuilding our crumbling infrastructure, combating climate change, making public colleges and universities tuition-free, criminal justice reform, comprehensive immigration reform and tax reform which demands that the

wealthy and large corporations start paying their fair share of taxes.

They traveled to the right places—Maine, Kentucky, Florida, Nevada, Utah, and Arizona—acknowledging the need for a fifty-state strategy. In a joint statement announcing the tour, Sanders and Perez sounded boldly progressive themes. "At a time of massive income and wealth inequality and a shrinking middle class, we need a government which represents all Americans, not just Wall Street, multinational corporations and the top 1 percent," they said.

Regardless of where they live or their political affiliations, most people understand that it is absurd for Republicans in Congress to support huge tax breaks for billionaires while pushing for cuts to Social Security, Medicare, and Medicaid. They understand that the recent Republican health care proposal that would have thrown 24 million Americans off of their health insurance, substantially raised premiums for older workers, and defunded Planned Parenthood while, at the same time, providing almost $300 billion in tax breaks to the top 2 percent is a disgraceful idea.

To have the Democratic Party speaking this language was a measure of the impact of the 2016 Sanders campaign on the party. Top democrats were now emulating the senator, and so were the people who proposed to lead the Democratic Party in 2020 and beyond. When Sanders challenged Trump's cabinet picks, social media flared up and cable news channels featured video of the clashes—especially a devastating exchange with secretary of education designee Betsy DeVos.

Reporters who had once neglected Sanders now sought his comments on the latest outrage during the first months of what the senator decried as "one-party, reactionary, right-wing rule in Washington." When Sanders renewed his proposal for a Medicare-for-All health care plan in September 2017, Democratic senators who were considering a 2020 presidential run—Elizabeth Warren of Massachusetts, Jeff Merkley of Oregon, Kamala Harris of California, Cory Booker of New Jersey, and Kirsten Gillibrand of New York—signed on as cosponsors.

On issue after issue, ideas that Sanders had popularized on the campaign trail were being accepted as mainstream. But Sanders was not satisfied. When we spoke about the Democratic Party, he invariably expressed frustration with an infrastructure that he saw as unresponsive to grassroots activism. "It needs revolutionary change," he said of the party.

> If you want to run for the United States Senate, you hire a consultant who will do polling for you, who will tell you the kinds of television ads you should run, who will tell you that most of the money you raise has got to go into TV. Raising money, and then putting that money into the hands of consultants, who then put on TV ads—that's more or less what campaigns are about. We've got to change that. The Democrats have got to open the door to young people. Welcome them in and understand that it will be messy, that many young people are not professional politicians. The Democratic Party is going to have to adjust itself to their reality, rather than force young people to be adjusted to the Democratic leadership's reality.

Campaigning with Ocasio-Cortez

It was this sensibility that led Sanders to celebrate the rise of a new generation of political leaders within the party— many of whom were veterans of his 2016 campaign. While prominent Democrats wrestled with the question of how to respond to the June 2018 New York primary victory of twenty-eight-year-old Alexandria Ocasio-Cortez over the fourth-ranking Democrat in the US House, Sanders embraced it, arguing, "What Alexandria did, in pulling off one of the great upsets in recent history, is show the folks in . . . states across this country that, yes, it can be done."

Within a month of the New York primary, Sanders was on the road with Ocasio-Cortez. The two democratic socialists headed to Kansas in mid-July to stump for congressional candidates James Thompson, a civil rights lawyer from Wichita, and Brent Welder, a labor lawyer from Bonner Springs. They were also out to prove a point about the viability of the aggressively progressive agenda in states far from Vermont and New York. Sanders and Ocasio-Cortez wanted to draw attention to the fact that the issues they were talking about had broad appeal—not just in blue states but in the reddest of red states. What sort of issues? Medicare-for-All health care reform, an expansive commitment to civil rights, women's rights, humane immigration policies, and an economic justice vision rooted in a commitment to working-class empowerment.

Standing up for unions and their members in Kansas—a so-called right-to-work state where Republican governors had shredded workplace protections and embraced the

antilabor program of the Wichita-based Koch family—
was, Sanders and Ocasio-Cortez argued, smart politics at a
time when plenty of Kansans were enraged by the scorch-
ing inequality that the Kochs had fostered in their state and
across this country. "I don't think the people of Kansas or
the people of Vermont or the people anywhere in this country think that it is appropriate that a handful of billionaires
like the Koch brothers can spend some $400 million in this
2018 election cycle to elect candidates to represent the
wealthy and the powerful," Sanders said as he discussed
Thompson's bid, "so I think a defeat of the Koch brothers,
if you like, would be a very symbolic victory." Ocasio-
Cortez was preaching the same gospel in Wichita, where
she thanked an enthusiastic crowd for showing her that
"girls from the Bronx are welcome everywhere." The New
Yorker brought thousands of Kansans to their feet with a
declaration that "wherever there [are] working-class
people, there is hope for the progressive movement."

What Sanders and Ocasio-Cortez talked about in Wichita
and Kansas City was a reversal of the equation the Koch
brothers and their fellow billionaires put in place after the
Republican "wave" election of 2010. Corporate-aligned
governors and legislators, elected with big bucks from the
Kochs, moved immediately to attack public-sector unions
and implement antilabor legislation—not just in
Republican-leaning states such as Kansas but in historically
progressive states like Wisconsin.

Sanders spent much of 2018 on the campaign trail. As a
national Harvard-Harris Poll identified him as the most popular prominent political figure in the United States, the outsider

was suddenly overwhelmed with invitations from Democratic
contenders who wanted the attention and energy that came
with a Sanders visit. In the last weeks before the election,
Sanders made a nine-state trek across the country, campaigning with candidates in some of the most closely contested races
of the fall. Many of the veteran Democrats with whom Sanders
campaigned won: Tony Evers, the Wisconsin educator who
upended Wisconsin governor Scott Walker; Gretchen
Whitmer, whose election as governor of Michigan ended eight
years of Republican rule in that state; Jacky Rosen, who
secured a Senate seat for the Democrats in Nevada. But
Sanders took particular interest in the next generation of political outsiders, especially those mounting uphill (and ultimately
unwinnable) races against noxious Republican incumbents:
Randy Bryce, the union ironworker whose Democratic challenge to Republican House Speaker Paul Ryan gained such
traction that Ryan finally quit; J.D. Scholten, the Democrat
who took on Congressman Steve King, a vicious anti-immigrant zealot, in the farm country of northwest Iowa; and
Ammar Campa-Najjar, who was crudely smeared as he challenged California congressman Duncan Hunter Jr.

Sanders ripped into Trump as "a demagogue" and "a
pathological liar." But, he added, "It's not good enough to
just beat up on Trump. You beat up on Trump and people
say, 'Yeah, you're right but so what? Why vote?' Here's
where I'm very proud, where I think the American people
should be very proud: What we have shown is that the
American people want bold ideas," he explained a few days
before the 2018 election.

A poll came out [in mid-October showing that] 70 percent of Americans support Medicare for All. The American people support making public colleges and universities tuition-free. The American people support raising the minimum wage. The American people support massive investments in our infrastructure. More and more people support transforming our energy system away from fossil fuels. Criminal justice reform. Immigration reform. All of those ideas are now kind of mainstream ideas. And our job right now, which is why I am here [on a college campus], is to get young people to understand that you have got to get involved. It's not good enough to believe in these ideas, support these ideas; you've got to make sure these ideas are implemented, and the only way you do that is by getting involved in politics.

Sanders was on the ballot himself in 2018, seeking a third term as Vermont's junior senator. In the August Democratic primary, he won 91 percent of the vote, but declined the nomination so that he could pursue reelection as he had in the past: as an independent, with support from Democrats and members of the state's Progressive Party. Though Sanders spent most of his time campaigning for others, such as Vermont lieutenant governor David Zuckerman, he swept to victory with almost 70 percent of the November vote. Even as the ballots were being counted, pundits and partisans speculated about whether Sanders would bid again for the presidency.

Sanders kept his own counsel through the last weeks of 2018 and into the start of 2019. He knew that if he made a second run for the White House, he would need to do it differently: with a larger and more experienced staff, more detailed strategies, and a broader message. And he understood that he would need to share more of himself. Where Sanders had in the past framed his remarks in stark policy terms, he had come to recognize that voters wanted more than statistics and platforms. They wanted to know where he was coming from. He had opened up some in 2016. He would need to open up more if he ran in 2020: to speak as the son of a Jewish immigrant who was profoundly concerned about the crude and divisive politics of those who targeted racial and ethnic and religious minorities; as a working-class kid who got ahead because he had access to education; as a husband, father and grandfather who recognized that existential challenges such as climate change and inequality needed to be addressed; as a veteran of the civil rights and antiwar struggles who still carried their passions within him; as a believer in movement politics who might lead a movement capable of upending the politics of the past and ushering in the next politics.

Running Again for the Presidency

When Sanders announced his first presidential bid with an email to supporters and a hastily scheduled press availability in April 2015, political and media elites characterized him as an outsider with radical ideas that would prevent him from ever being taken seriously by Democratic primary and caucus voters. When he launched his second bid in February 2019, with a series of huge events and high-profile interviews, the same political and media aristocrats speculated about whether Sanders would have a hard time distinguishing himself in a field of candidates who had begun to echo many of his positions. As he put it in the formal announcement of his 2020 bid on February 19, 2019:

> Three years ago, during our 2016 campaign, when we brought forth our progressive agenda we were told that our ideas were "radical" and "extreme." We were told that Medicare for All, a $15-an-hour minimum wage, free tuition at public colleges and universities, aggressively combating climate change, demanding that the wealthy start paying their fair share of taxes were all concepts that the American people would never accept. Well, three years have come and gone. And, as a result of millions of Americans standing up and fighting back, all of these policies and more are now supported by a majority of Americans.

Now everyone in the party—well, just about everyone—wanted to identify as a progressive. Sanders, pundits announced, was a victim of his own success. He had so expanded the range of debate in the Democratic Party, it was said, that he himself was no longer viable.

Just as media and political elites misunderstood what made Sanders stand out in 2016, they were now misunderstanding what would make him stand out in 2020. As a democratic socialist, Sanders had been the most ideologically engaged Democratic presidential contender four years earlier, and he would be the most ideologically engaged Democratic contender in 2020. Until his 2016 campaign jumpstarted the debate, the "S-word" was often relegated to the fringe. Now, however, a new generation of democratic socialists was winning seats in Congress, state legislatures and city halls across the country. Sanders would seek in 2020 to bring the movement to the next level of our politics. This would continue to distinguish him—not as an extreme and "unelectable" figure, but as the popularizer of big ideas that extended from, built upon and modernized the "Economic Bill of Rights" that FDR had proposed in his 1944 State of the Union address.

When Sanders ran in 2016, he got credit for proposing bold responses to the health care, education, economic, environmental, and social challenges that the country had so neglected. His ideas proved to be popular, but they weren't particularly new. For the most part, Sanders was calling for an American embrace of policies and programs that were implemented long ago in Canada, Britain, Germany, and, of course, the social democracies of Scandinavia. Sanders's identification as a democratic social-ist was not a liability in 2016—it was a strength. It made him an intellectually dynamic and exciting contender who addressed America's anxieties and its hopes, not merely with the solutions he proposed but in the way he put the pieces together, by comfortably talking about doing battle with "oligarchy" and "plutocracy" and "the billionaire class."

At a time when Americans were sick and tired of the political "competition" between right-wing dogma and centrist double-talk, Sanders raised fundamental questions and provided fundamental answers. Ending austerity and addressing inequality strengthens the economy in the ways that matter most, he argued; taxing the rich will help to balance the books; a comprehensive response to climate change will save the planet and usher in a sustainable economy.

It was common sense, rooted in the democratic socialist agenda Sanders had embraced and articulated for the better part of six decades. Unlike most of the other candidates, who were still evolving toward the positions he had long held, Sanders simply had to be his authentic self—the guy who started working with civil rights groups as a student at the University of Chicago and who joined the 1963 March on Washington for Jobs and Freedom that was organized by A. Philip Randolph and another democratic socialist, Bayard Rustin. Sanders was running in a potential New Deal moment, a potential Great Society moment. Bigger ideas, bolder approaches, better answers were needed if the country was going to respond in a meaningful way to climate change, to economic and racial injustice, to the dislocation caused by the collapse of the old economy, and to the reality that the "new economy" looks like a new Gilded Age.

Truly bold ideas are always red-baited in American politics. Social Security was described as a "socialist" program, but FDR fought for and implemented it. Medicare was attacked as a "socialist" program, but LBJ fought for and implemented it. Major strides on behalf of racial justice, gender equity, disability rights, environmental protection and progressive taxation were often decried by the right as "socialist" initiatives—as backers of a Green New Deal are now learning.

As Sanders emerged as a leading contender to win the

2020 Democratic nomination, the attacks began in earnest, including a *New York Times* article questioning his Central American solidarity efforts three decades ago. As Chuck Todd of NBC's *Meet the Press* put it, "The Right's going to hammer-and-sickle you to death." Sanders replied,

> I worked hard, as a young man, against the war in Vietnam. I don't apologize for that. As a member of the United States House, I helped lead the effort against the war in Iraq, which turns out to have been the worst foreign policy blunder in the modern history of the United States. As a United States senator, I led the effort to pass a bipartisan resolution to get America out of the war in Yemen, led by Saudi Arabia. And I've got to tell you something, Chuck. I hope you guys pay attention to Yemen. What's going on in Yemen now is the worst humanitarian disaster in the world. We're talking about hundreds of thousands of people, children, dying. And I'm doing my best to get the U.S. out of that war. And if Trump wants to go to war in Iran, that will make the war in Iraq look like a cakewalk . . . so we've got to do everything we can to stop that.

Sanders has always maintained a deep aversion to war and militarism, and he was not about to back down on his opposition to past and new conflicts. But Sanders has never been so doctrinaire as his critics have imagined, nor so idealistic as his champions have suggested. He's a practical former mayor who ran his state's largest city ably. He's been in the U.S. House and the U.S. Senate for the better part of thirty years. He is a serious thinker and policy analyst who is prepared to consider prospects that others dismiss. He is familiar with social democracy as it has been practiced in the past in the United States and as it is currently practiced in Norway, Sweden, Germany, and Canada. And he is certain that Americans are ready to learn from other countries—so certain that he once organized town meetings in Vermont with Denmark's ambassador to the United States.

Being America's most prominent democratic socialist is not something Sanders sees as a political burden. Polling suggests that social-democratic responses to contemporary challenges—like providing health care as a right, not a privilege, or taxing the rich to fund job creation and green infrastructure—are popular, especially with young voters and with the historically dispossessed voters who must be mobilized to forge new and necessary coalitions.

Sanders bet, with his decision to mount a second bid for the presidency, that the longing for such policies is sufficient to secure him the Democratic presidential nomination. This prospect terrified Donald Trump. That's why the president used his 2019 State of the Union address to target Sanders and the growing number of elected officials such as Ocasio-Cortez who identify as democratic socialists. "Here, in the United States, we are alarmed by the new calls to adopt socialism in our country," the president announced. "America was founded on liberty and independence—not government coercion, domination, and control. We are born free, and we will stay free. Tonight, we renew our resolve that America will never be a socialist country."

Trump understands *socialism* as a scare word, and many prominent Democrats do indeed get scared when it is referenced. But Sanders has always been comfortable discussing democratic socialism. "Do they think I'm afraid of the word? I'm not afraid of the word," he says. "I happen to believe that, if the American people understood the significant accomplishments that have taken place under social-democratic governments, democratic socialist governments, labor governments throughout Europe, they would be shocked to know about those accomplishments," the senator told me several years ago.

> How many Americans know that in virtually every European country, when you have a baby, you get guaranteed time off and, depending on the country, significant financial benefits as well. Do the American people know that? I doubt it. Do the American people even know that we're the only major Western industrialized country that doesn't guarantee healthcare for all? Most people don't know that. Do the American people know that in many countries throughout Europe, public colleges and universities are either tuition-free or very inexpensive?

What has always made Bernie Sanders stand out as a mayor, a congressman, a senator and a presidential contender is an ability to move the discussion forward by educating voters rather than trying to frighten or divide them.

> Let me define for you, simply and straightforwardly, what democratic socialism means to me. It builds on what Franklin Delano Roosevelt said when he fought for guaranteed economic rights for all Americans. And it builds on what Martin Luther King Jr. said in 1968, when he stated that, "this country has socialism for the rich and rugged individualism for the poor."

Sanders presented this explanation at a critical stage in his 2016 campaign. "It's time we had democratic socialism for working families, not just Wall Street, billionaires and large corporations. It means that we should not be providing welfare for corporations, huge tax breaks for the very rich, or trade policies which would boost corporate profits as workers lose their jobs," he said, echoing a line that he frequently repeats in his standard campaign speech across the country. "It means that we create a government that works for all of us, not just powerful special interests. It means that economic rights must be an essential part of what America stands for. It means that health care should be a right of all people, not a privilege."

That was blunt language for an American presidential contender. Four years later, Sanders would speak an even blunter language. He opened his campaign with a promise of a new politics that was more detailed and aggressive than what he had offered in 2016. "Today," Sanders declared,

> I want to welcome you to a campaign which says, loudly and clearly, that the underlying principles of our government will not be greed, hatred, and lies. It will not be racism, sexism, xenophobia, homophobia, and religious bigotry. That is going to end. The principles of our government will be based on justice: economic justice, social justice, racial justice, and environmental justice.

Candidates who have mounted insurgent campaigns in one election cycle often return as more cautious and calculating contenders in the next, imagining that a softer focus might prevail. But when Sanders decided to run again, he chose a different course. He would pull no punches. He would join more picket lines, call out more corporations like Walmart, and infuse his talks with the movement language of solidarity. He would campaign for the White House as an outsider, proposing what he had started talking about decades before: the political revolution that might transform the United States and the world.